IMAGES
of Sports

NEW YORK GIANTS
A BASEBALL ALBUM

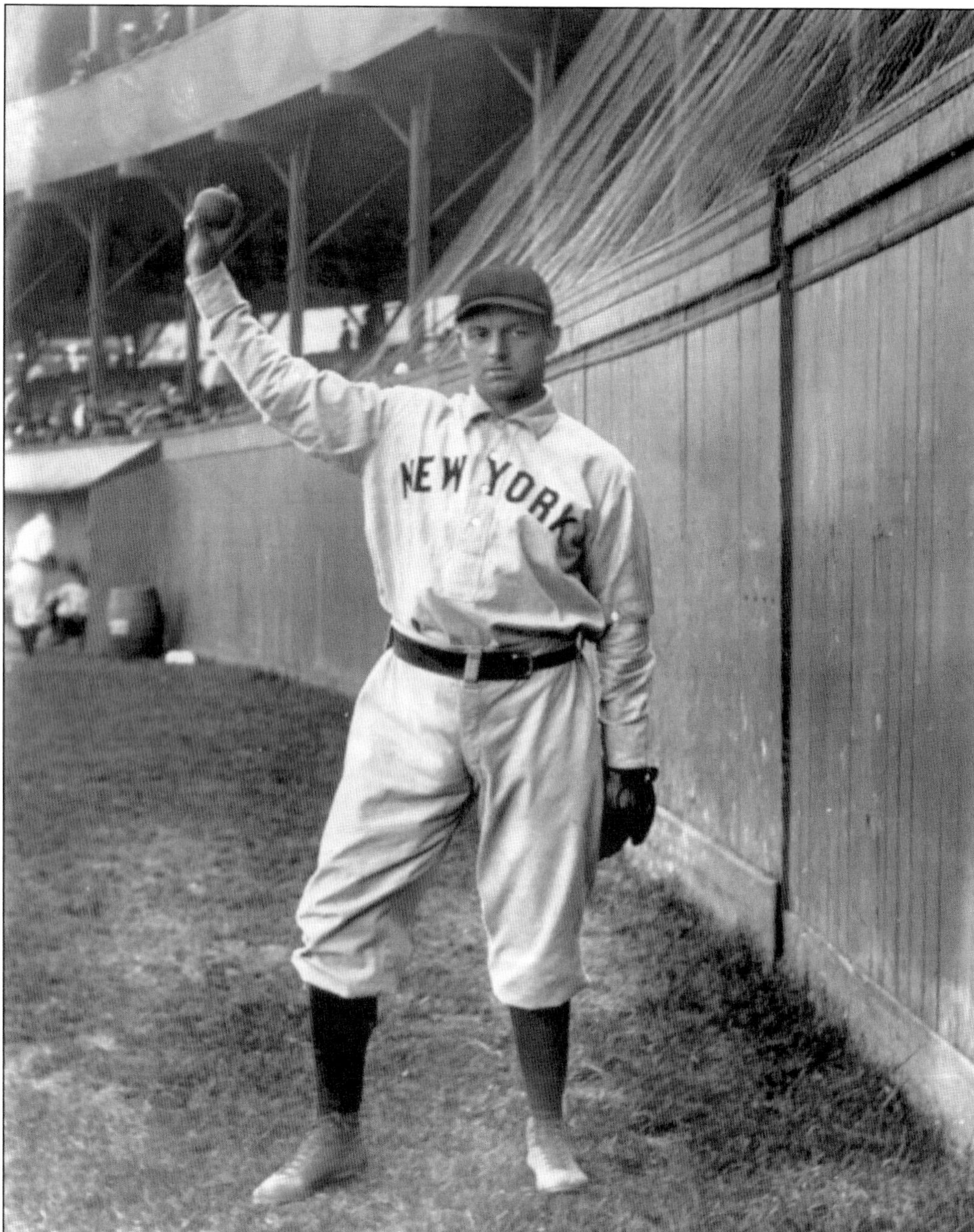

MADE OF IRON. Joe McGinnity was dubbed "Iron Man" McGinnity because of his off-season job as a foundry worker, but the moniker also perfectly described his remarkable pitching exploits. During his ten big-league seasons (1899-1908) the stocky right-hander from Illinois led the league in victories and innings five times apiece and topped the circuit in games pitched seven times. On five separate occasions he started and completed both ends of a doubleheader, including three times in the month of August 1903. An iron man, indeed!

IMAGES
of Sports

NEW YORK GIANTS
A BASEBALL ALBUM

Richard Bak

ARCADIA
PUBLISHING

ISBN 978-0-7385-0337-0

Published by Arcadia Publishing
Charleston, South Carolina

Printed in the United States of America

Library of Congress Catalog Card Number: 2007938822

For all general information contact Arcadia Publishing at:
Telephone 843-853-2070
Fax 843-853-0044
E-mail sales@arcadiapublishing.com
For customer service and orders:
Toll-Free 1-888-313-2665

Visit us on the Internet at www.arcadiapublishing.com

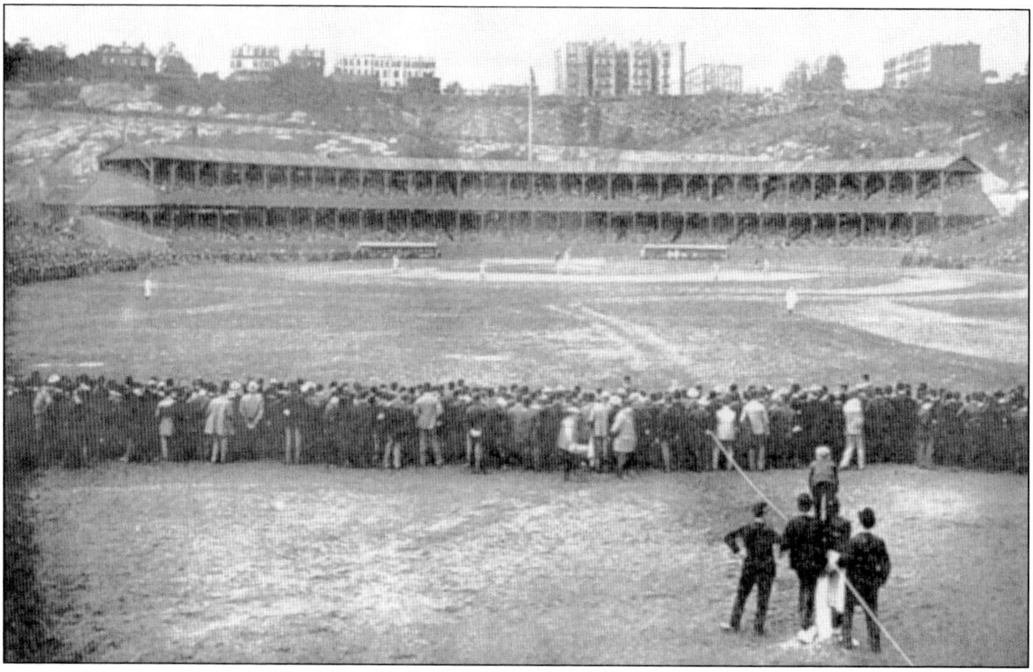

POLO GROUNDS, 1901. The New York Giants square off against St. Louis at the Polo Grounds on Memorial Day (then known as Decoration Day), May 30, 1901.

CONTENTS

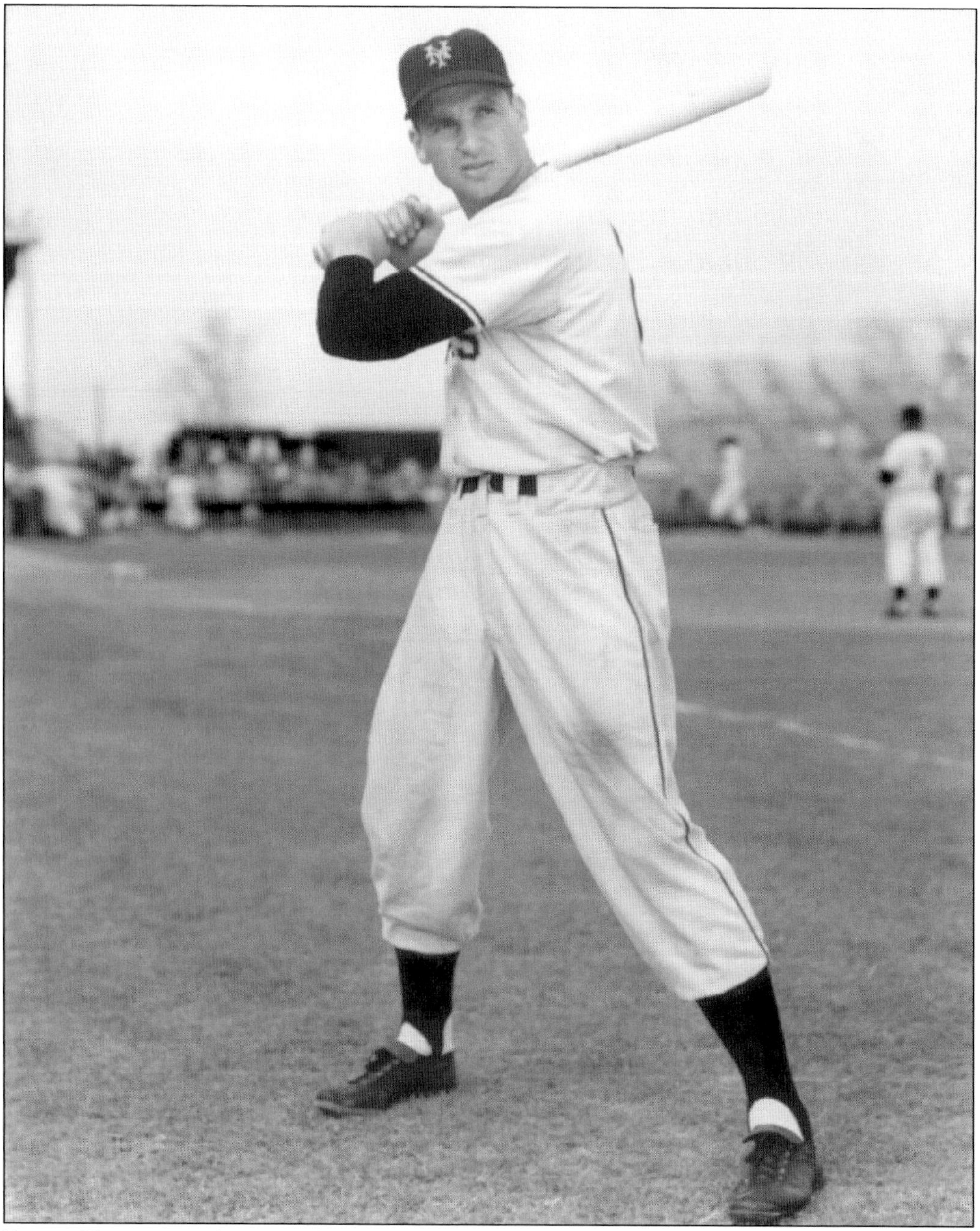

BOBBY THOMSON. The man who delivered the most famous home run in baseball history was a 27-year-old third baseman named Bobby Thomson, who on an overcast October afternoon in 1951 won the pennant for the Giants with an impossibly dramatic blast off Brooklyn's Ralph Branca. "Bobby's feat was totally unexpected," said teammate Monte Irvin. "It was sudden and stunning, came under the greatest pressure imaginable, and was the most unbelievable experience for everyone involved with it."

INTRODUCTION

SEVENTY-FIVE SUMMERS

The New York Giants have sent more men to the Baseball Hall of Fame than any other team, a distinction that only begins to hint at the place this storied franchise holds in the long history of America's national pastime.

Between 1883 and 1957, a span of 75 summers, the Giants were one of professional sports' great dynasties. Aside from the 17 National League pennants and eight world championships (in 1888, 1889, 1894, 1905, 1921, 1922, 1933, and 1954) the team won during this period, there were the unique personalities and imperishable moments that remain so much a part of the lore of the game: John McGraw's pugnacity, Christy Mathewson's fadeaway, Fred Snodgrass's muff, Mel Ott's leg kick, Carl Hubbell's scroogie, Bobby Thomson's home run, Willie Mays' catch. Even the Giants' ballpark, the Polo Grounds, had a personality of its own, with a center field that seemed as expansive as Utah and abbreviated foul lines that turned many an ordinary fly ball into a mighty home run.

This illustrated chronicle uses nearly 190 vintage photographs, period advertisements, and historic scorecards to recapture 75 years of memories provided by the New York Giants, a team that—with apologies to Tony Bennett—may have moved to San Francisco but left its heart in Manhattan.

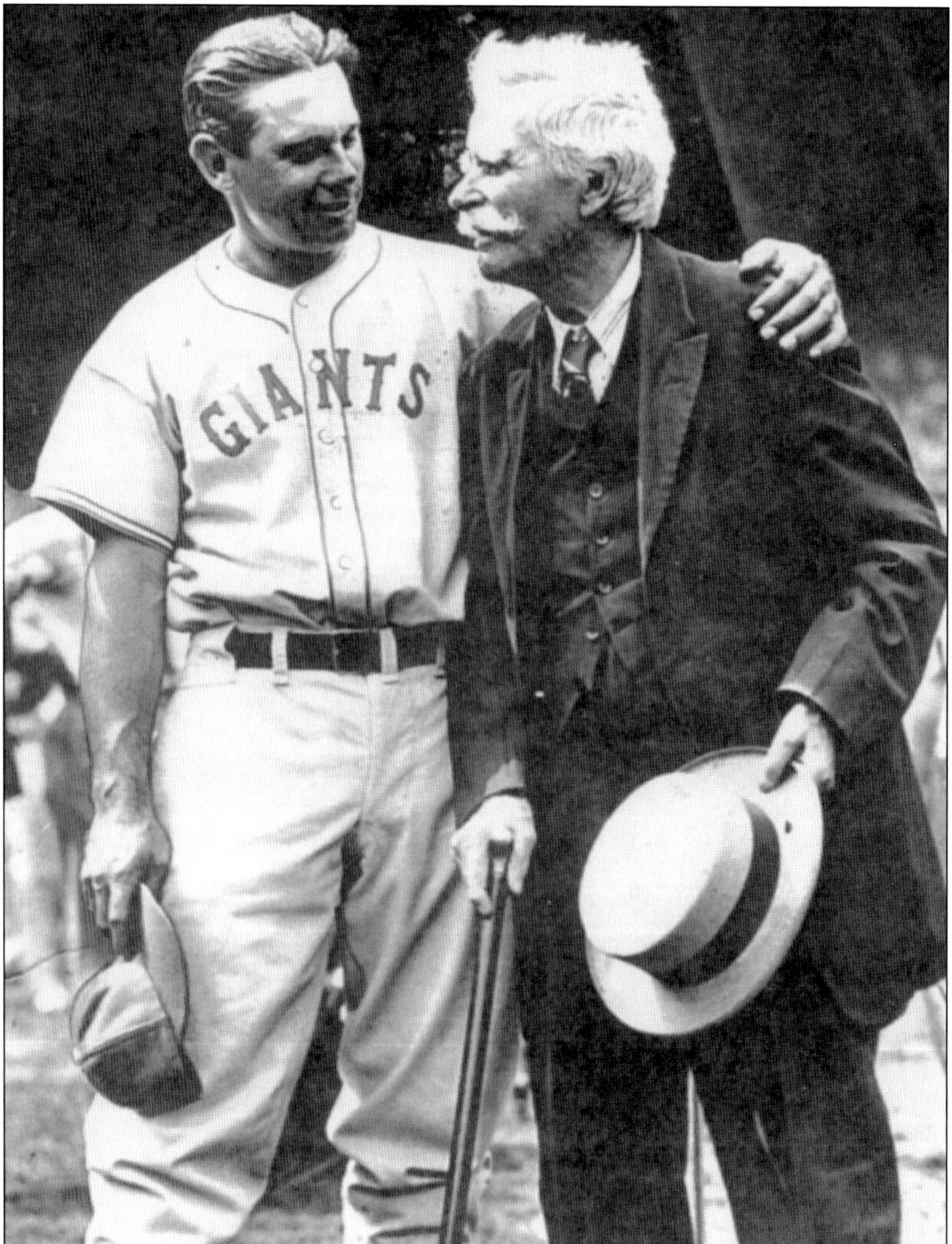

THE OLD AND THE NEW. Jim Mutrie and Bill Terry exchange pleasantries in 1933, on the 50th anniversary of the Giants' debut in the National League. The octogenarian Mutrie had been one of the Giants' original owners and the 34-year-old Terry was in his first full season as the club's manager.

One

My Strong Fellows

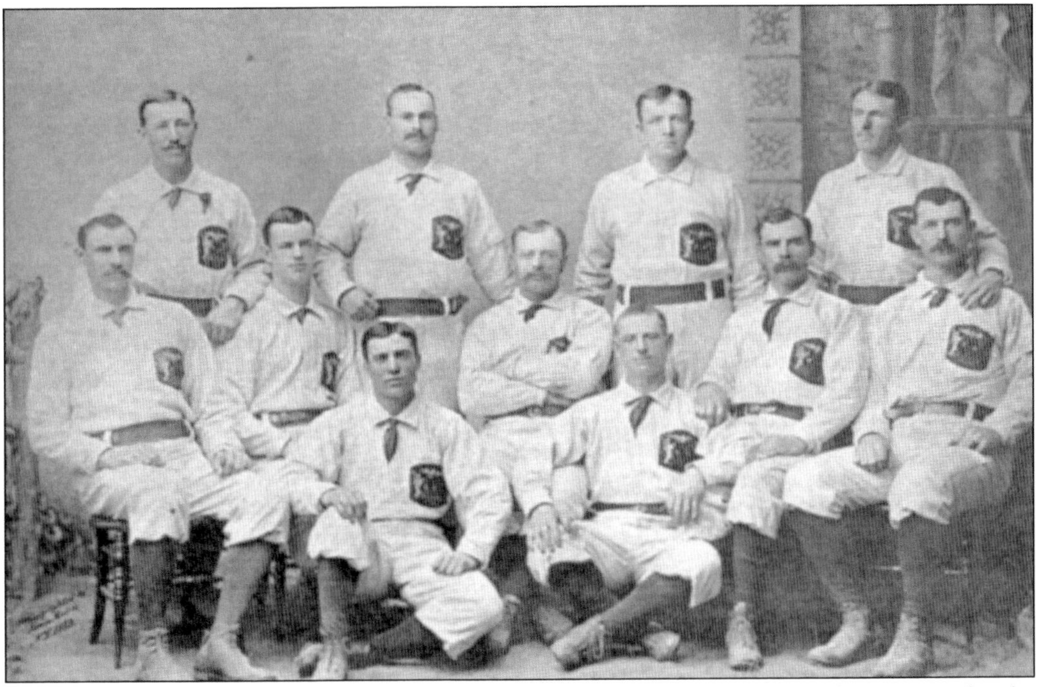

The 1883 Gothams. Seen here is the inaugural edition of the New York Giants, who for their first few seasons were known as the Gothams. Pictured, from left to right, are (front row) Mickey Welch and Dasher Troy; (middle row) Pat Gillespie, Tip O'Neill, John Clapp, Ed Caskin, and Roger Connor; (back row) Buck Ewing, Frank Hankinson, Mike Dorgan, and Monte Ward. New York opened up league play on May 1, 1883. A crowd of 15,000, including former President U.S. Grant, watched New York beat Boston, 7-5.

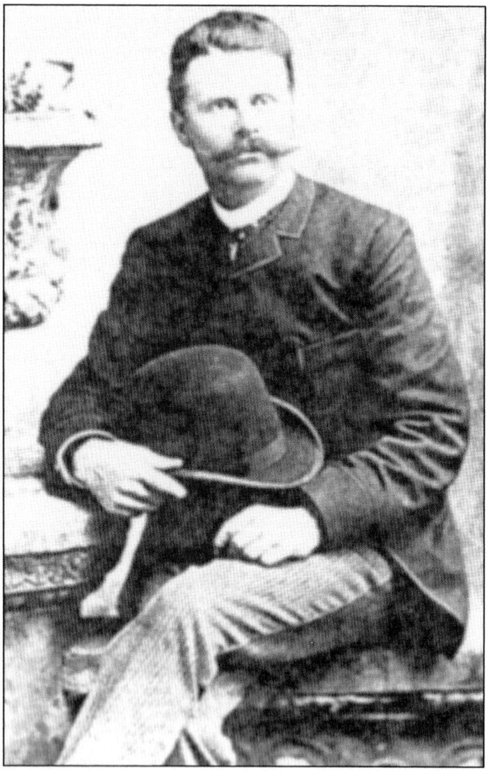

THE MAN WHO NAMED THE GIANTS. Sports promoter Jim Mutrie owned and managed New York entries in the National League and American Association, frequently upgrading the former with top-notch players from the latter. After his National League team finished a close second to Cap Anson's Chicago White Stockings in 1886, Mutrie exclaimed, "My big fellows! My giants!" The name stuck.

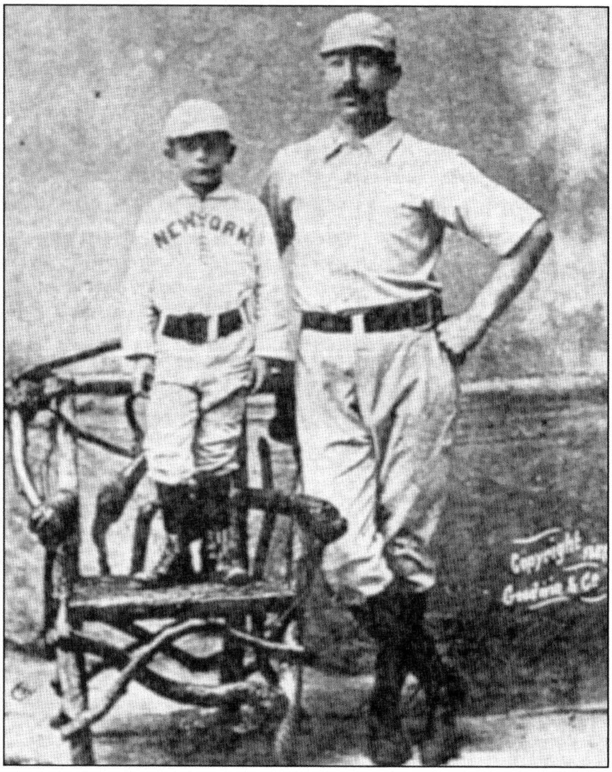

BUCK EWING. The first catcher to use a "pillow" glove was Buck Ewing, a future Hall of Famer widely regarded as one of the brainiest men in the game. Ewing was one of several players used to stock the Giants from the failed Troy franchise after the 1882 season. Ewing hit ten home runs for the sixth-place Giants in 1883, at the time a major league record. The versatile Ewing played all nine positions during his career and displayed surprising base running ability, stealing 53 bases in 1888, the season he batted lead-off for the Giants' first pennant winner.

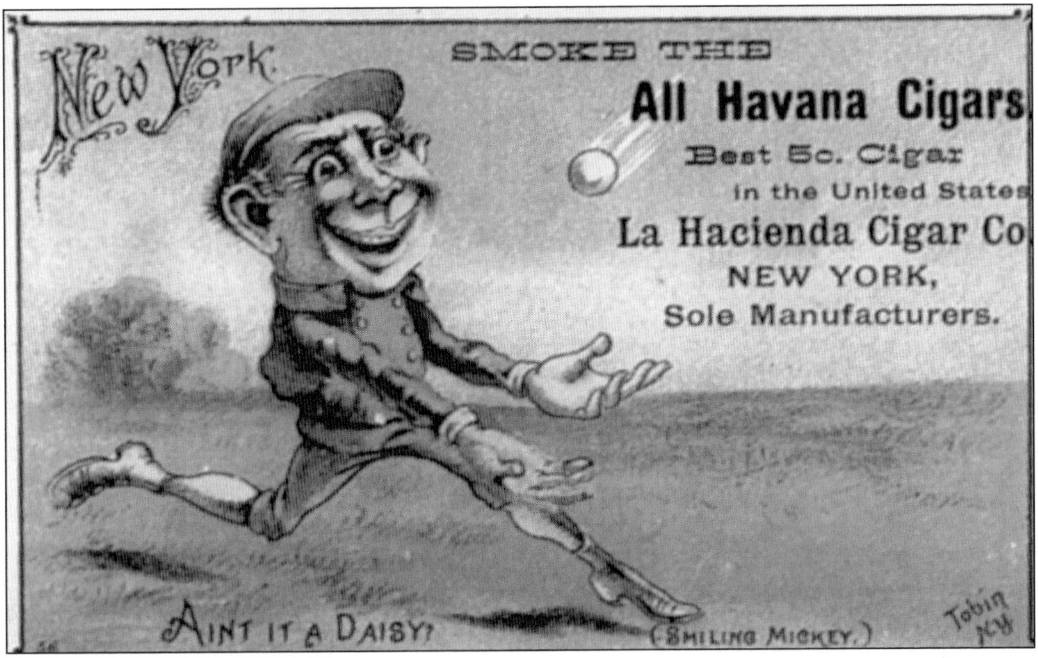

TOBACCO CARD, C.1887. The historic connection between nicotine and the national pastime was never stronger than in the 19th century, when most American males either chewed or smoked tobacco. In the 1880s, New York's La Hacienda Cigar Company issued colorful trade cards featuring several major league stars, including the Giants' Hall of Fame pitcher, "Smiling Mickey" Welch.

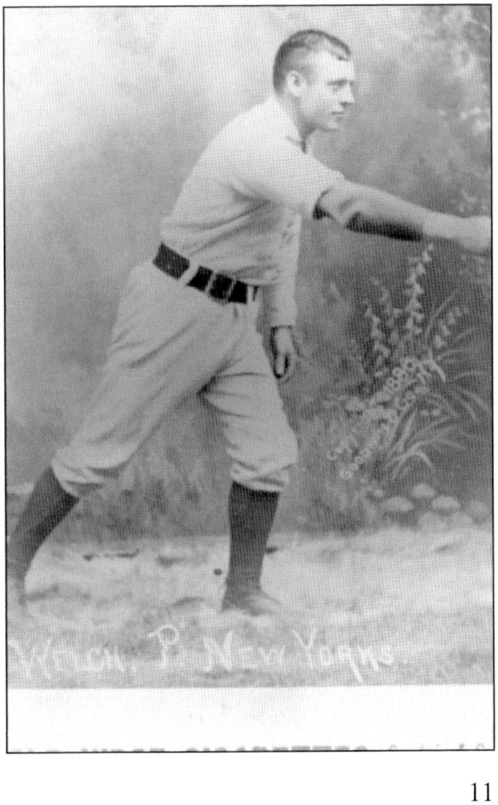

SMILING MICKEY. Good-humored Mickey Welch gave New York fans something to smile about, winning 311 games during a big-league career that stretched from 1880 to 1892. His ten years with the Giants included a 44-11 record in 1885, a season in which the diminutive Brooklyn native won 17 in a row. Welch, who once pitched 105 straight complete games, attributed his success to his favorite beer, for which he wrote the following jingle: "Pure elixer of malt and hops/Beats all the drugs and all the drops."

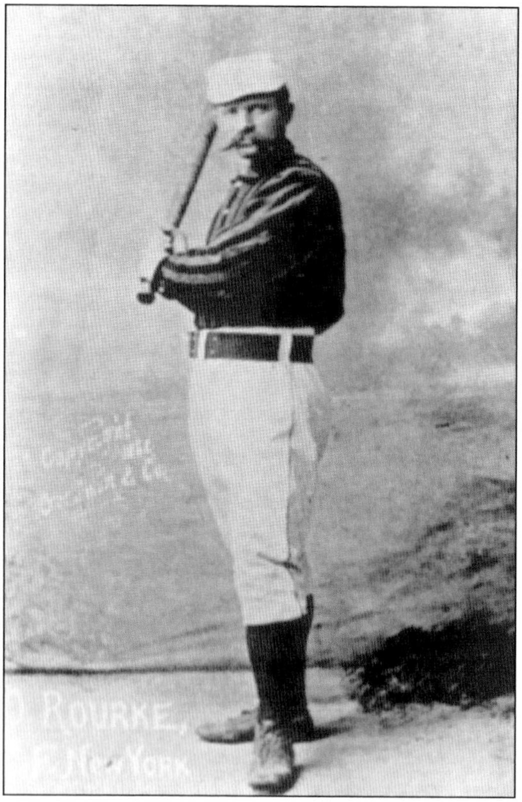

ORATOR O'ROURKE. Jim O'Rourke, the product of a poor Connecticut farm family, grew into one of baseball's great ambassadors during his half-century as player, activist, and executive. The eloquent O'Rourke had a law degree from Yale and was a major contributor to New York's 1888–89 pennant winners. Principally an outfielder, he batted .310 during his Hall of Fame career, which included one last game in 1904 as a 52-year-old catcher for John McGraw's Giants.

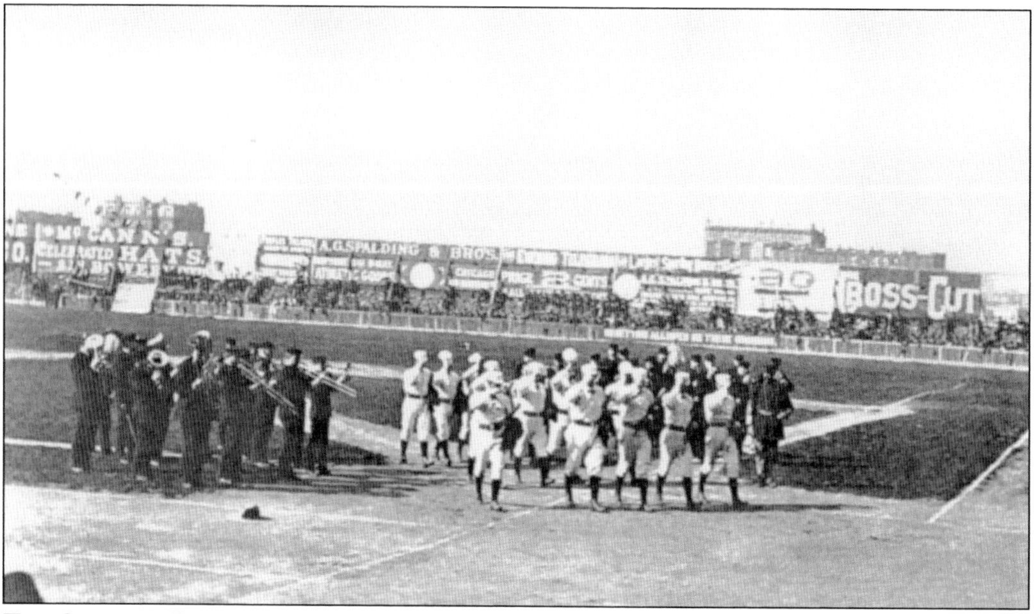

THE ORIGINAL POLO GROUNDS, 1886. Between 1883 and 1888 the Giants played home games at a former polo grounds at 110th Street between Fifth and Sixth Avenues. The festivities at the 1886 opener included the Giants, accompanied by Cappa's Seventh Regiment Band, marching from the clubhouse to home plate.

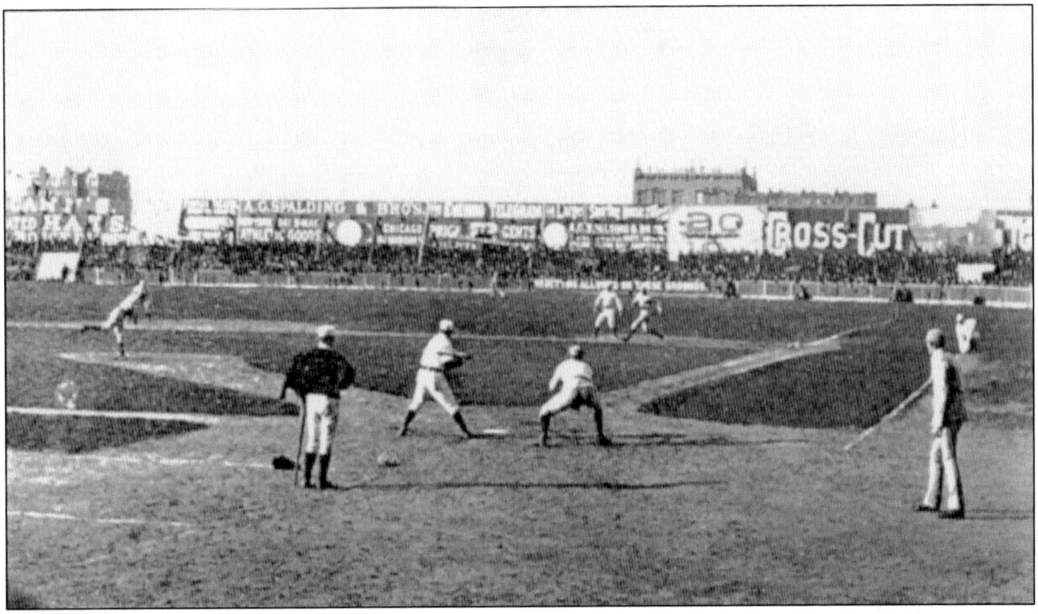

OPENING DAY, 1886. Two more views depict the Giants' home opener on April 29, 1886. Above, an action shot shows Mickey Welch batting against Boston's Hoss Radbourn. Below, players from both sides are assembled for the traditional team photo. The man in the top hat is Jim Mutrie, who was known to climb into the Polo Grounds stands and whip up cheers for the home nine.

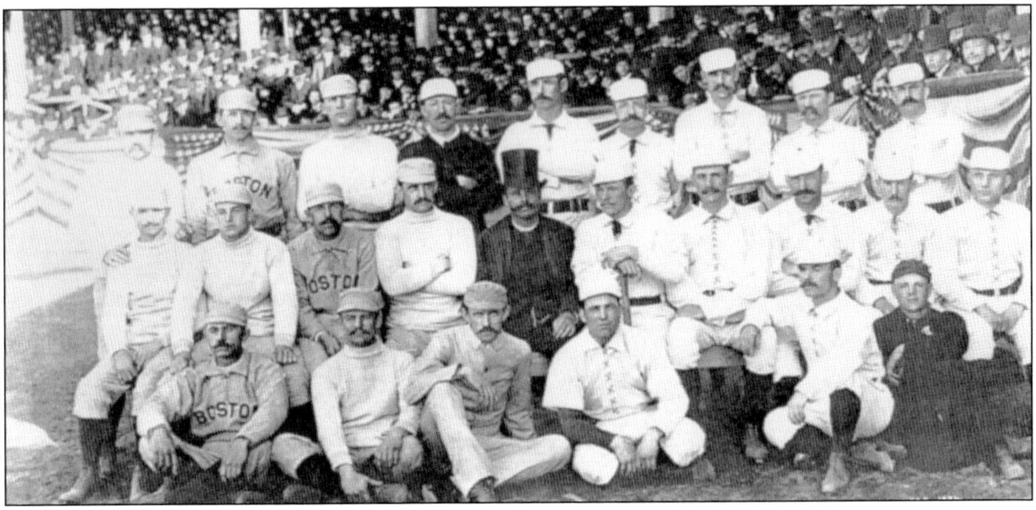

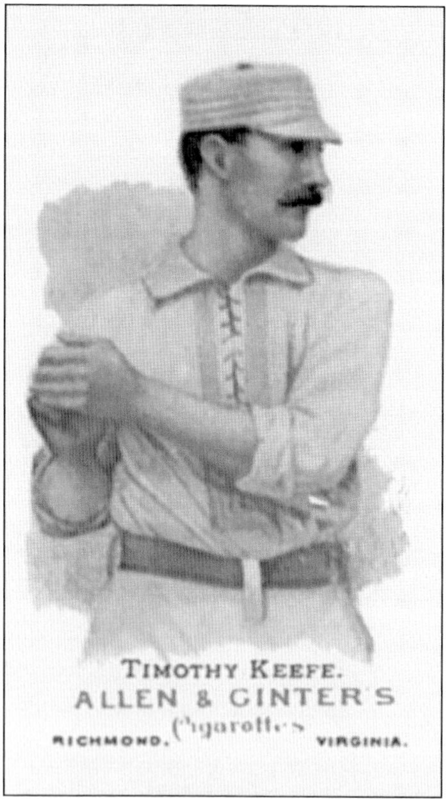

KEEFE WAS A KEEPER. Tim Keefe was one of several players Jim Mutrie transferred from his American Association team, the Metropolitans, to the Giants. After winning a collective 78 games in two seasons for the Metropolitans, Keefe notched 32 victories in 1885 for the Giants, leading the league with a 1.58 earned run average. Using an underhanded delivery and pioneering the use of the change-up, Keefe led the loop with 42 wins in 1886 and 35 wins, 1.74 ERA, and 333 strikeouts in 1888. Keefe wrapped up his 14-year Hall of Fame career in Philadelphia, retiring in 1893 with 344 lifetime wins.

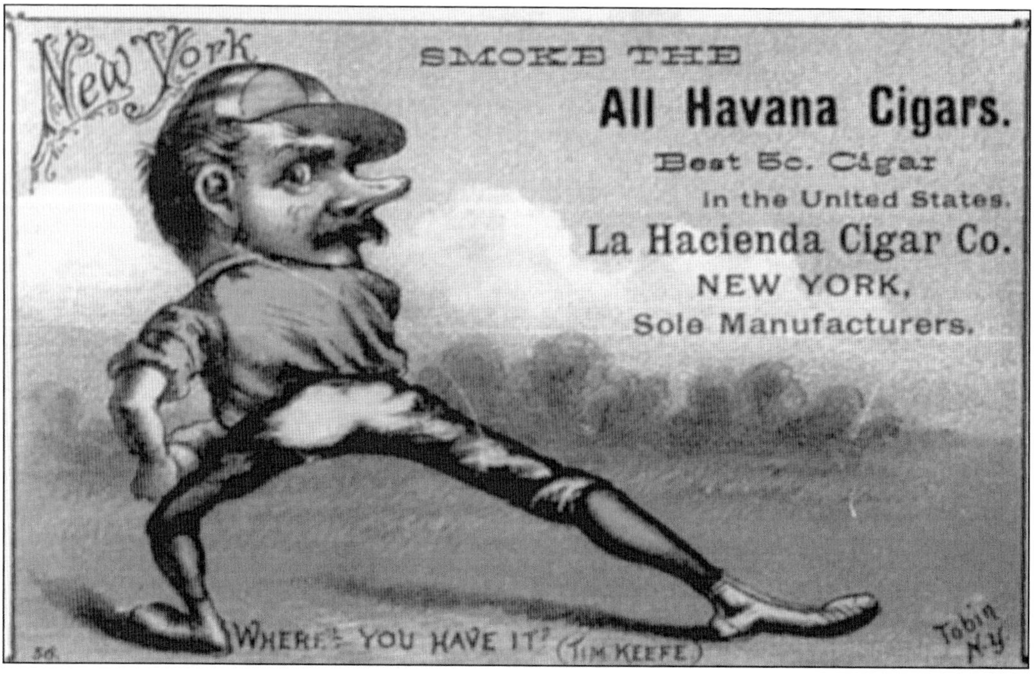

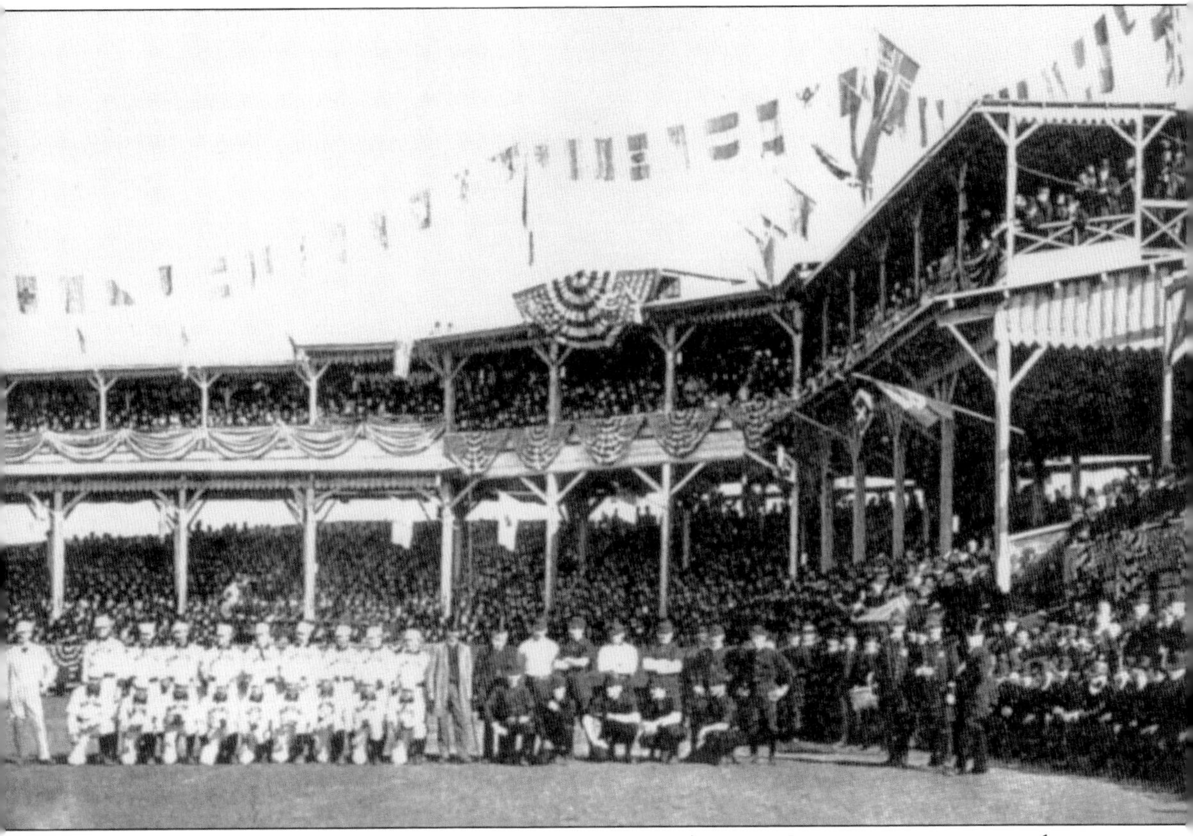

THE 1888 OPENER. Two traditional rivals, the Giants and Boston Beaneaters, are pictured at the flag-bedecked Polo Grounds before the start of the 1888 home opener. The Giants finished 84-47 to win their first flag that summer, then defeated St. Louis of the American Association, six games to four, in the ensuing "world's series" between the two leagues. The Giants repeated as champs in 1889, finishing 83-43 and then beating Brooklyn, six games to three, in the post-season tournament.

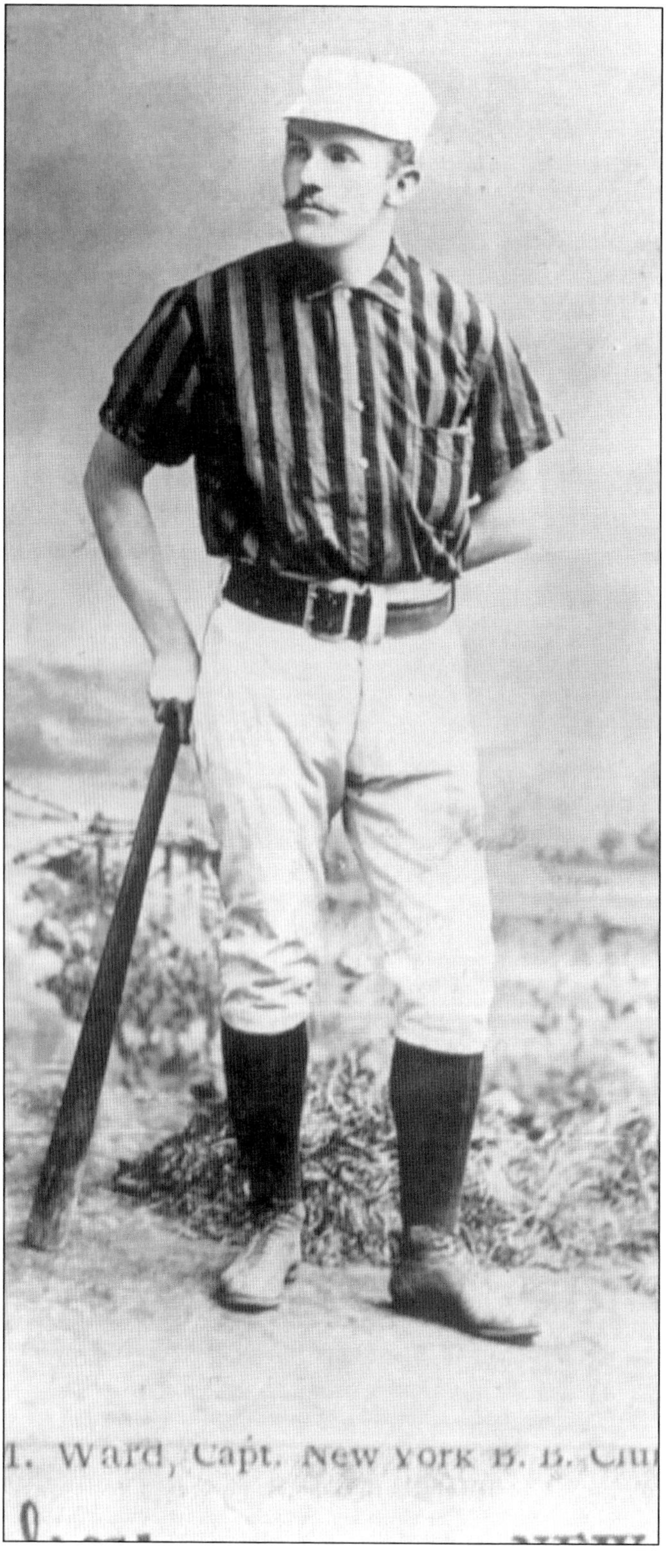

MONTE WARD. John Montgomery Ward was one of baseball's true pioneers, a versatile and controversial figure whose place in the Hall of Fame wasn't secured until 1964, 39 years after his death. Born into a well-to-do Pennsylvania family, Ward was an outstanding young pitcher for Providence, winning 158 big-league games (including a perfect game) until an arm injury forced him to switch to shortstop. In 1887 he batted .338 and led the league in stolen bases while leading the Giants to the first of two championships. The first player to openly challenge baseball's reserve clause, he formed the Players League in 1890, taking 100 of the National League's top players with him. Ward, who had a law degree from Columbia, successfully defended himself in court when the Giants issued an injunction against his leaving. The upstart league collapsed after a year and Ward ultimately rejoined the Giants, playing and managing them to a Temple Cup victory in 1894. Only 34, he then retired from baseball to open a successful law practice.

SPEEDBALL KING. Amos Rusie joined the Giants in 1890. The "Hoosier Thunderbolt" won 239 games in eight seasons with New York and led the loop in strikeouts five times. In one three-year period he averaged 527 innings and 328 strikeouts, Hall of Fame numbers that failed to impress Giants owner Andrew Freedman. When Freedman fined the ace right-hander $200 for "indifferent work" on the final day of the 1895 season, the protesting Rusie sat out the entire 1896 season. Finally, the league made up the money Rusie had lost during his holdout. In 1899 Freedman traded him to Cincinnati for an unknown pitcher named Christy Mathewson.

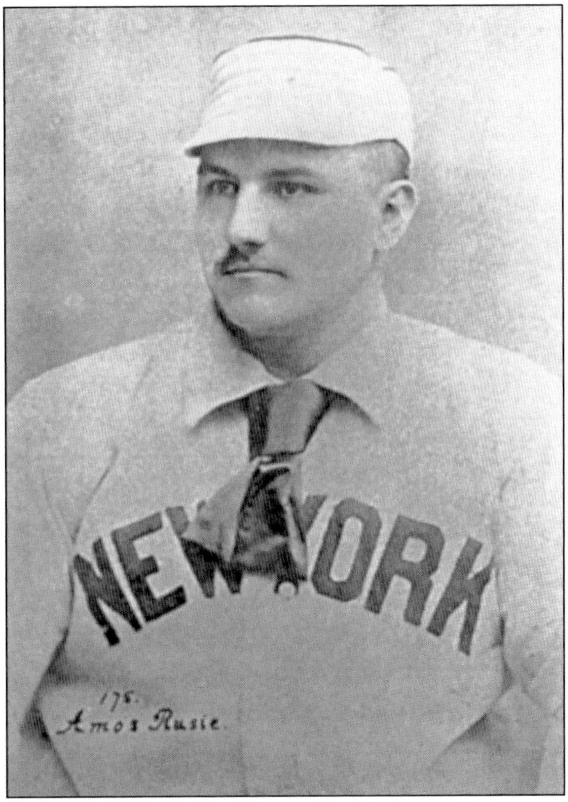

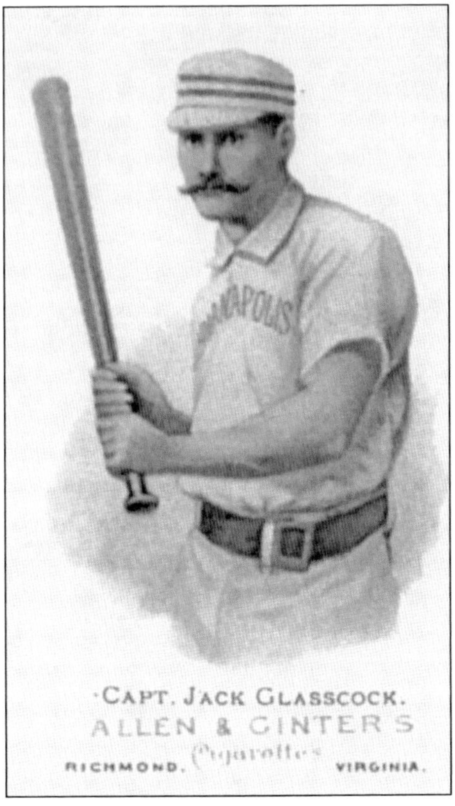

JACK GLASSCOCK. Second baseman Jack Glasscock was obtained from Indianapolis in 1890 and won the batting title with a .336 average. He was one of the few bright spots as the Giants finished sixth.

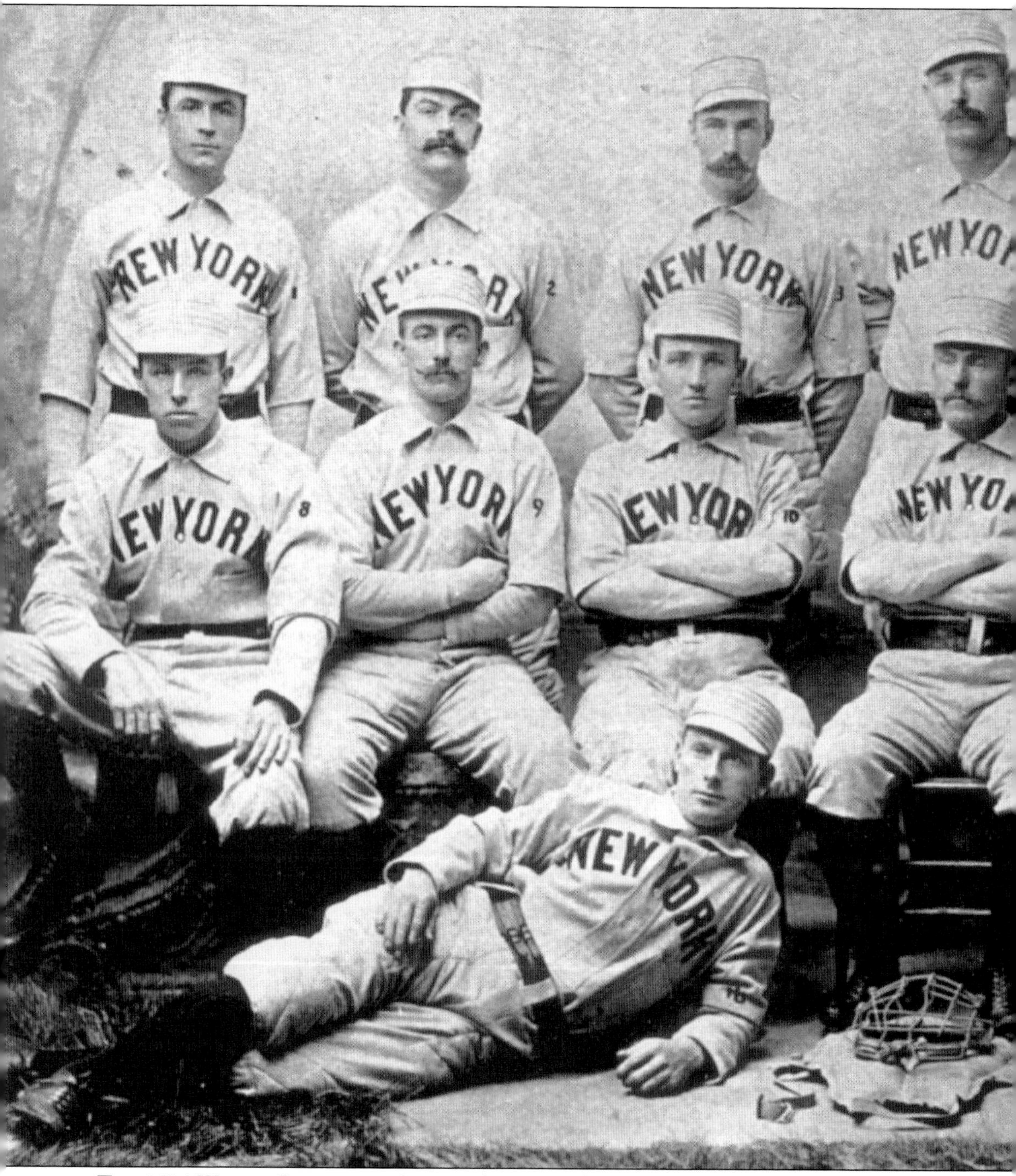

THE 1894 WORLD CHAMPIONS. In 1894 the Giants finished second in the National League but still won the world championship, defeating first-place Baltimore in a post-season tournament. The roster included, from left to right, (front row) James Stafford and Yale Murphy; (middle row) W.H. Clark, Lester German, John J. Doyle, Monte Ward, Mike Tiernan, George S. Davis, W.B. Fuller, and Edward Burke; (back row) Park Wilson, Charles Farrell, George Van Haltren, Roger Connor, Jouett Meekin, Huyler Westervelt, and Amos Rusie. The hulking Connor

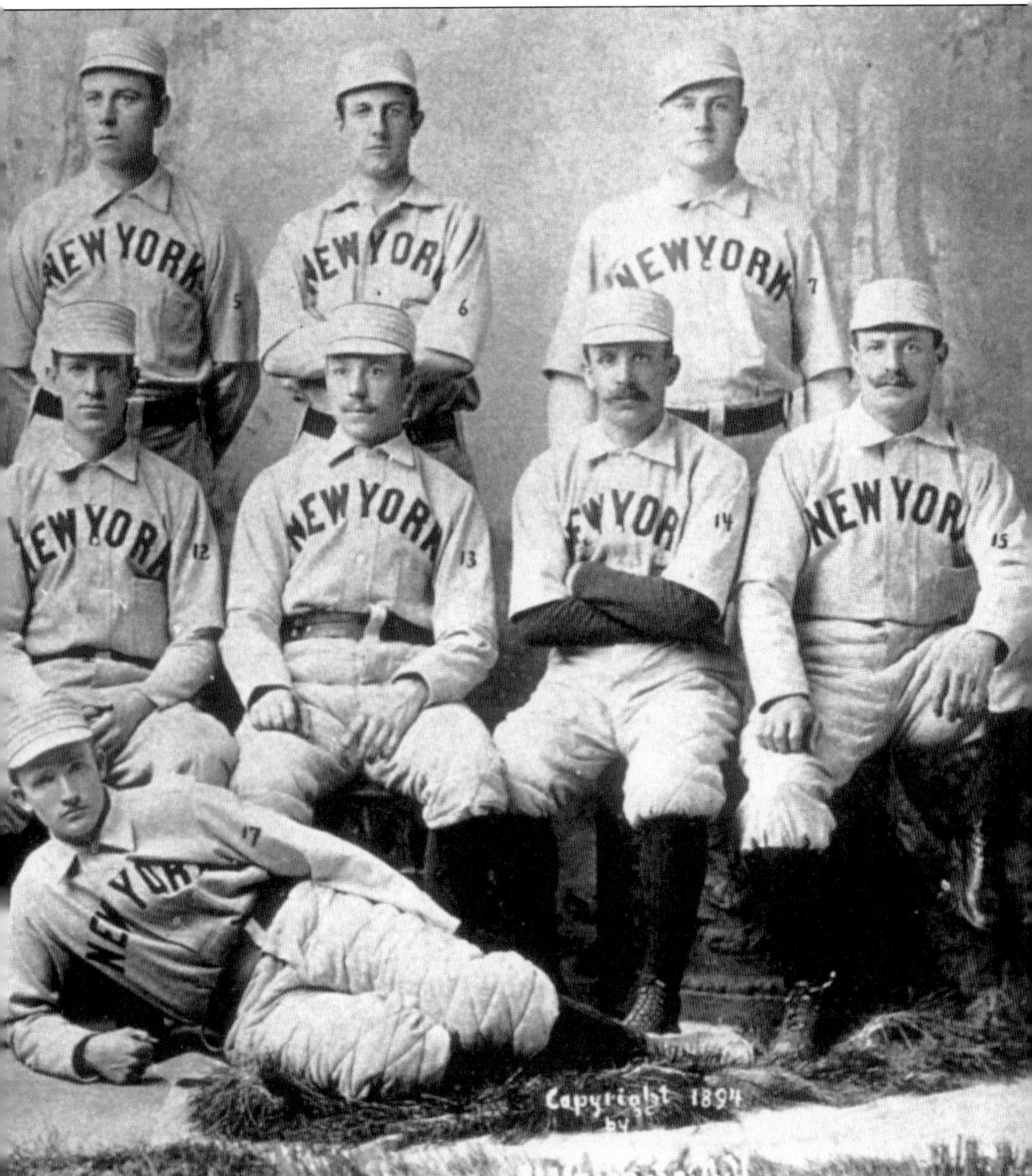

deserves special mention. Swinging from the left side of the plate, the 6-foot-3, 210-pound first baseman was the premier long-ball hitter of the 19th century. Until Babe Ruth came along a generation later, the muscular, mustached Connor held the record for most career home runs with 136. Connor played for the Giants in 10 of his 18 big-league seasons and was voted into the Hall of Fame in 1976.

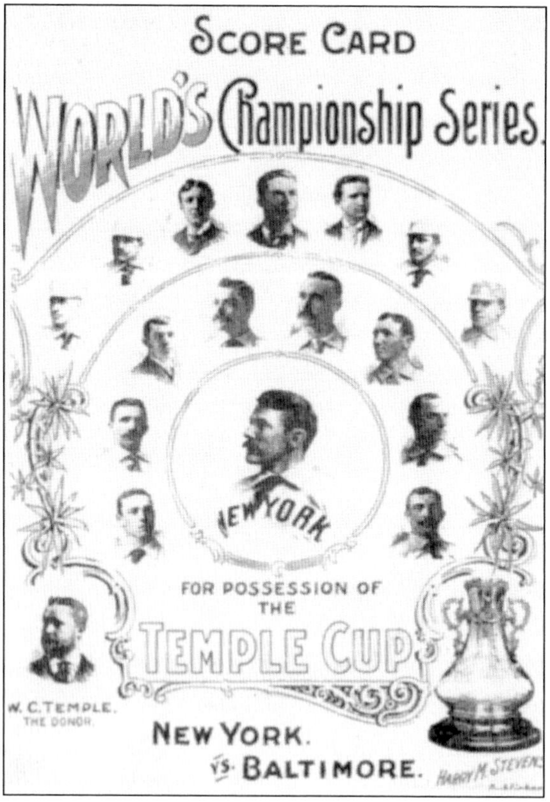

1894 TEMPLE CUP PROGRAM. Beginning in 1894, the first- and second-place finishers in the National League vied in a post-season tournament for the Temple Cup, a trophy put up by Pittsburgh sportsman William C. Temple. The Giants won the first Temple Cup, sweeping the heavily favored Baltimore Orioles in four straight games. The star of the series was Jouett Meekin, who pitched two complete-game victories and batted .556.

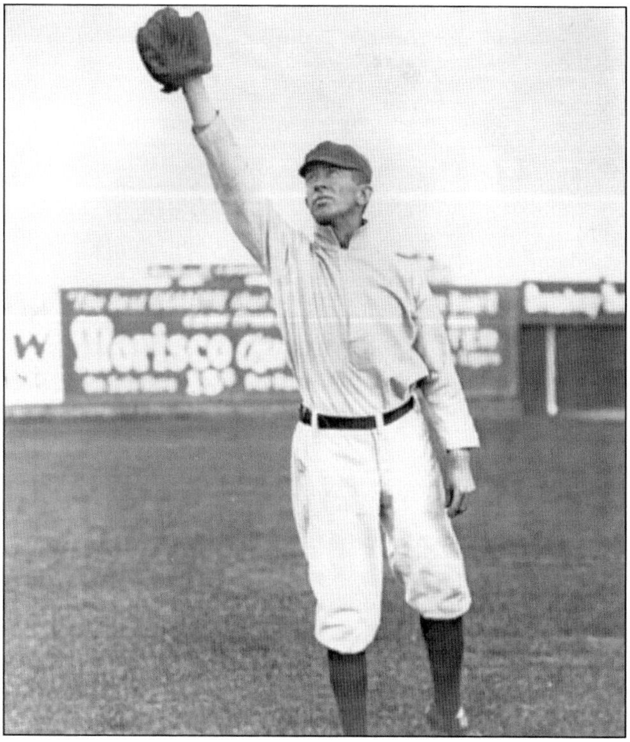

WEE WILLIE KEELER. The proponent of "hitting 'em where they ain't," outfielder Willie Keeler played two abbreviated seasons for the Giants before joining the Baltimore Orioles in 1894, where he became famous. One of his teammates was a rambunctious third baseman named John McGraw. In 1910, McGraw, now manager of the Giants, brought Keeler back to the Polo Grounds for a swan song. There the 38-year-old Keeler gathered the final three base hits of his Hall of Fame career.

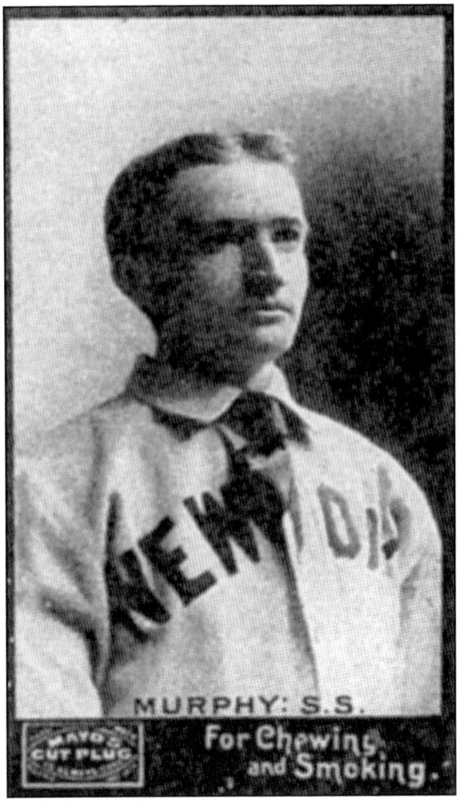

COVER BOY. During the mid 1890s the face of Giants infielder Yale Murphy graced tobacco cards and magazine covers, though such exposure probably owed more to playing in the media capital of the United States than to anything Murphy—a career .239 hitter with no home runs—accomplished on the field.

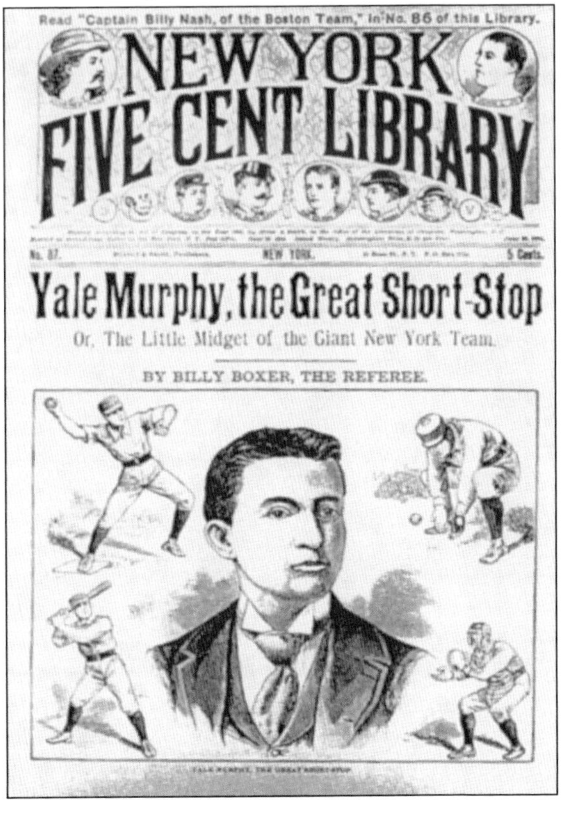

Read "Captain Billy Nash, of the Boston Team," in No. 86 of this Library.

NEW YORK FIVE CENT LIBRARY

No. 87. NEW YORK. 5 Cents.

Yale Murphy, the Great Short-Stop

Or, The Little Midget of the Giant New York Team.

BY BILLY BOXER, THE REFEREE.

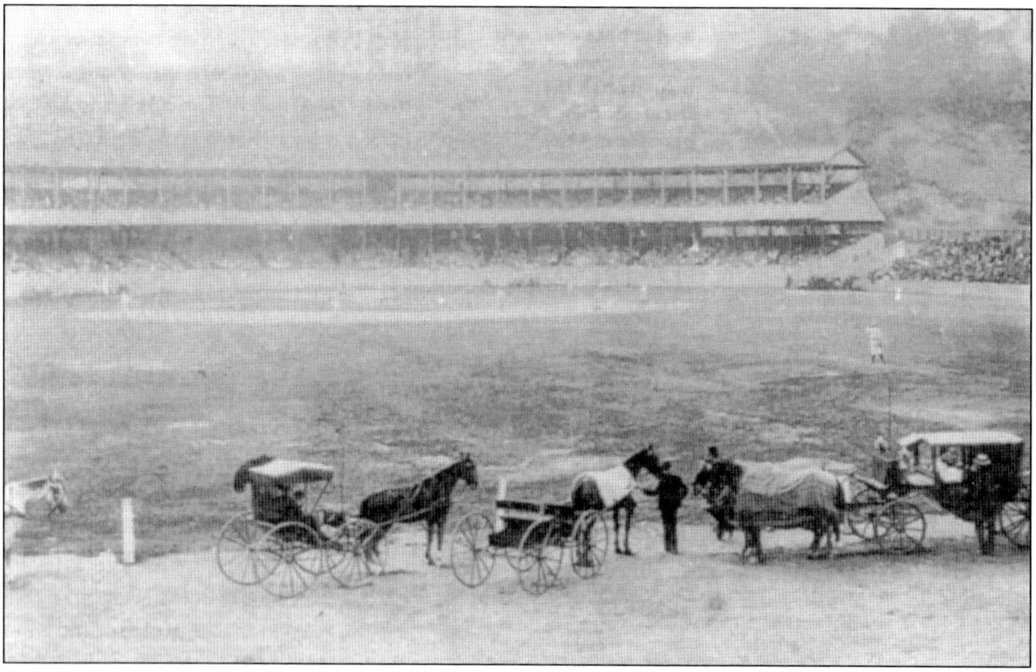

THE PLACE TO BE. Beginning in 1891, the Giants played at a wooden park erected on a grassy meadow between 157th and 159th Streets in Upper Manhattan. Although polo was never actually played there, it was called the Polo Grounds. The importance of horses in everyday life during the 1890s can be gleaned from the top photo of carriages watching a game from deep center field and from the cardboard cutout of a horse-drawn trolley car. Note the advertisements for that afternoon's game at the Polo Grounds.

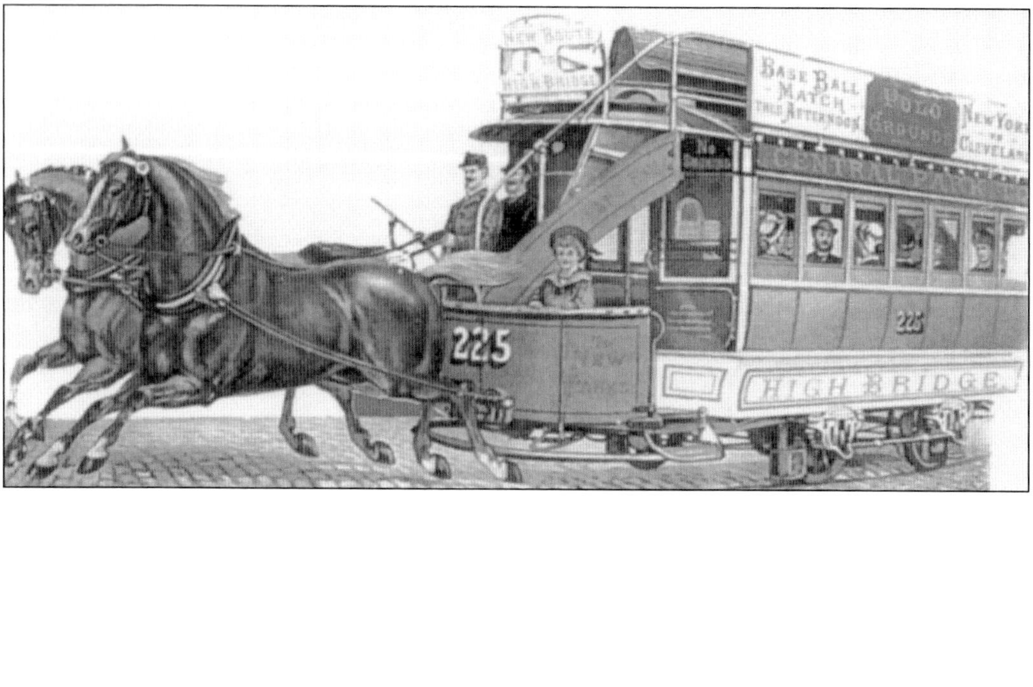

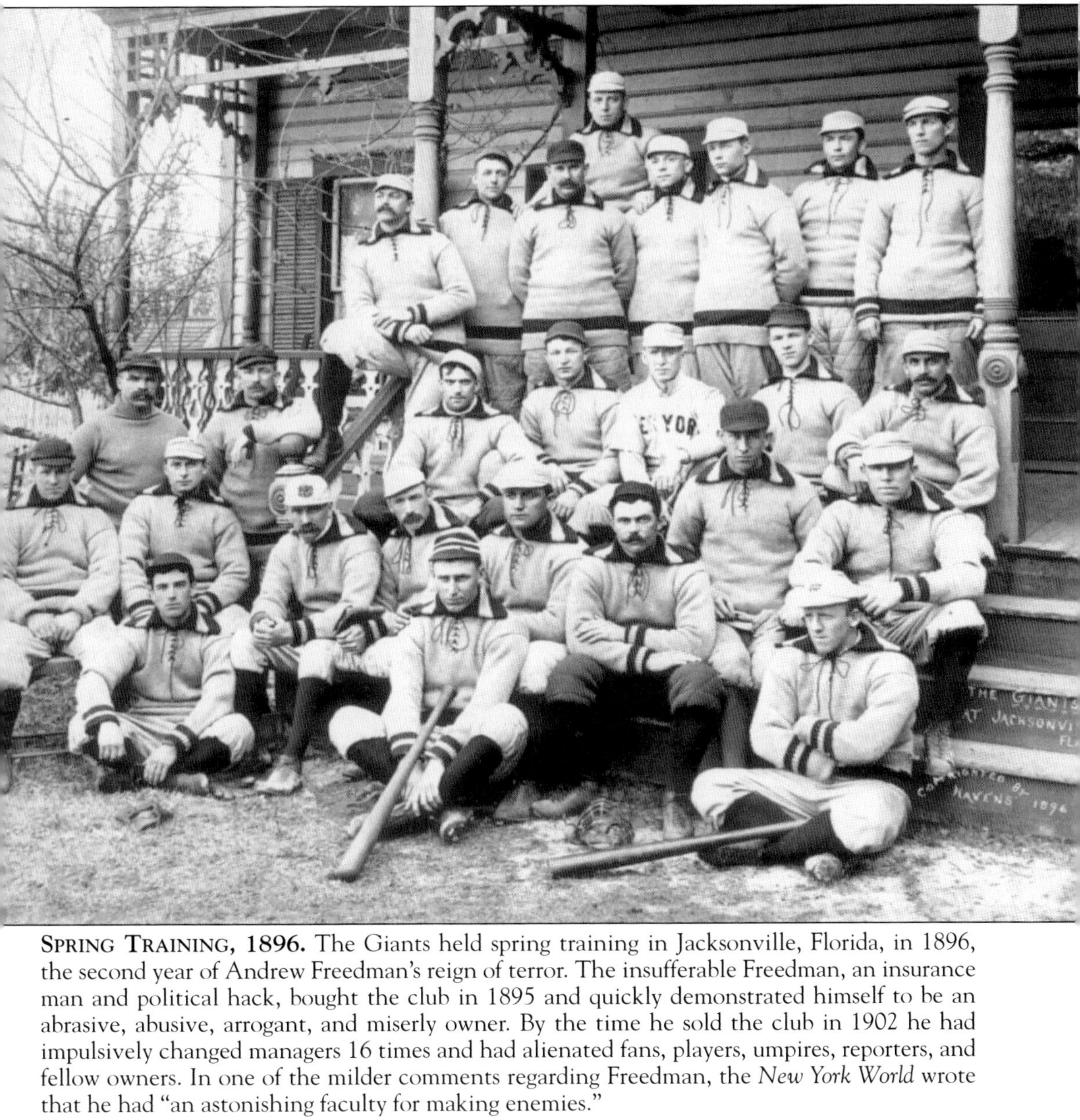

SPRING TRAINING, 1896. The Giants held spring training in Jacksonville, Florida, in 1896, the second year of Andrew Freedman's reign of terror. The insufferable Freedman, an insurance man and political hack, bought the club in 1895 and quickly demonstrated himself to be an abrasive, abusive, arrogant, and miserly owner. By the time he sold the club in 1902 he had impulsively changed managers 16 times and had alienated fans, players, umpires, reporters, and fellow owners. In one of the milder comments regarding Freedman, the *New York World* wrote that he had "an astonishing faculty for making enemies."

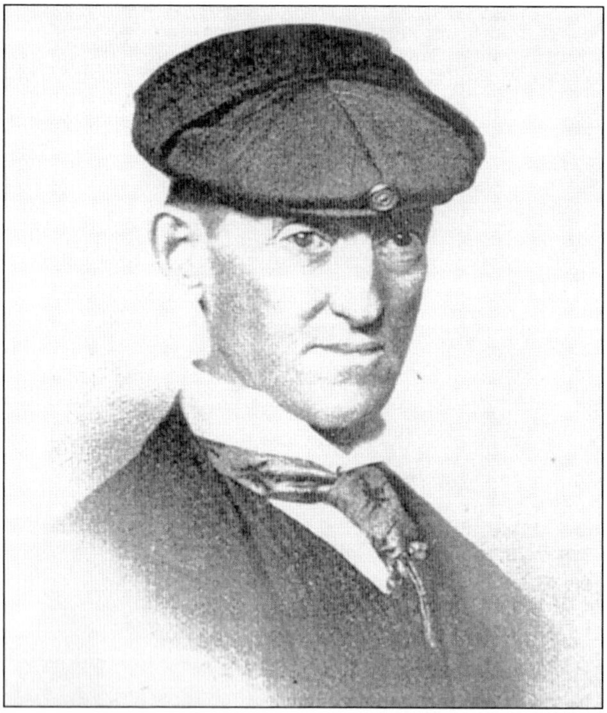

BRUSH AND MCGRAW. After Andrew Freedman had succeeded in running the once-proud Giants franchise into the ground, a pair of saviors appeared in 1902. That year partner John T. Brush, who also had a controlling interest in the Cincinnati Reds, took over the Giants. In the bottom photograph Brush sits in an automobile alongside John McGraw, the brash 29-year-old infielder he imported from Baltimore to breathe life into the moribund team. One of McGraw's first acts was to release nine Giants players over Freedman's protests. Despite McGraw's presence, the Giants finished last in 1902. "But look out for us next year," he warned.

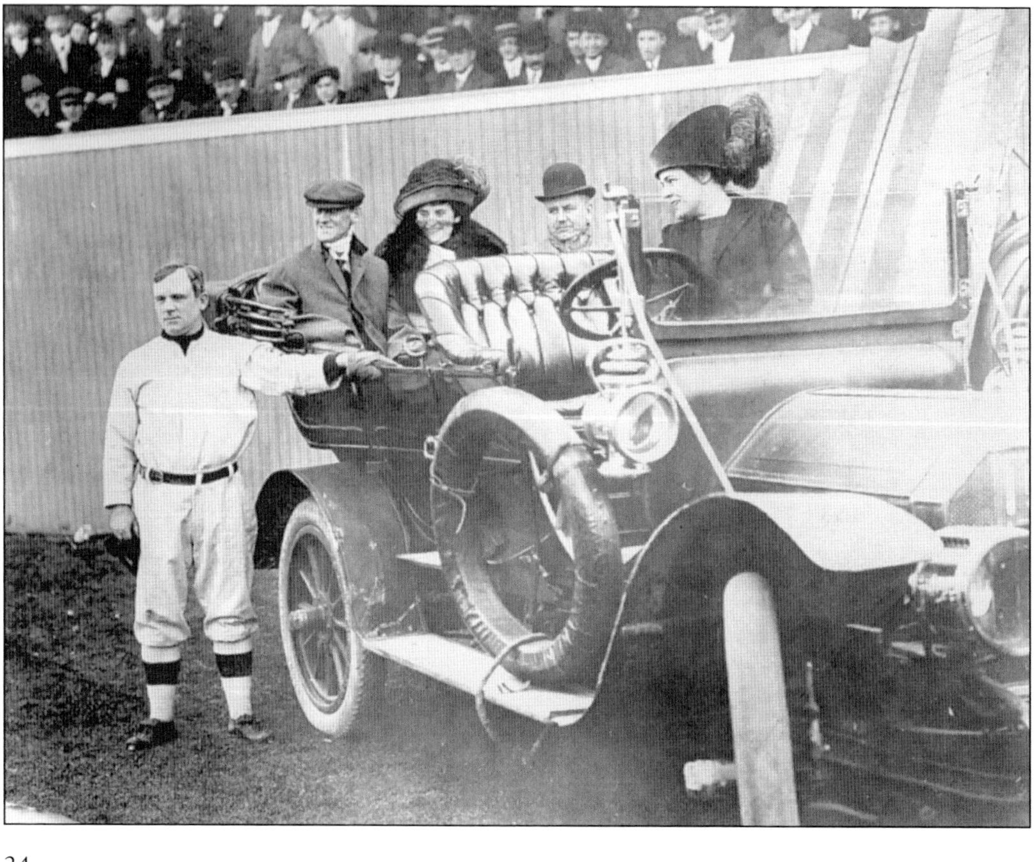

Two

IT'S GREAT TO BE YOUNG AND A GIANT

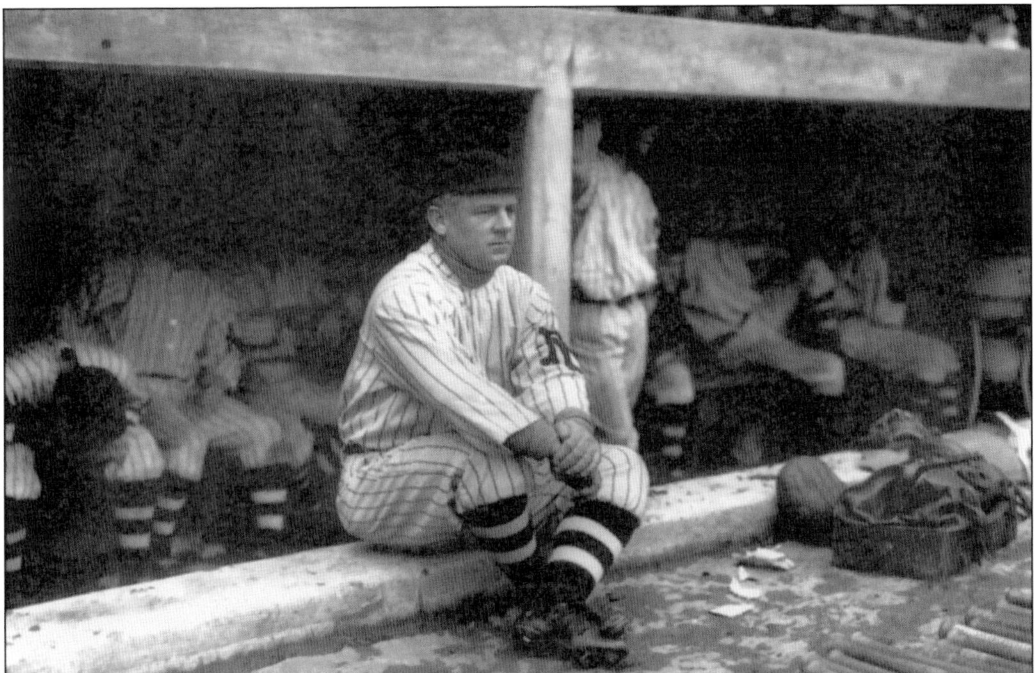

JOHN MCGRAW IN 1912. John J. McGraw managed the Giants from 1902 to 1932. Two-fisted, acid-tongued, and roundly reviled, McGraw "was wise enough to realize that hate is as strong an attraction as love," observed one sportswriter. Such hate made the Giants as big a draw on the road as at home. "His very walk across the field in a hostile town is a challenge to the multitudes," wrote Grantland Rice.

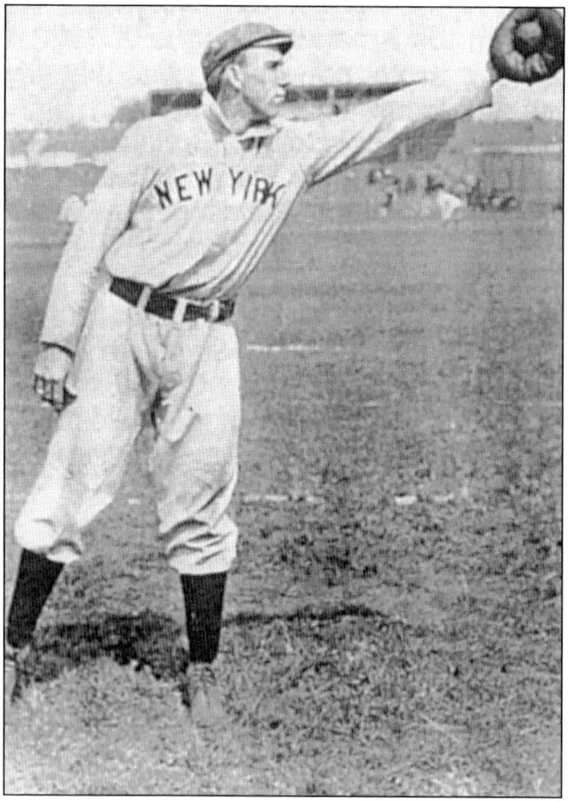

THE TRAGIC DAN MCGANN. McGraw's early Giants teams fielded several players acquired from his former club, Baltimore, including Dan McGann. The first baseman served as captain before being traded to Boston after the 1907 season. One December day in 1910, McGann, evidently upset over his brother's suicide, put a bullet through his heart.

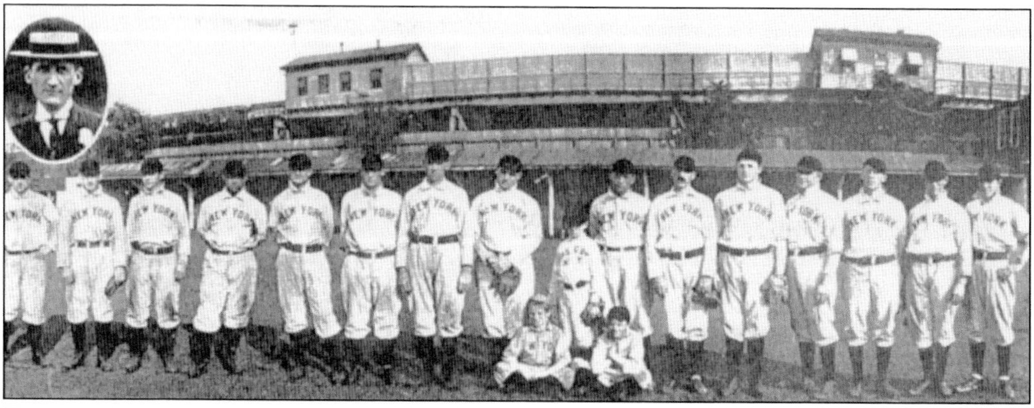

THE 1903 GIANTS. New York improved to second place in 1903, McGraw's first full season at the Polo Grounds. A leg injury limited McGraw, a .334 lifetime hitter, to just 12 games and prevented him from becoming the field leader he had hoped to become in New York. It didn't matter, for he quickly was recognized as being equally brilliant on the bench. "The Giants are a second-division team with a first-division manager," Chicago second baseman Johnny Evers once said. "Without McGraw they wouldn't be heard of."

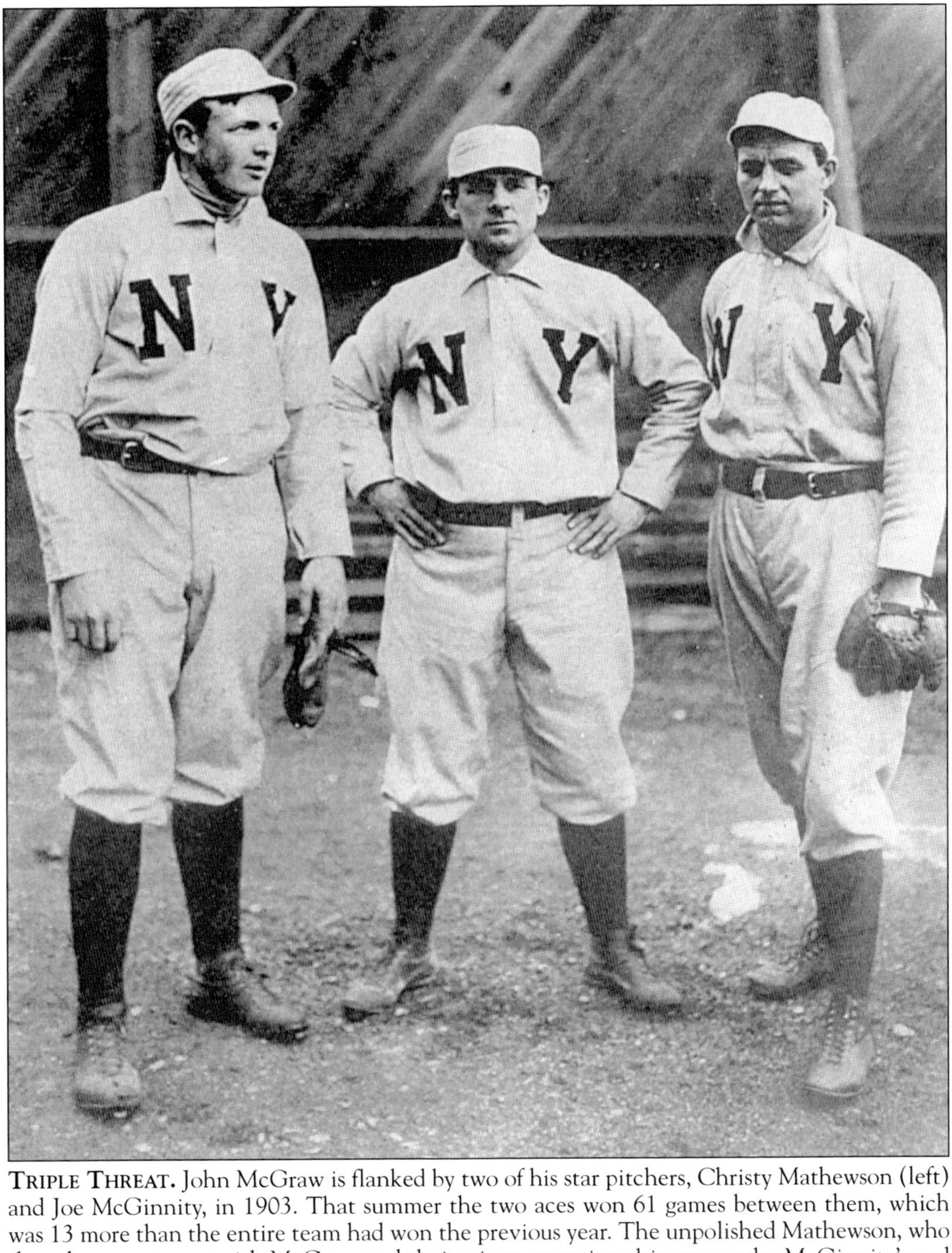

TRIPLE THREAT. John McGraw is flanked by two of his star pitchers, Christy Mathewson (left) and Joe McGinnity, in 1903. That summer the two aces won 61 games between them, which was 13 more than the entire team had won the previous year. The unpolished Mathewson, who shared an apartment with McGraw and their wives, came into his own under McGinnity's and McGraw's tutelage. He learned to pace himself, reserving that little extra for tight, late-game situations. He called it "pitching in a pinch."

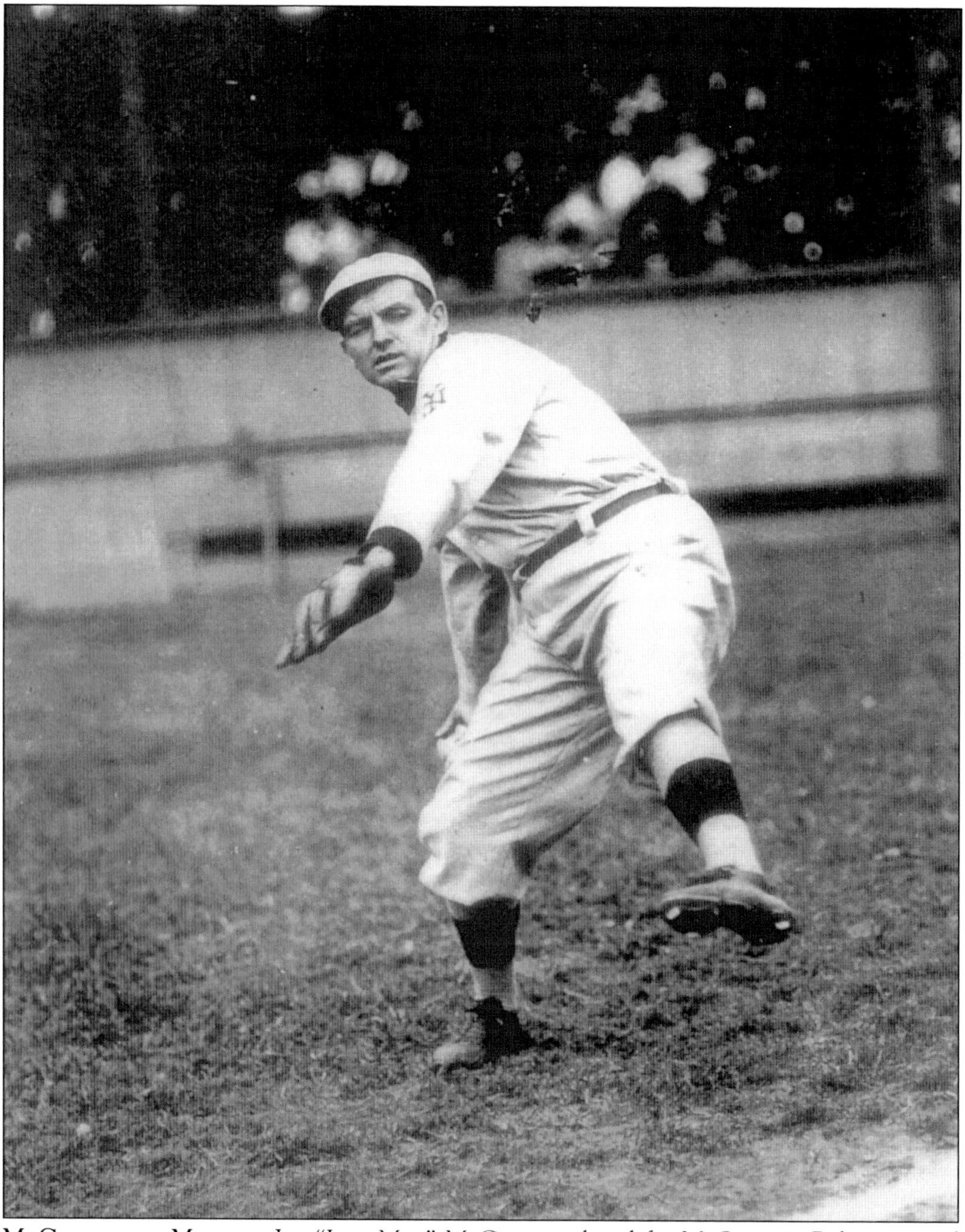

McGinnity in Motion. Joe "Iron Man" McGinnity played for McGraw in Baltimore and Brooklyn before both found a home at the Polo Grounds in 1902. The following season he pitched and won both ends of a doubleheader three times, an exhibition of durability that could be attributed to an underhand delivery that reduced the stress on his arm. McGinnity, elected to Cooperstown in 1946, won 247 games in the majors and was still pitching minor-league ball when he was 54.

DUMMY TAYLOR. On July 23, 1902, Luther "Dummy" Taylor beat Brooklyn, 4-1, to hand John McGraw the first of his 2,658 regular-season managerial wins with the Giants. The entire team learned sign language to please Taylor, a deaf mute who "took it as an affront if you didn't learn to converse with him," remembered Fred Snodgrass. "If we went to the vaudeville show, he wanted to know what the joke was, and somebody had to tell him. So we all learned."

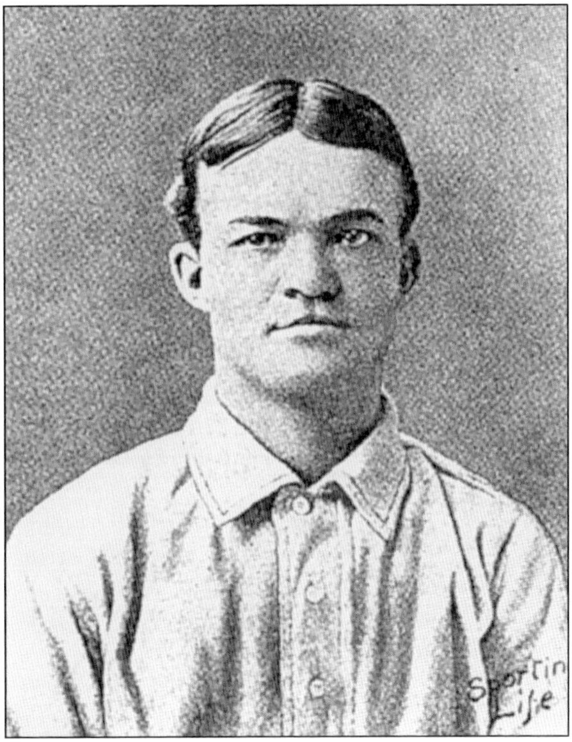

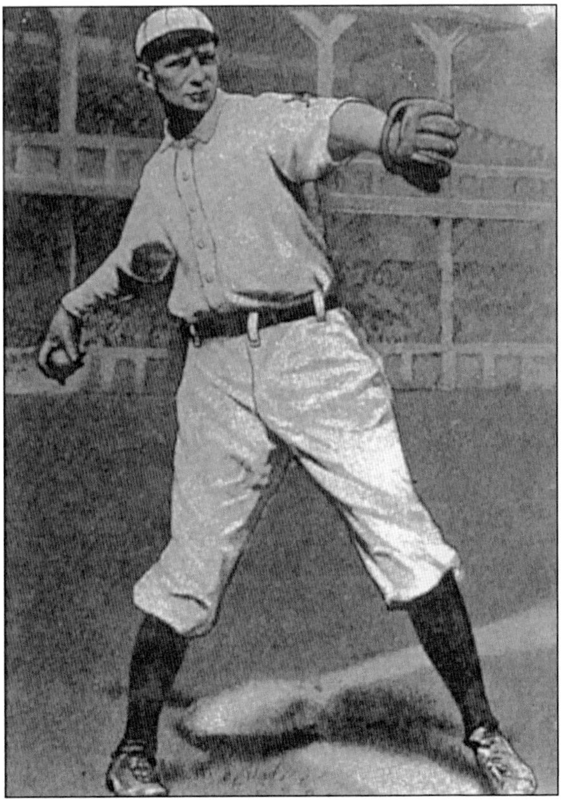

MCGRAW'S KIND OF GUY. Art Devlin, who attended Georgetown University before coming to the Giants in 1904, led the league with 59 steals in 1905, one of the few times the slim third baseman stood out statistically. Not that the aggressive and baseball-savvy Devlin cared about numbers—he was only concerned with winning, which made him one of McGraw's favorites.

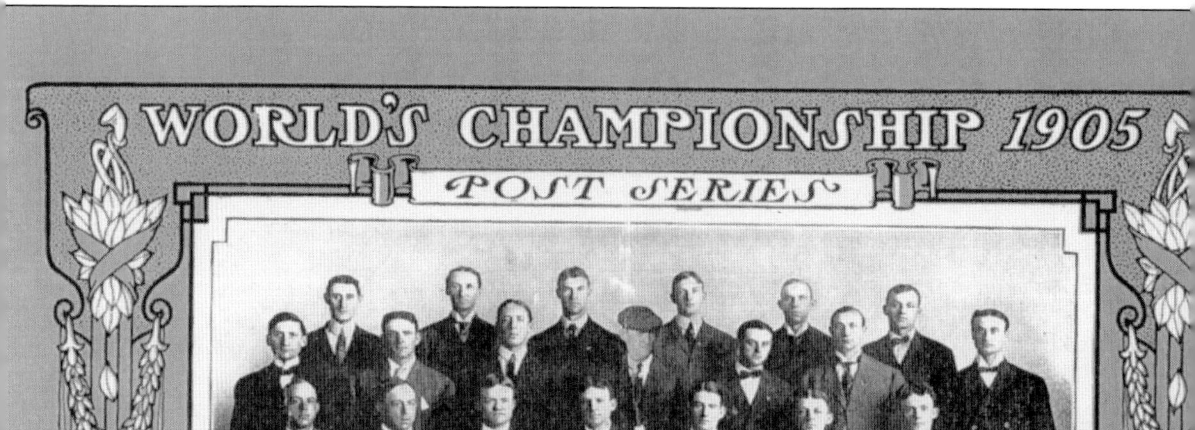

THE 1904–05 CHAMPIONS. The program from the 1905 World Series featured a photograph of the 1904–05 National League champions on the cover. In 1904 the Giants won the pennant, their first of ten under McGraw, with a record of 106-47. But because of lingering bad blood between the American League and Giants owner John Brush, New York refused to play the Boston Pilgrims in the World Series that October. In 1905 the Giants repeated as National League champs with a 105-48 record. This time, because of a formal agreement that created the World Series as a permanent and official post-season tournament between the two rival circuits, McGraw's Giants played the Philadelphia Athletics.

RED AMES, C.1905. Leon "Red" Ames broke in with the Giants in 1903 and two years later contributed 22 victories to McGraw's pennant winners. Between 1905 and 1907 he had the highest strikeout percentage in the National League.

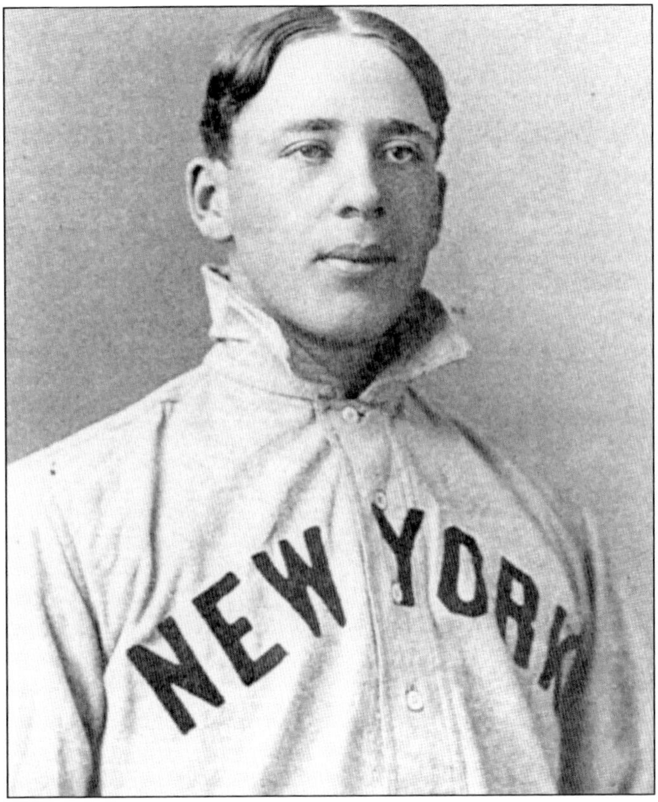

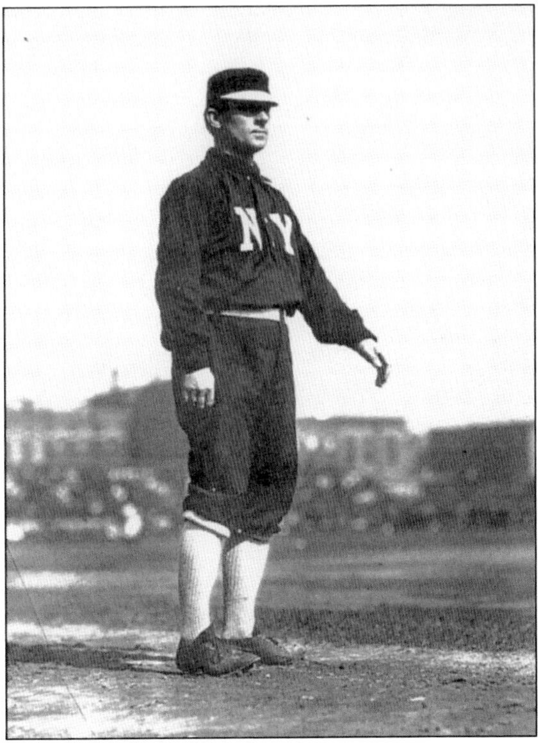

THE MAN IN BLACK. John McGraw dressed his team in spiffy black uniforms for the 1905 World Series, which opened October 9th in Philadelphia. "I will never forget the thrill I got when the Giants trotted out from their dugout clad in uniforms of black flannel," McGraw later said. "Hundreds of Giant fans had escorted us to Philadelphia." New York rooters were rewarded with a 3-0 victory, as Christy Mathewson shut out Philadelphia on four hits.

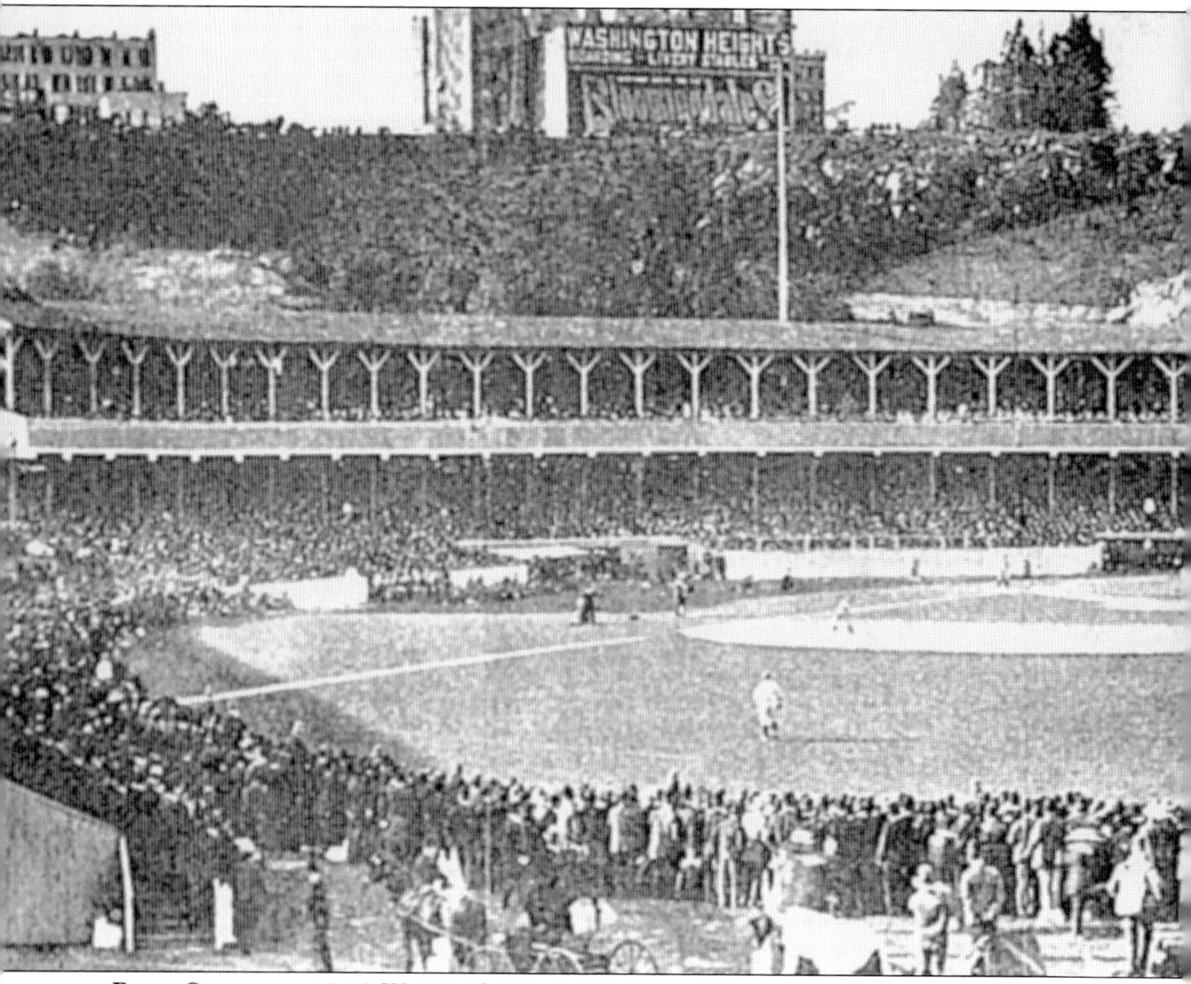

POLO GROUNDS, 1905 WORLD SERIES. The 1905 World Series was unique in that all five games were shutouts—one by Philadelphia and four by New York. The Athletics' sole victory (seen here) was a 3-0 whitewashing by Chief Bender in game two at the Polo Grounds.

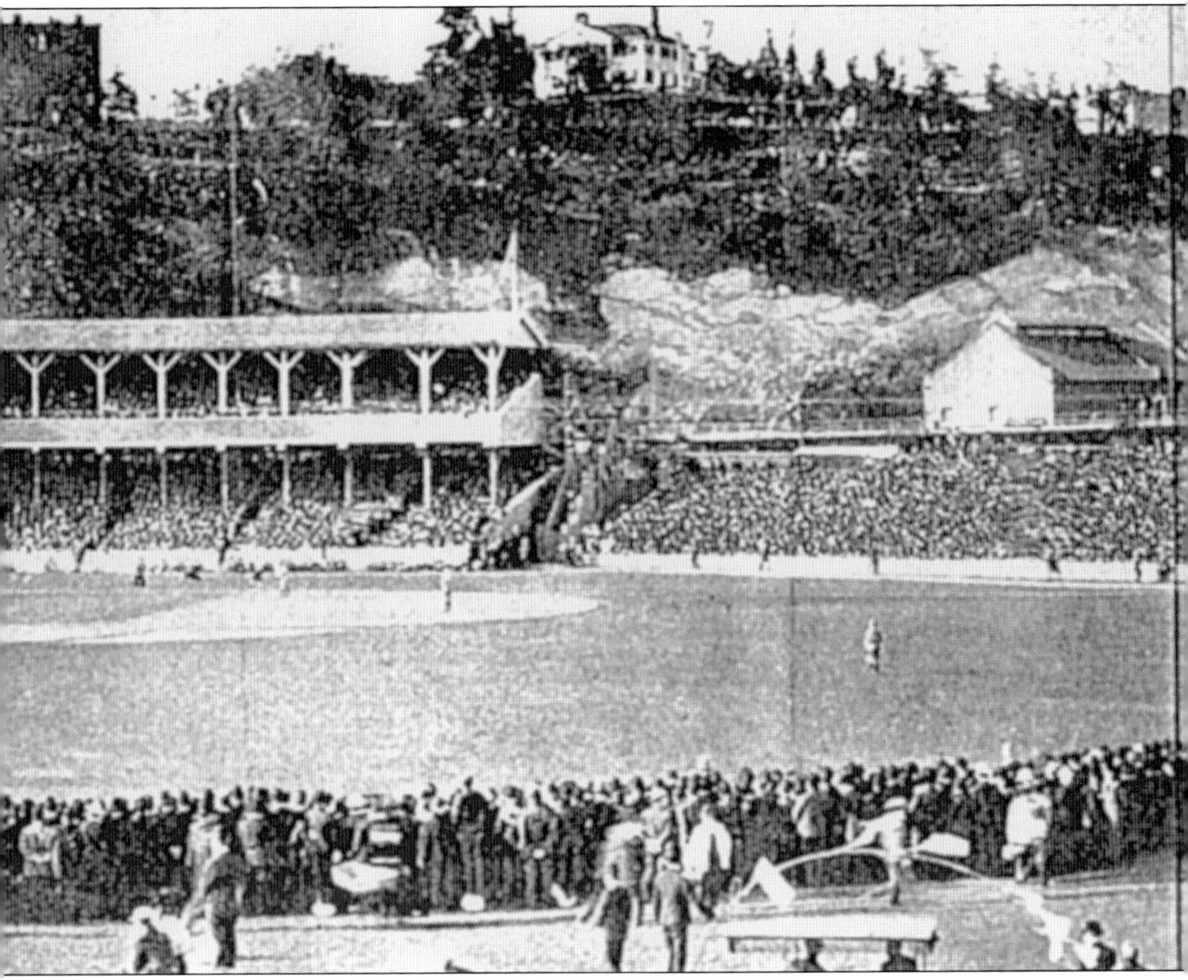

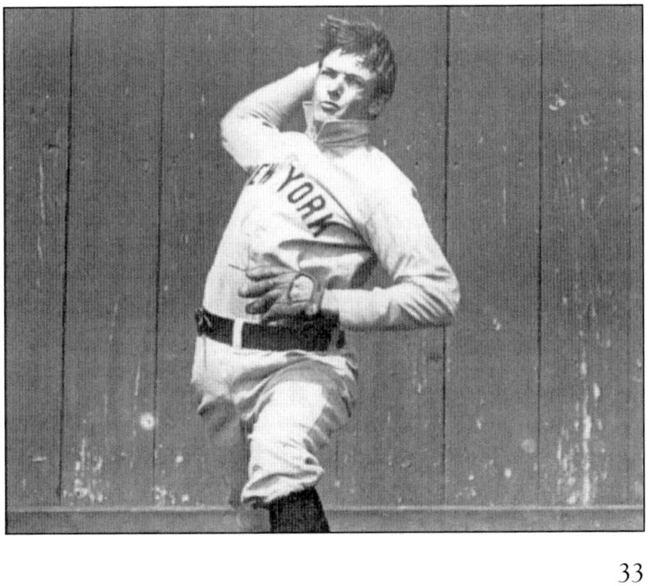

NOTHING BUT GOOSE EGGS. Christy Mathewson blanked the Athletics in games one, three, and five of the 1905 World Series. Employing a pitch known as the "fadeaway" that broke out and away from left-handed batters and down and in on right-handers, he allowed a paltry 14 hits and 1 walk in 27 innings. It was perhaps his greatest moment in a career filled with highlights.

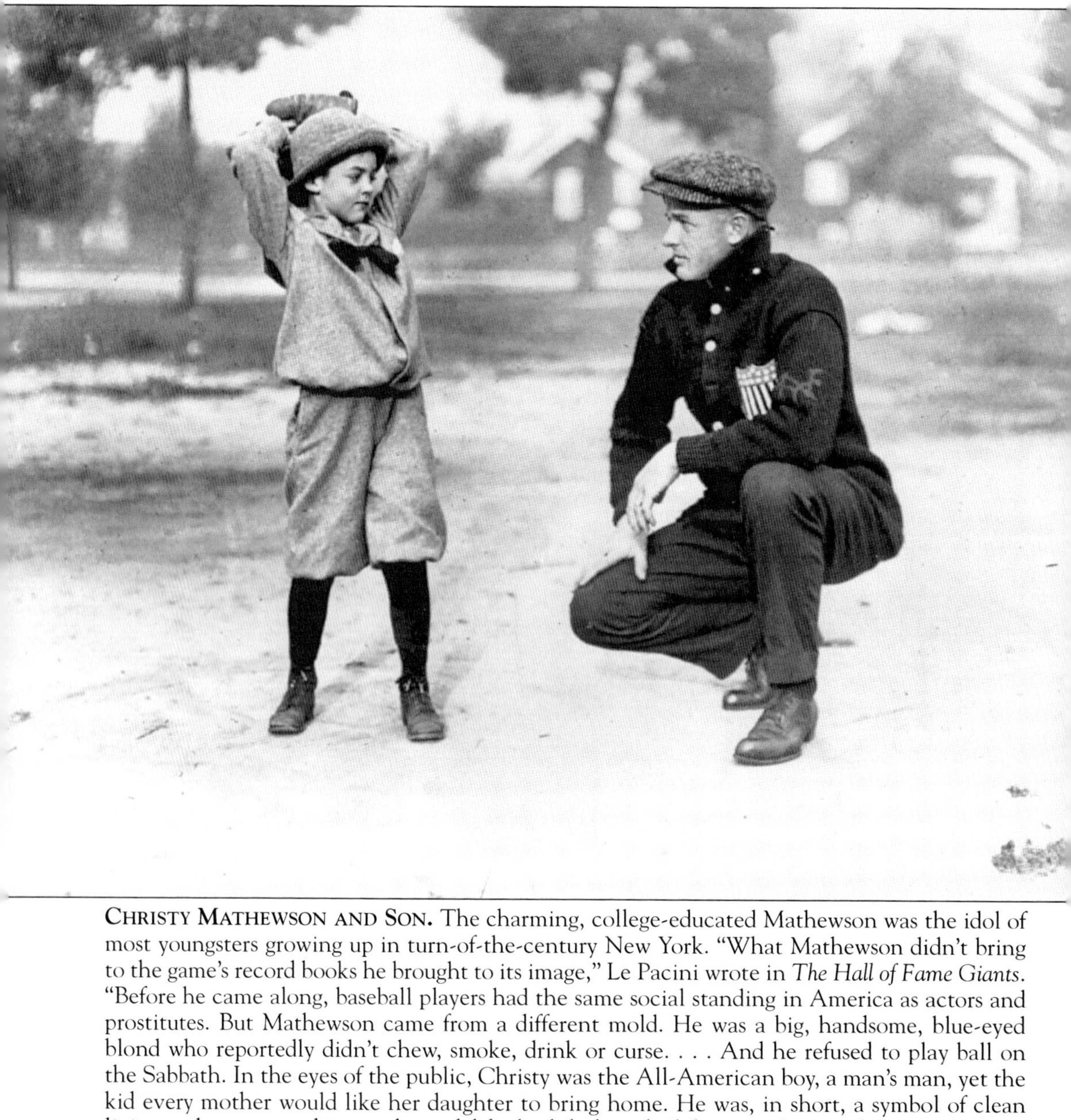

CHRISTY MATHEWSON AND SON. The charming, college-educated Mathewson was the idol of most youngsters growing up in turn-of-the-century New York. "What Mathewson didn't bring to the game's record books he brought to its image," Le Pacini wrote in *The Hall of Fame Giants*. "Before he came along, baseball players had the same social standing in America as actors and prostitutes. But Mathewson came from a different mold. He was a big, handsome, blue-eyed blond who reportedly didn't chew, smoke, drink or curse. . . . And he refused to play ball on the Sabbath. In the eyes of the public, Christy was the All-American boy, a man's man, yet the kid every mother would like her daughter to bring home. He was, in short, a symbol of clean living and sportsmanship, a role model for both kids and adults, a perfect amalgamation of guts and gentleness."

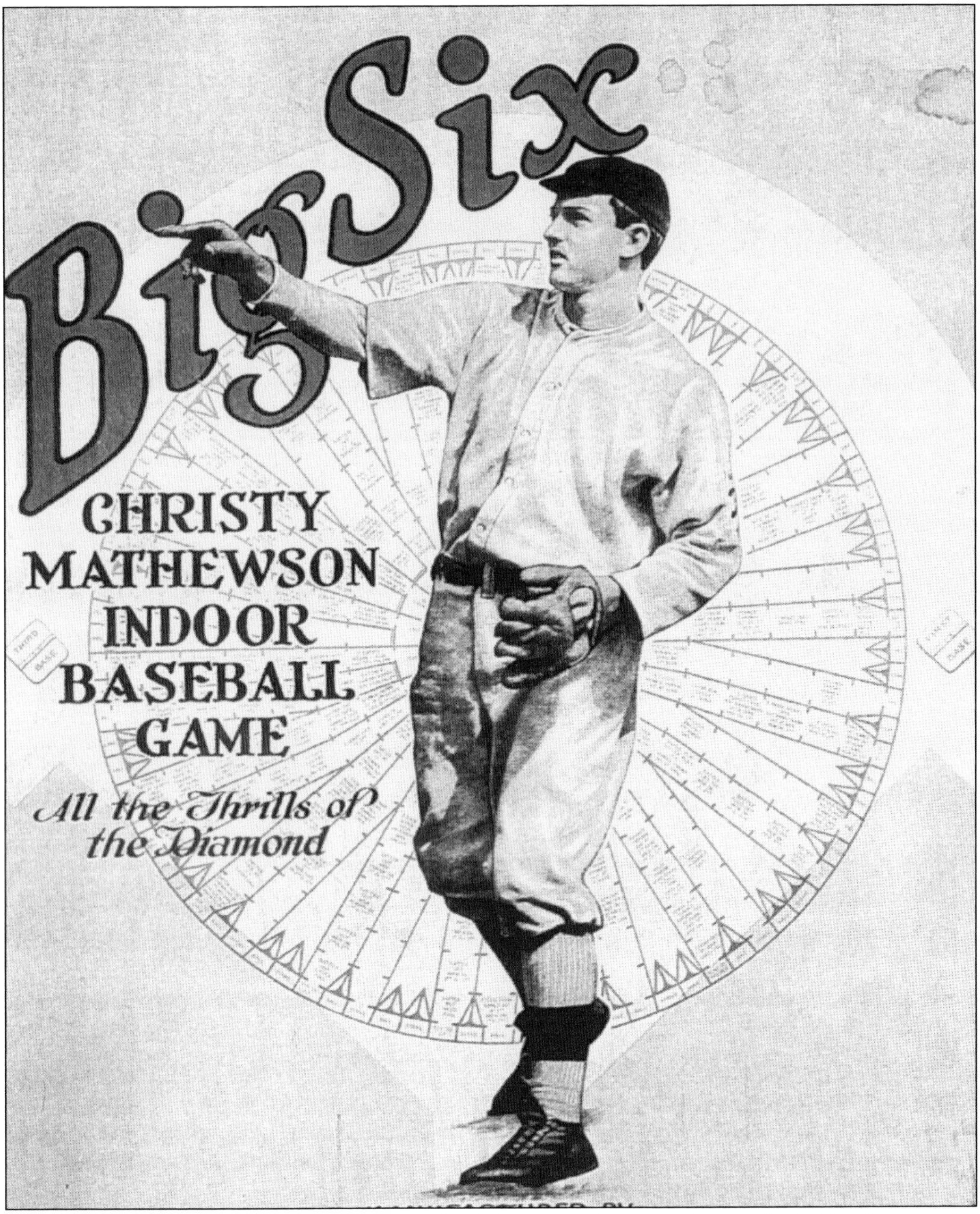

BIG SIX. For those who couldn't get enough of the Giants' ace pitcher at the ballpark or on the sports pages, there was the Big Six Christy Mathewson Indoor Baseball Game to which to turn. The game, manufactured by the Piroxloid Products Corporation, promised "All the Thrills of the Diamond." Mathewson (who was dubbed "Big Six" after a powerful locomotive of that name) would retire in 1916 after winning 372 games for New York and one more for Cincinnati, to whom he was traded in order to manage that team. He died prematurely of tuberculosis in 1925, the result of an accidental gassing he suffered while serving in the chemical corps during World War I. Mathewson was a member of the first class of inductees at the Baseball Hall of Fame.

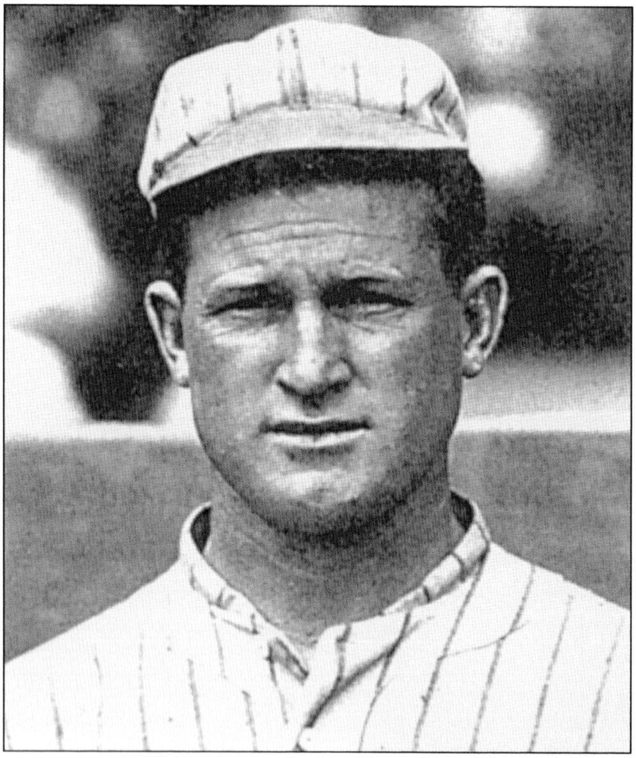

A Costly Homer. Outfielder Jack "Red" Murray led the loop with seven home runs in 1909. Once Murray ignored McGraw's instructions to bunt in a tight game with Pittsburgh. Instead he swung away, hitting a game-winning home run off Howie Camnitz. "You told me to bunt," he explained afterwards. "But you know what happened, Mac. Camnitz put one right in my gut, so I cow-tailed it." McGraw responded, "Well, I'm fining you $100, and you can try putting that right in your gut, too!"

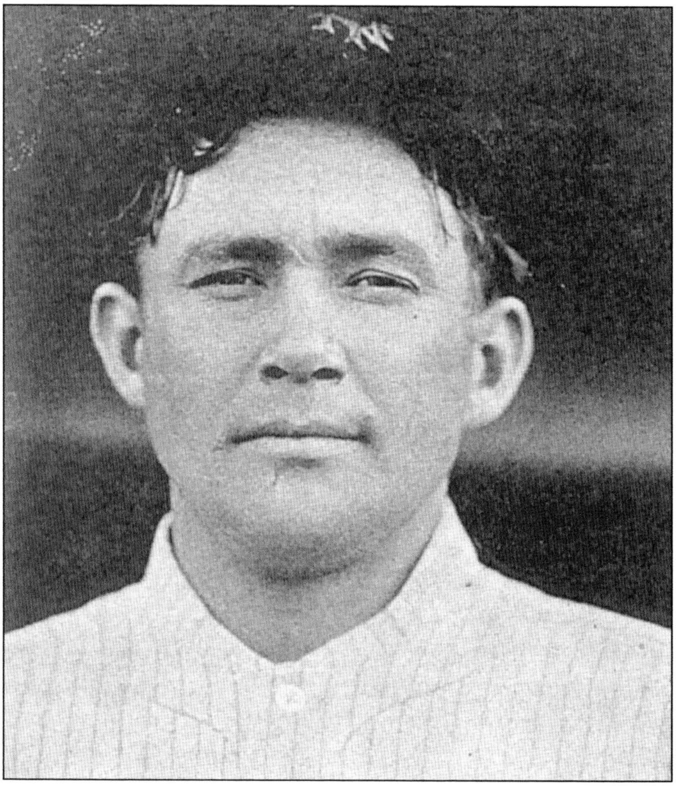

Al Bridwell in 1908. John McGraw acquired Al Bridwell from the Boston Braves in 1908, and the pugnacious shortstop fit right in with McGraw's style of play. The reason McGraw was a great manager "was because he knew how to handle men," said Bridwell, who once earned a two-week suspension for punching McGraw in the nose. "Some players he rode, and others he didn't. He got the most out of each man."

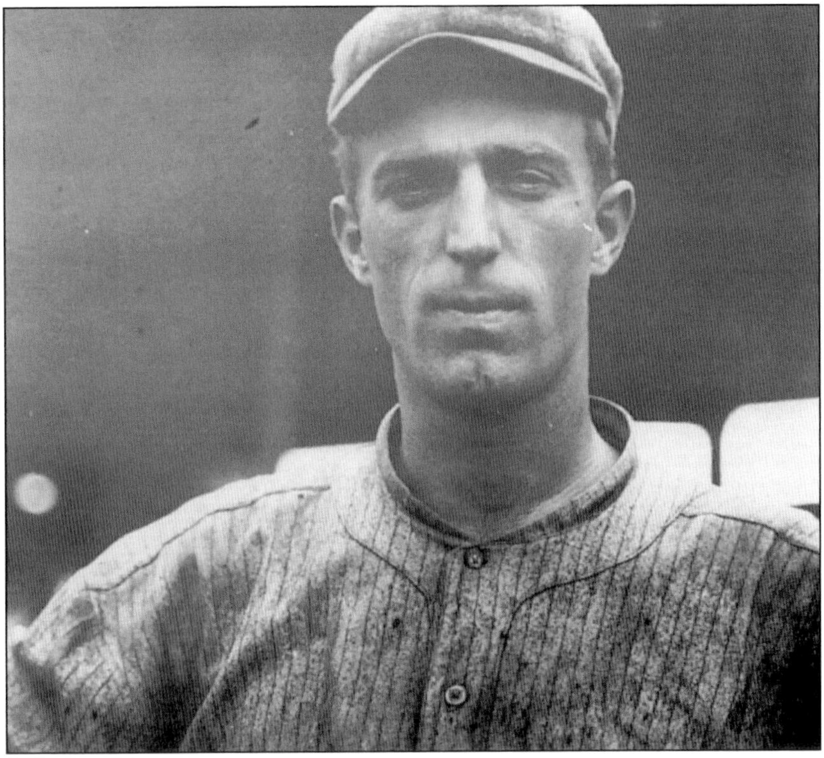

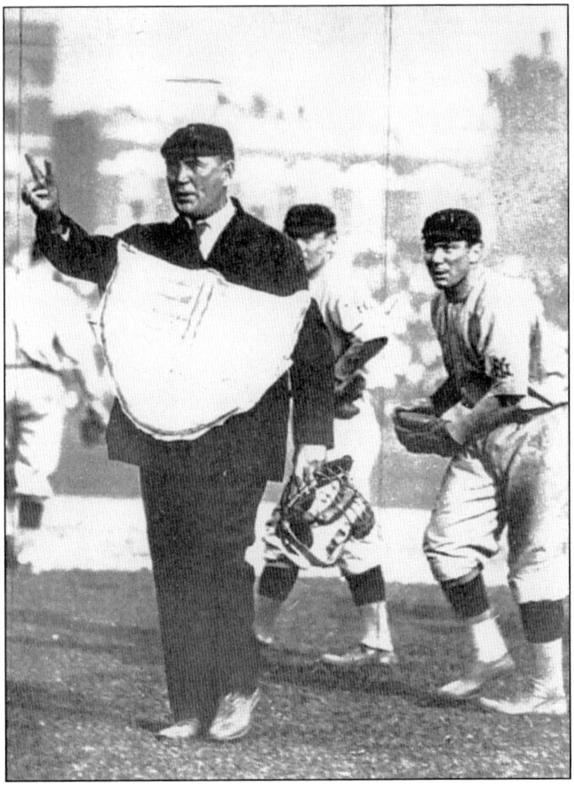

BONEHEAD MERKLE. Fred Merkle is best remembered for a base running blunder that cost the Giants the 1908 pennant. In the bottom half of the ninth inning in a game played September 23, 1908, with Moose McCormick on third base and rookie Merkle on first, Al Bridwell singled in what appeared to be the winning run against Chicago. Merkle, anxious to avoid the crush of jubilant fans pouring onto the field, went halfway to second base before running to the centerfield clubhouse. "I think that under the circumstances any ballplayer on any ball club would have done the same thing Merkle did," insisted Bridwell. "They did it all the time in those days." But on this occasion Chicago second baseman Johnny Evers somehow found a ball in the throngs of spectators, stepped on second base, and argued for the forceout. Umpire Hank O'Day (left), a former Giants player, agreed with the Cubs' appeal. He called Merkle out, negating the run and setting off a firestorm of controversy.

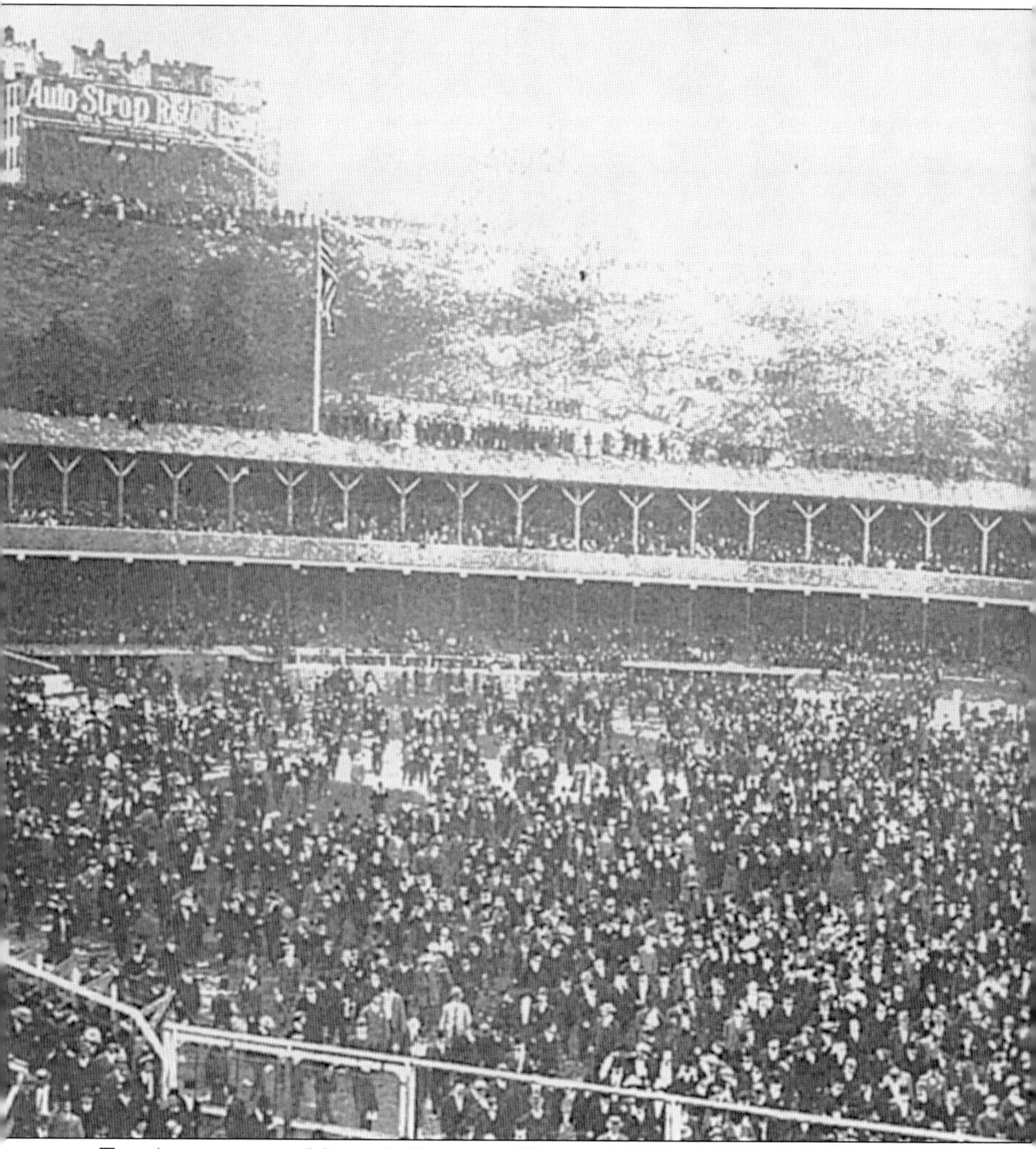

The Aftermath of Merkle's Blunder. Thousands of fans mill around the Polo Grounds in the confusing aftermath of the infamous New York-Chicago game of September 23, 1908. The Giants ran off the field believing they had won, 2-1, while the Cubs insisted that either the game should be forfeited to them because the Giants couldn't clear their own field, or that it had ended in a 1-1 tie and should be replayed. In the midst of the pandemonium, umpire Hank O'Day finally ruled that the game had ended in a tie. After three days of debate, league officials upheld O'Day's decision. They also announced that the game would only be replayed if the two contenders were deadlocked at the end of their 154-game schedule. Remarkably, that

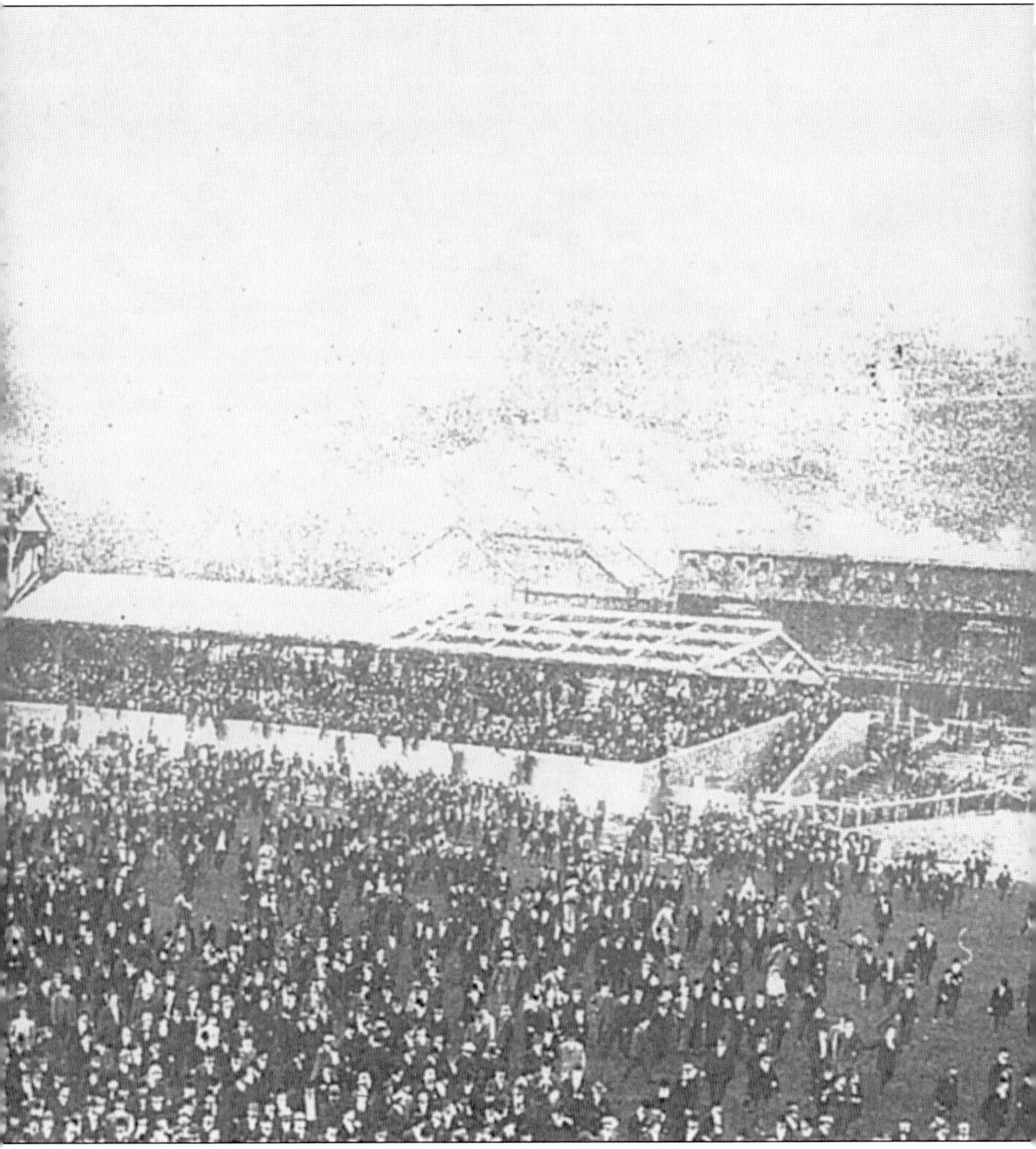

is what happened. The Giants lost five games to finish in a flat-footed tie with the Cubs. The teams met on October 8th at the Polo Grounds to decide who would advance into the World Series against Detroit. With Chicago roughing up Christy Mathewson for four runs in the third inning, the Cubs won the game, and the pennant, by a 4-2 score. "It is very unfair to put all the blame on Merkle for our losing the pennant in 1908," the Giants' Fred Snodgrass told Larry Ritter many years later. "McGraw never did, and neither did the rest of us. It was mostly the newspapers. They were the ones who invented the term 'bonehead'."

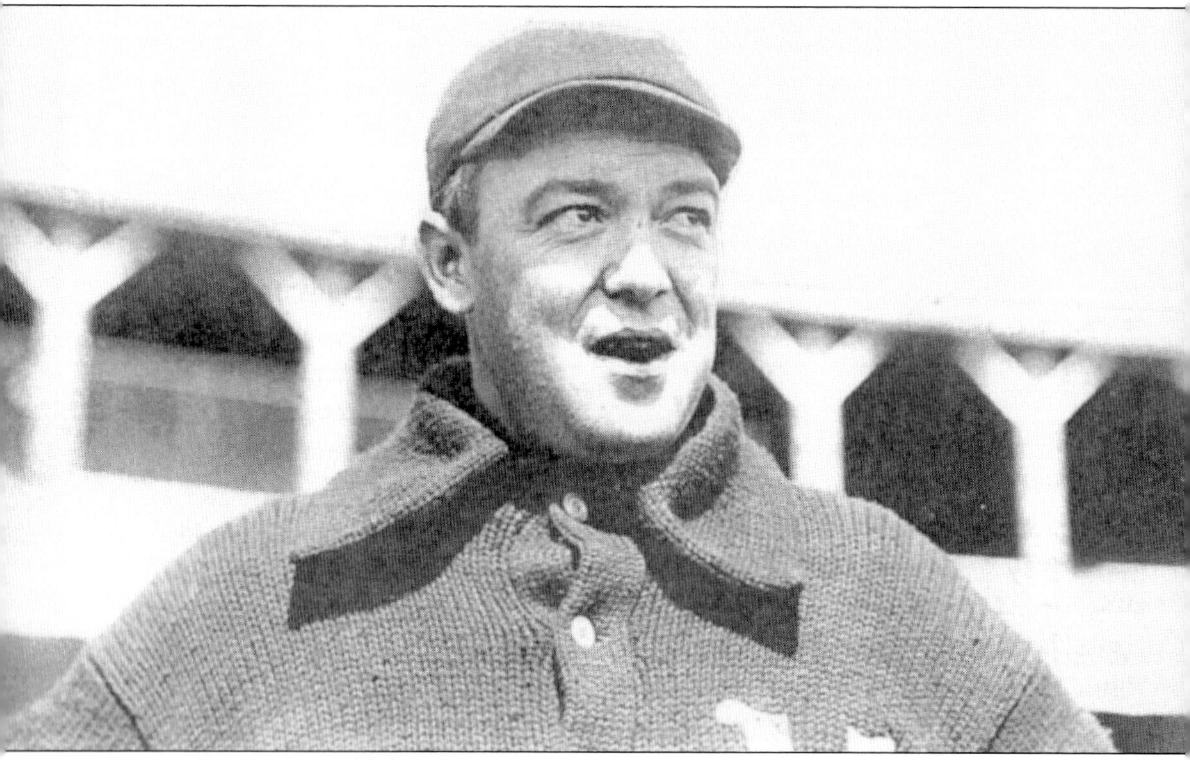

Boozy Bugs. One of John McGraw's most exasperating players was his wayward alcoholic pitcher, Arthur "Bugs" Raymond. "What a terrific spitball pitcher he was," teammate Rube Marquard recalled. "Bugs drank a lot, you know, and sometimes it seemed like the more he drank the better he pitched. They used to say he didn't spit on the ball; he blew his breath on it, and the ball would come up drunk." The limit of McGraw's patience was reached in an important 1911 game. Told to go down to the bullpen to warm up, Raymond snuck out of the Polo Grounds for a few quick drinks at a neighborhood bar. When he finally entered the game in relief, he was obviously drunk. McGraw immediately released him. Raymond drifted into poverty and despair. Separated from his wife, and with his two small daughters dead from an influenza epidemic, he was only 30 when he drank himself to death inside a seedy Chicago hotel room.

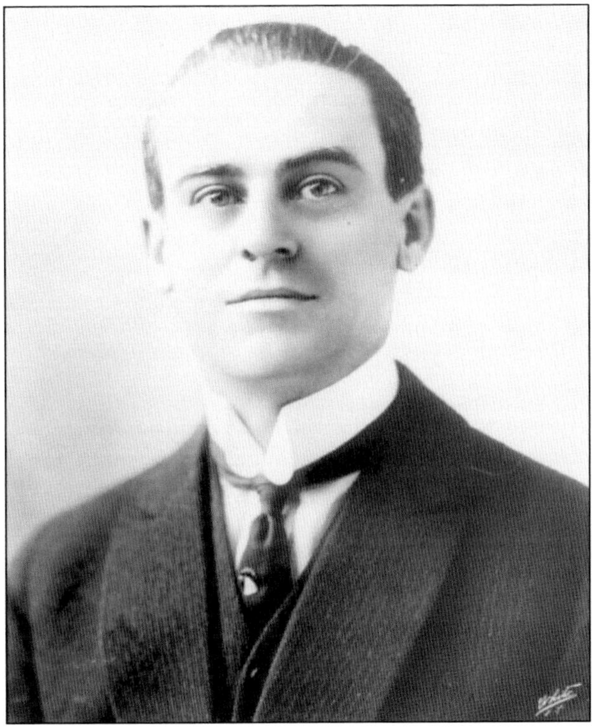

TURKEY DONLIN. Mike Donlin was a gifted batsman who was nicknamed "Turkey" for the way he strutted around the field. He hit as high as .356 in a season for McGraw and .333 overall in a dozen big-league seasons. The handsome outfielder was married to Broadway actress Mabel Hite and had four tours of duty with New York, all of them interrupted by contract disputes and regular forays into show business. His entertainment credits included stage plays, silent movies, and songs like "My Brudda Sylvest."

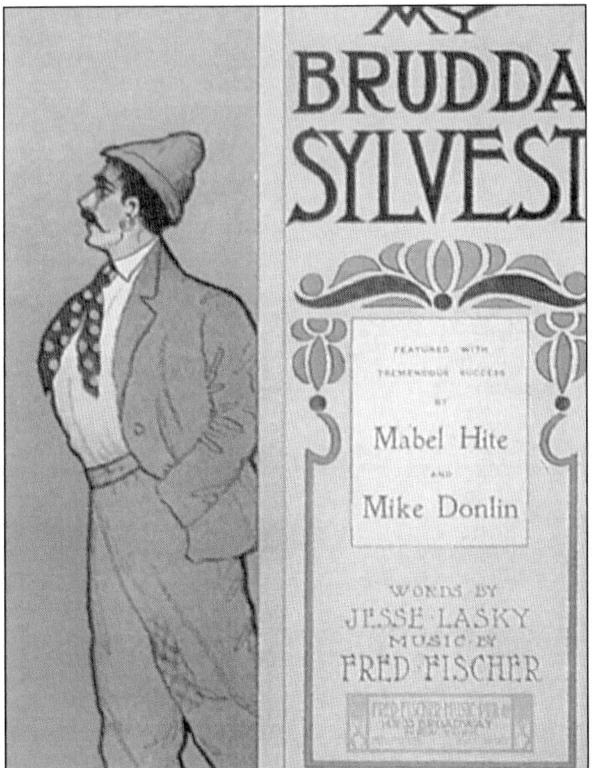

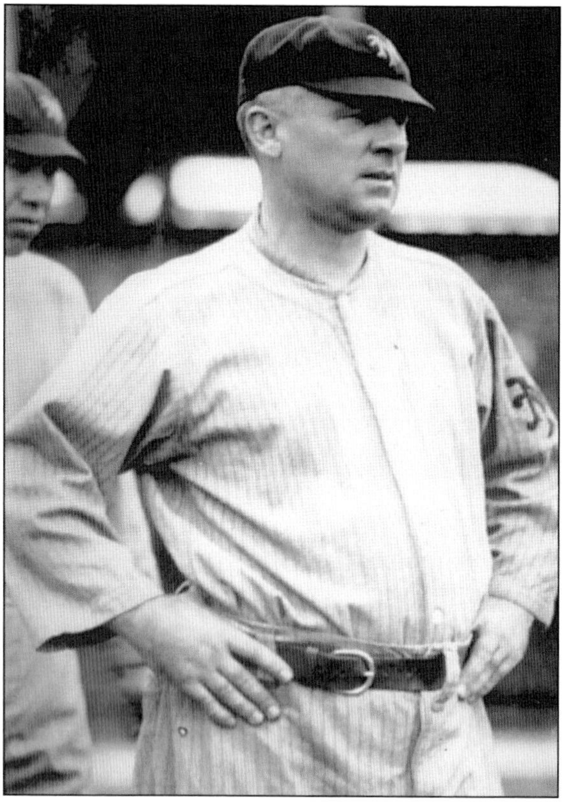

THE LITTLE ROUND MAN. John McGraw grew pudgy with the passing years, causing some to refer to him as "the little round man." Despite his roly-poly appearance, he had a commanding presence, in and out of uniform. "We respected him in every way," said catcher Chief Meyers. "According to Mr. McGraw, his ball team never lost a game; he lost it, not his players. He fought for his ballplayers and protected them. You couldn't come around and second-guess McGraw's players in his presence without having a fight on your hands right there. He stood up for us at all times."

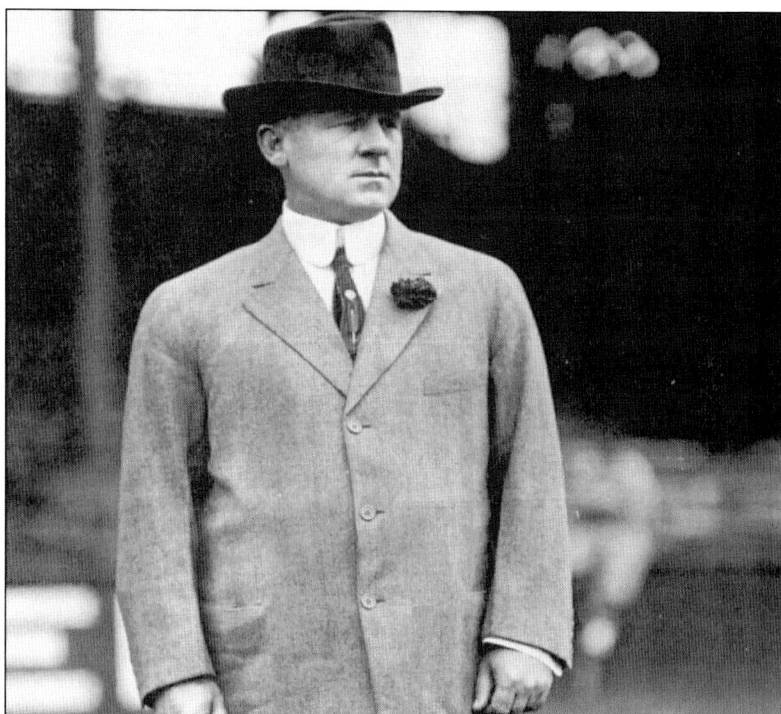

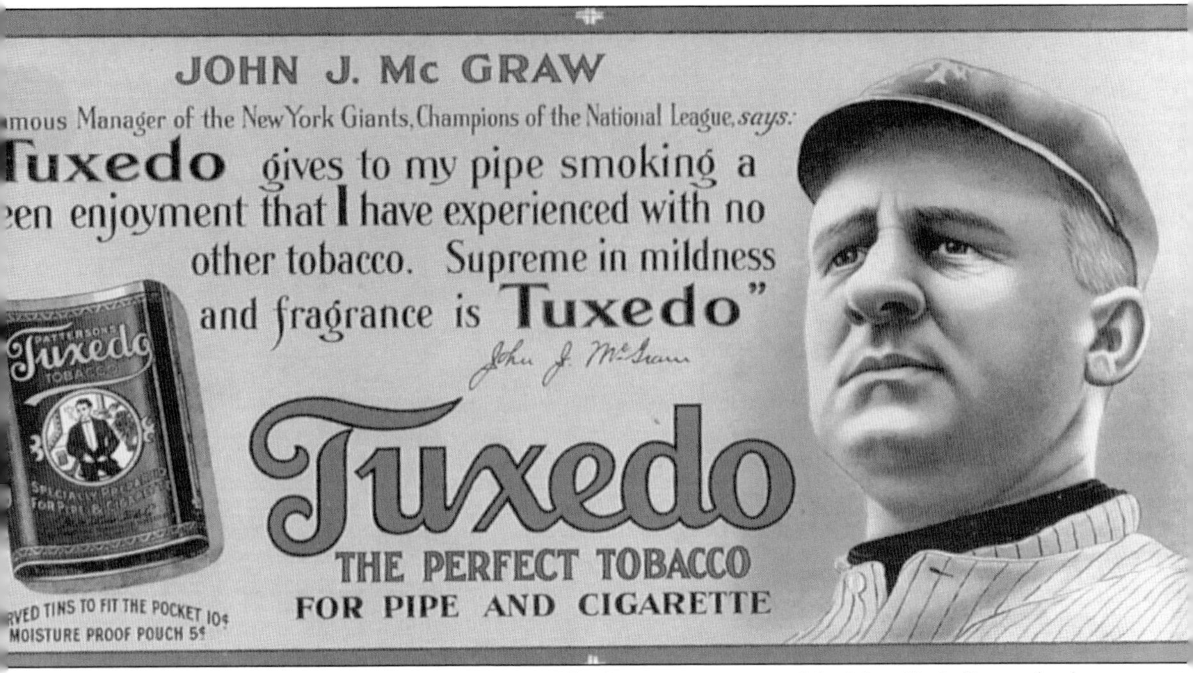

TUXEDO TOBACCO ADVERTISEMENT, C.1912. The famous manager of the New York Giants had no compunction about endorsing Tuxedo, "The Perfect Tobacco." After all, Christy Mathewson did, at no harm to his public image. Like many other sporting figures, John McGraw capitalized on his notoriety to add to his income. For example, after the 1912 season he embarked on a 15-week vaudeville tour, appearing on stage with such acts as "Odiva the Goldfish Lady." Later he played the role of an Irish gumshoe in a forgettable silent movie called *The Detective*. Including salary and endorsements, McGraw was making roughly $60,000 a year by 1912, a considerable amount at a time when a quality cigar cost a nickel.

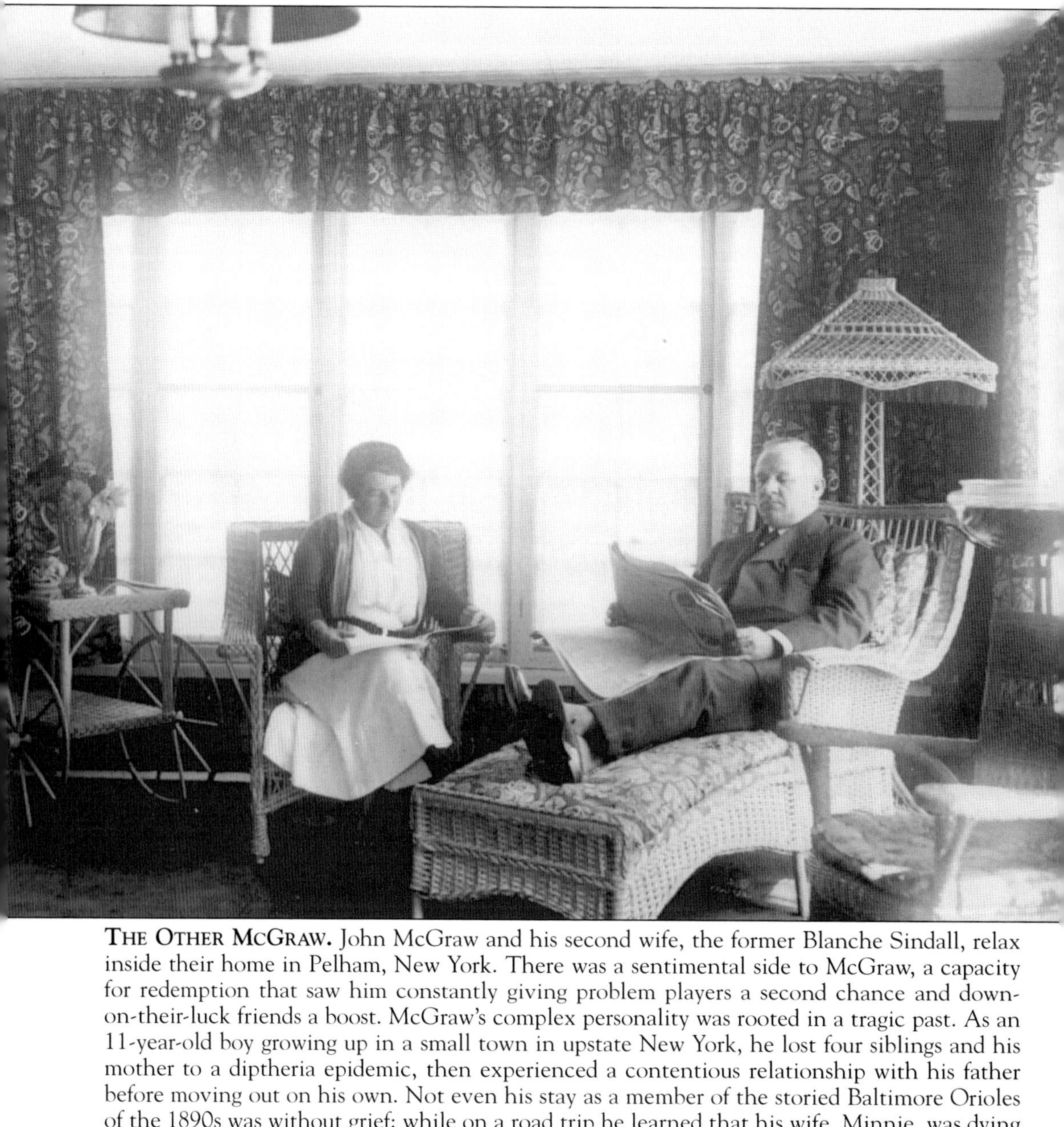

THE OTHER MCGRAW. John McGraw and his second wife, the former Blanche Sindall, relax inside their home in Pelham, New York. There was a sentimental side to McGraw, a capacity for redemption that saw him constantly giving problem players a second chance and down-on-their-luck friends a boost. McGraw's complex personality was rooted in a tragic past. As an 11-year-old boy growing up in a small town in upstate New York, he lost four siblings and his mother to a diptheria epidemic, then experienced a contentious relationship with his father before moving out on his own. Not even his stay as a member of the storied Baltimore Orioles of the 1890s was without grief; while on a road trip he learned that his wife, Minnie, was dying of a ruptured appendix. Although frequently cantankerous, McGraw also "was a very fair man," remembered Fred Snodgrass, "and it was only when you really had it coming to you that you got it. And once he'd bawled you out good and proper, and I do mean proper, then he'd forget it."

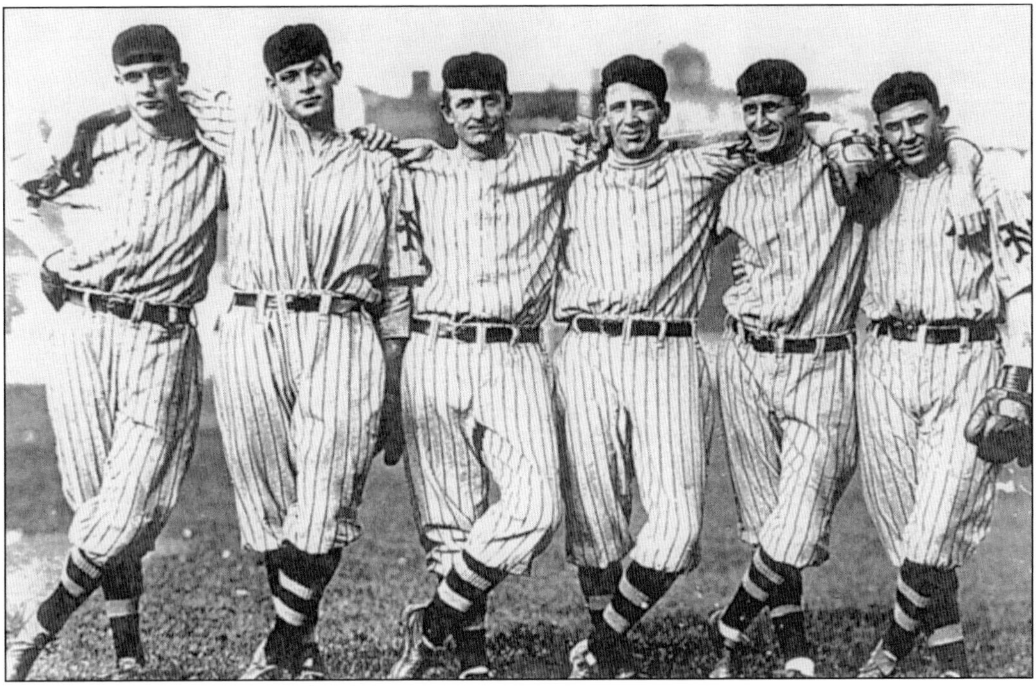

A CALL TO ARMS, 1912. The Giants boasted one of the deepest pitching staffs in the majors in the years leading up to World War I. Pictured, from left to right, are Rube Marquard, Jeff Tesreau, Christy Mathewson, Red Ames, George "Hooks" Wiltse, and Jim "Doc" Crandall. McGraw knew how to get the most of his hurlers, employing Crandall as one of the game's early relief specialists.

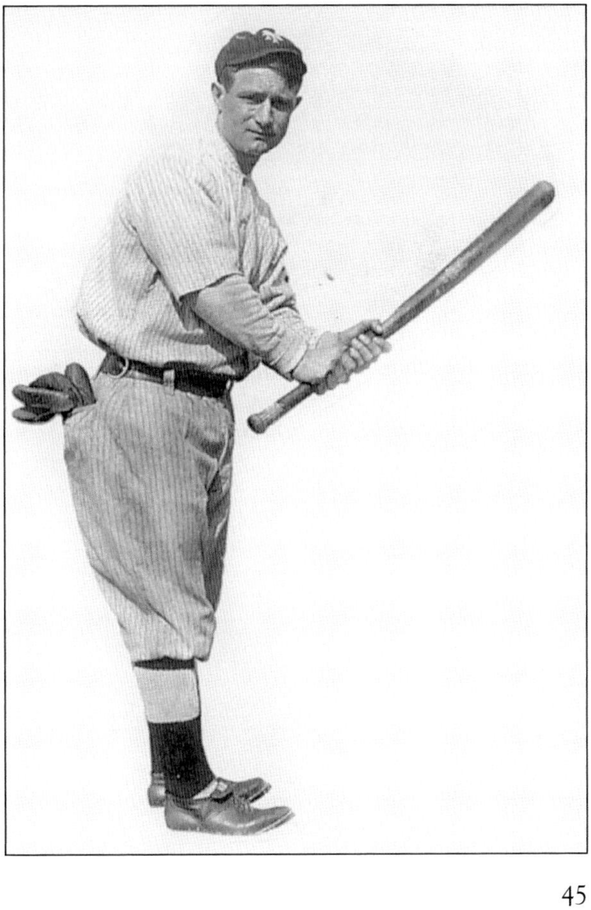

JACKRABBIT JOSH. McGraw's Giants were a running team, leading the league in stolen bases 11 times during his tenure. The 1911 squad stole a record 347 bases, including 61 by outfielder and leadoff man Josh Devore. The following year Devore stole four bases in a single inning!

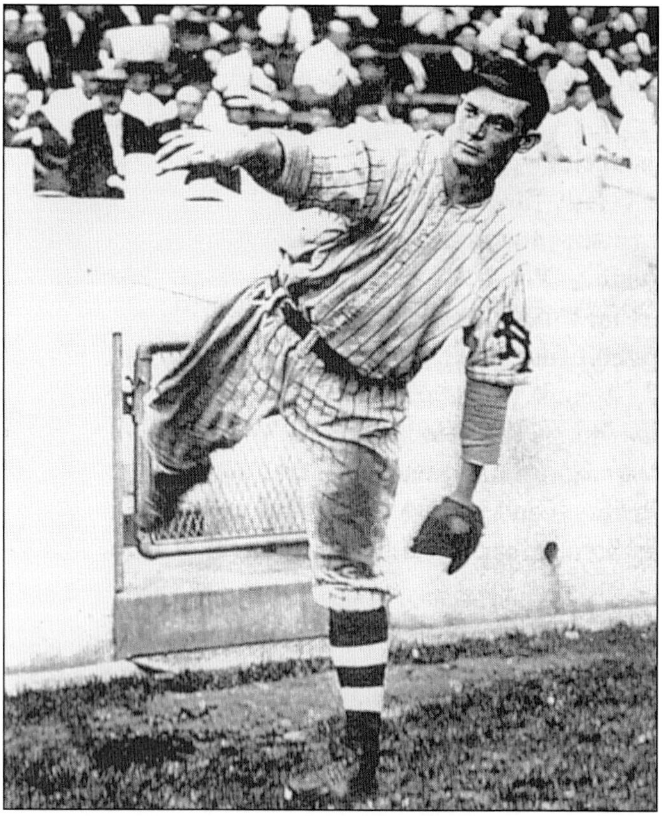

BIG JEFF. Jeff Tesreau was a strapping, handsome spitball pitcher from Missouri who resembled heavyweight fighter Jim "Big Jeff" Jeffries. Tesreau led the loop with a 1.96 ERA as a rookie in 1912, then followed up with 22- and 26-win seasons in 1913–14.

TWO CHIEFS. A couple of Native American stars, John Meyers of the Giants (left) and Charlie Bender of the Athletics, pose for the cameras at the 1911 World Series. Both Meyers, a Cahuilla Indian, and Bender, a Chippewa, were inevitably nicknamed "Chief." Note Meyers' dark uniform. "Superstitious McGraw," he recalled, "he had us dressed in black uniforms, because that's the way the Giants had been dressed when they beat the A's in the 1905 World Series."

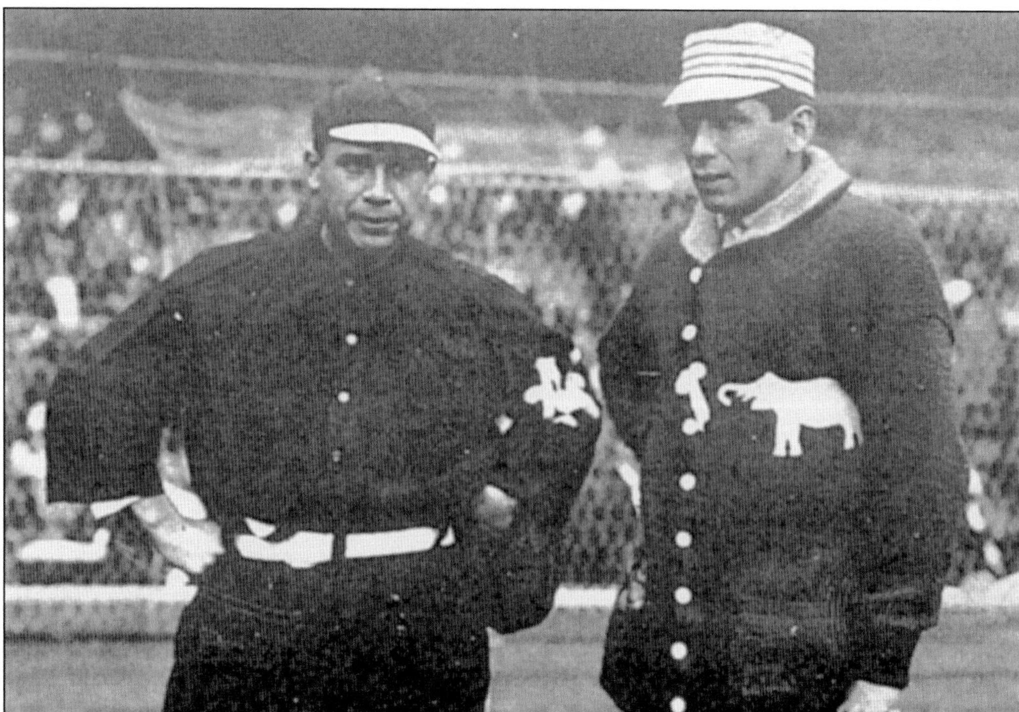

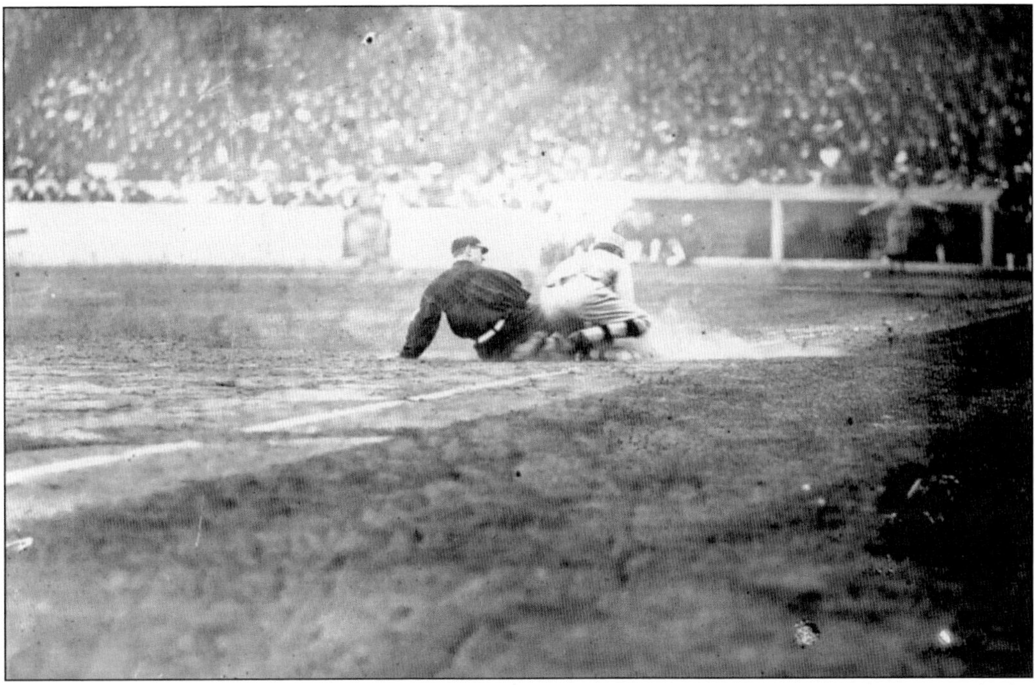

THE SNODGRASS-BAKER INCIDENT. Philadelphia third baseman Frank Baker earned the sobriquet "Home Run" Baker with a pair of timely home runs in the 1911 World Series against the Giants. In the tenth inning of the third game, Fred Snodgrass slid hard into Baker, ripping Baker's knickers and cutting his thigh. Philadelphia players and fans thought Snodgrass had deliberately tried to put Baker out of the series and vowed revenge. These two photographs show Snodgrass's controversial slide and the aftermath. The A's won, 3-2, scoring an unearned run off Christy Mathewson in the 11th. The series was then interrupted by six days of rain, which gave inflamed passions a chance to cool off.

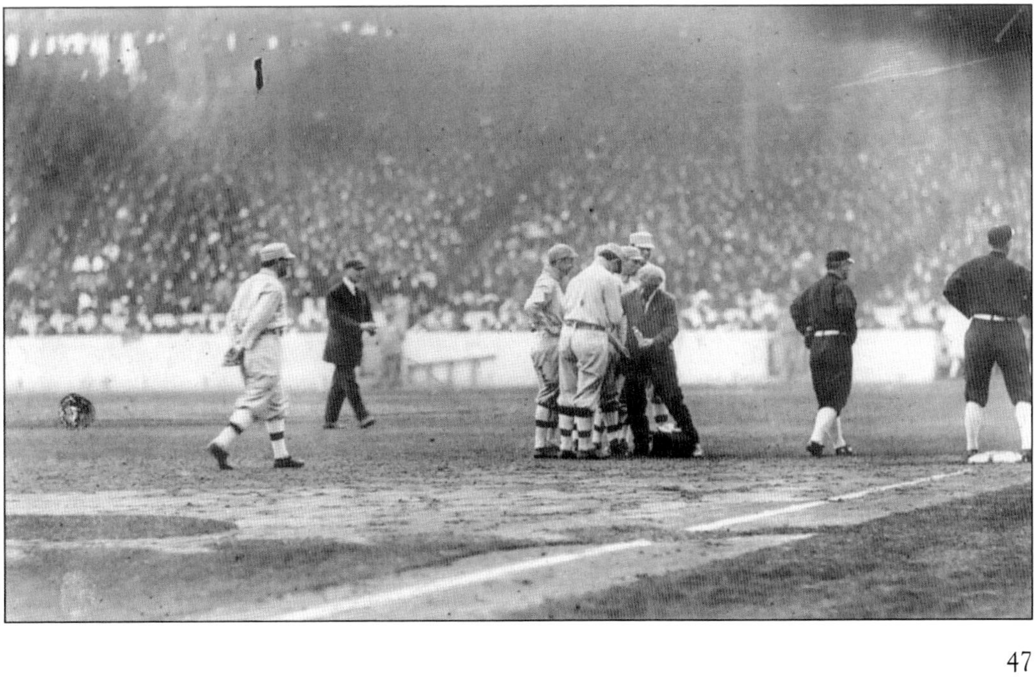

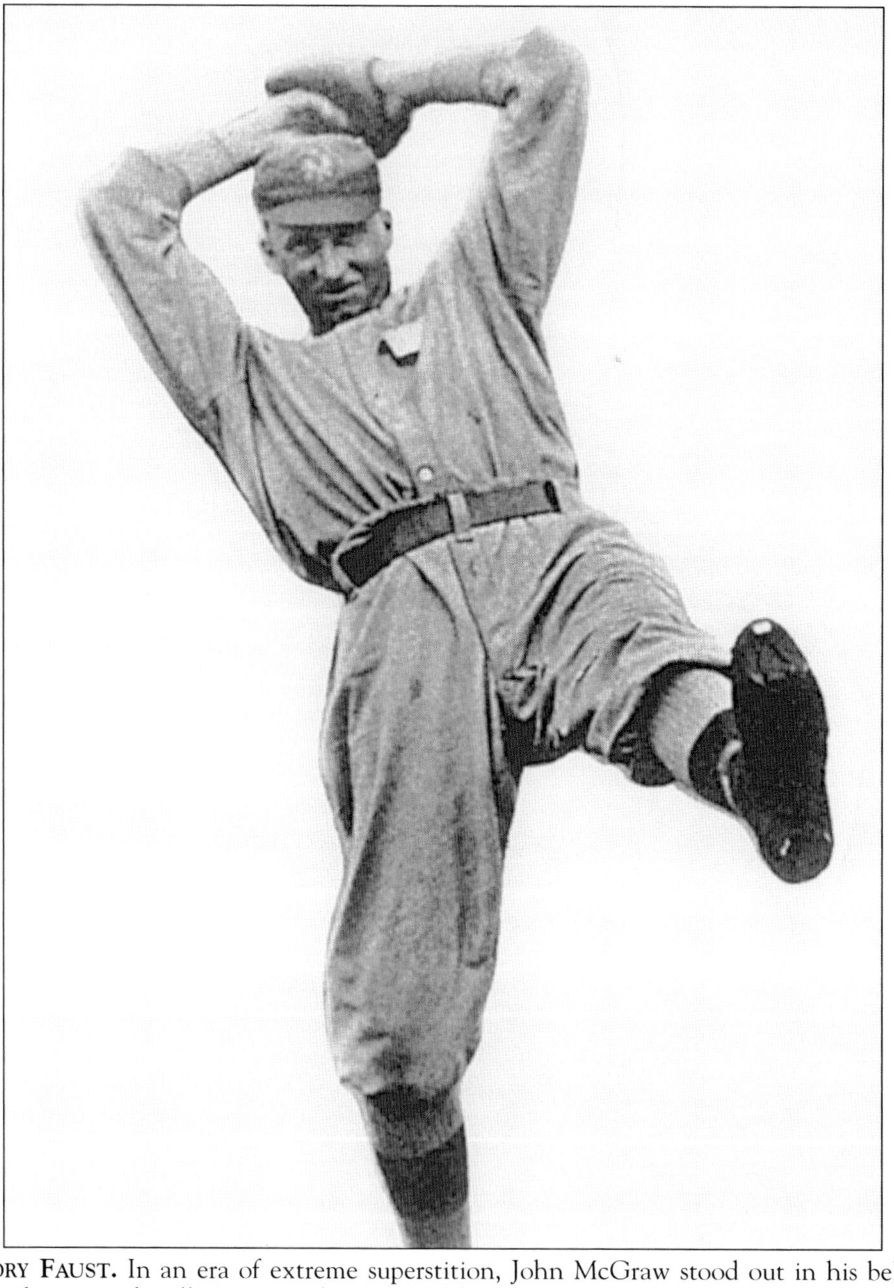

VICTORY FAUST. In an era of extreme superstition, John McGraw stood out in his belief of omens, charms, and spells. His most famous good-luck charm was an unbalanced Kansas hayseed named Charles Faust, whose middle name of Victor was changed to "Victory" after a string of victories was attributed to his presence around the club. McGraw, looking to keep players and fans loose, often had Faust warm up using his bizarre windmill windup. In the ninth inning of the final game of the 1911 season, he actually inserted Faust in the lineup. Brooklyn players, playing along with the farce, swung half-heartedly at Faust's feeble pitches, then let him steal his way around the bases in his only at-bat. Faust "helped" the Giants to three straight pennants, but his magic failed in the World Series, as New York lost in the post-season each time. Faust died in a hospital for the insane in 1915. That year the Giants finished last.

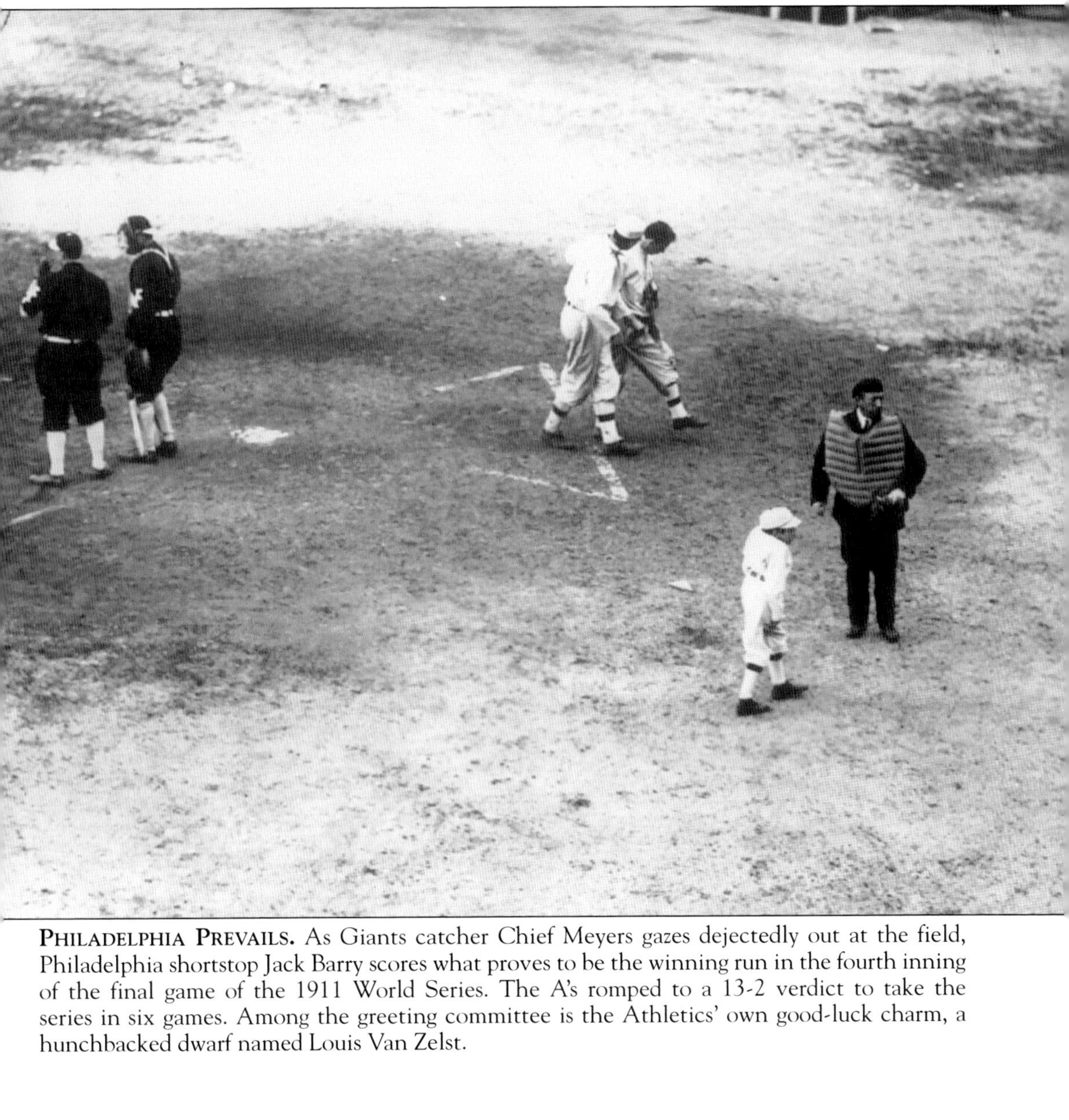

PHILADELPHIA PREVAILS. As Giants catcher Chief Meyers gazes dejectedly out at the field, Philadelphia shortstop Jack Barry scores what proves to be the winning run in the fourth inning of the final game of the 1911 World Series. The A's romped to a 13-2 verdict to take the series in six games. Among the greeting committee is the Athletics' own good-luck charm, a hunchbacked dwarf named Louis Van Zelst.

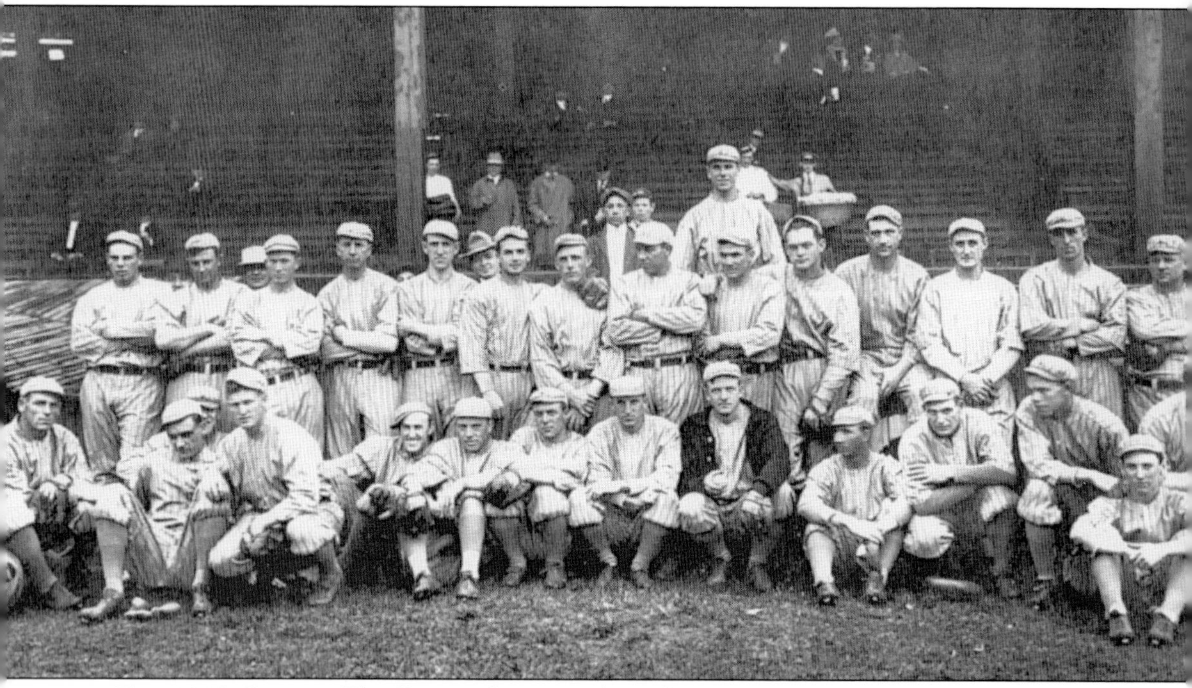

THE 1912 GIANTS. The Giants, the toast of Manhattan, captured a second straight National League flag in 1912 with a record of 103-48. "John McGraw had a good, tough ball club that year," remembered an opponent. "I would say they were probably the most famous team in baseball. I mean, people who didn't know anything about baseball might have heard of John McGraw and the Giants, just like years later they heard of Babe Ruth and the Yankees."

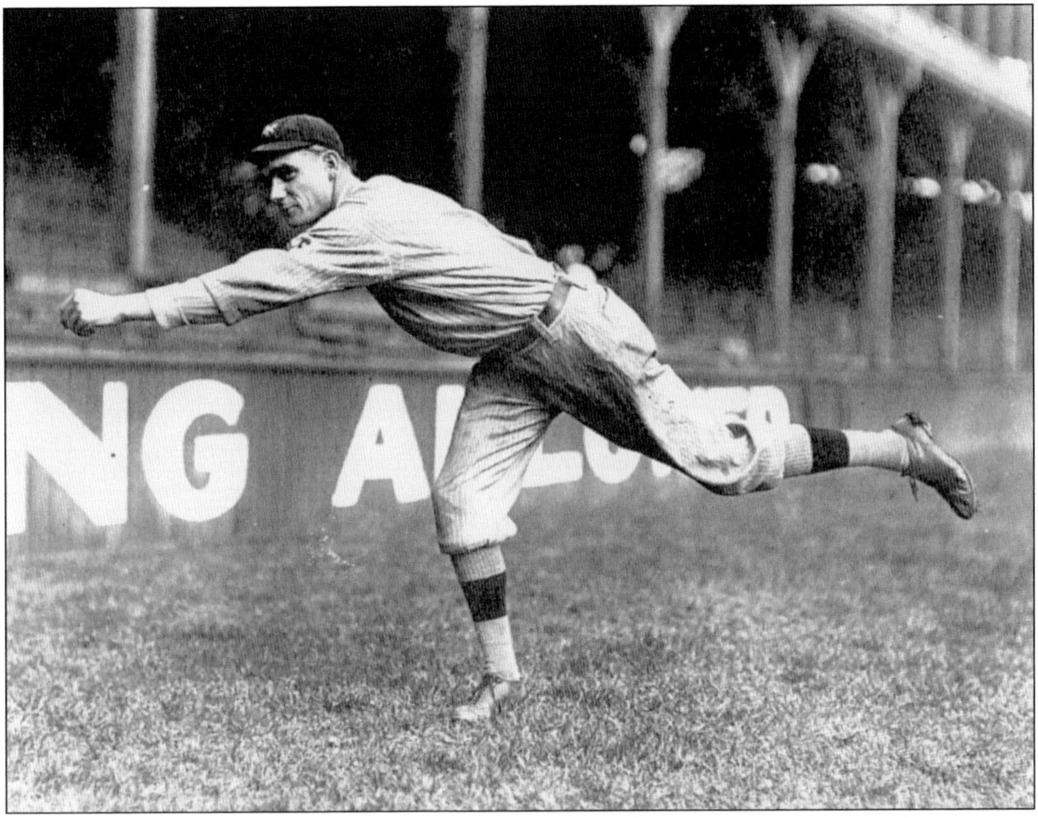

RUBE MARQUARD. Richard "Rube" Marquard, the son of Cleveland's chief engineer, disappointed his father by running off to play pro ball. But he made Giants fans happy, winning a total of 73 games during the pennant-winning seasons of 1911–13. The urbane curveballer, who was pinned with the nickname "Rube" for his resemblance to pitcher Rube Waddell, had the greatest season of his Hall-of-Fame career in 1912. He won a record 19 straight games, beat the Red Sox twice in the World Series, and launched a vaudeville act with his first wife, Broadway actress Blossom Seely. Together they performed a number called "The Marquard Glide." Marquard later divorced his wife but reconciled with his father.

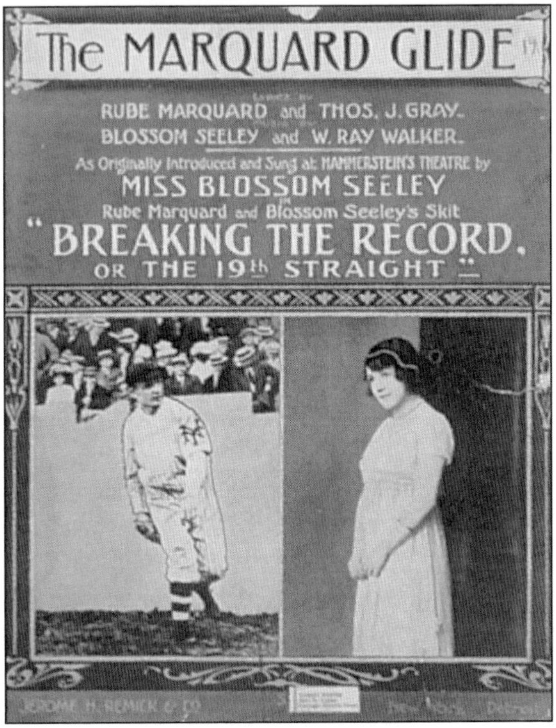

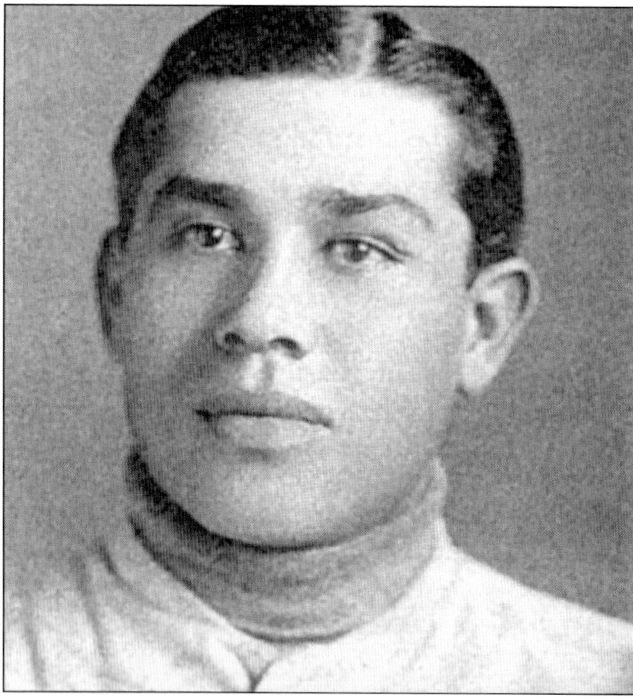

CHIEF MEYERS. John "Chief" Meyers, the Giants' regular catcher from 1909 to 1915, batted .358 in 1912. Meyers was born in California and attended Dartmouth, but his mother's illness and his ineligibility to play college ball (he was banned for having already played organized ball) prompted him to drop out of school. He was 28 when he was signed by the Giants. "I liked playing ball, and I was good at it," he reflected in his old age. "But I do wish I had finished my college education."

WORLD SERIES ACTION, 1912. Giants catcher Chief Meyers beats Boston's Tris Speaker to first base to record the putout in this action shot from the 1912 World Series.

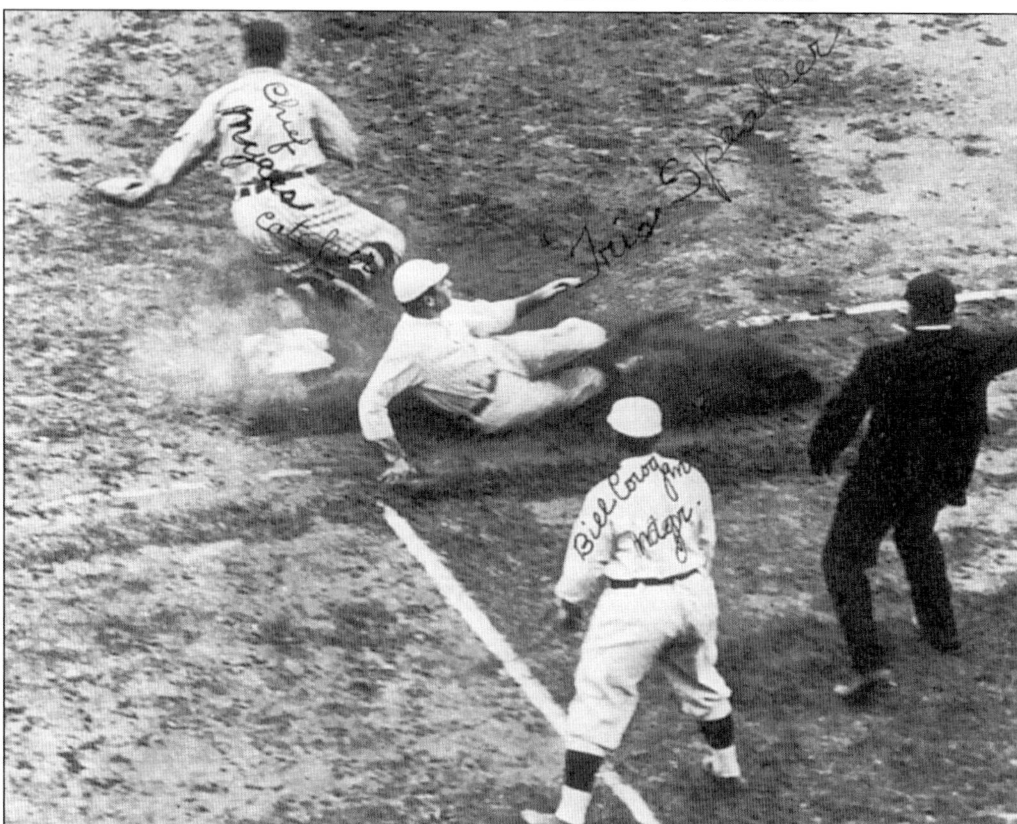

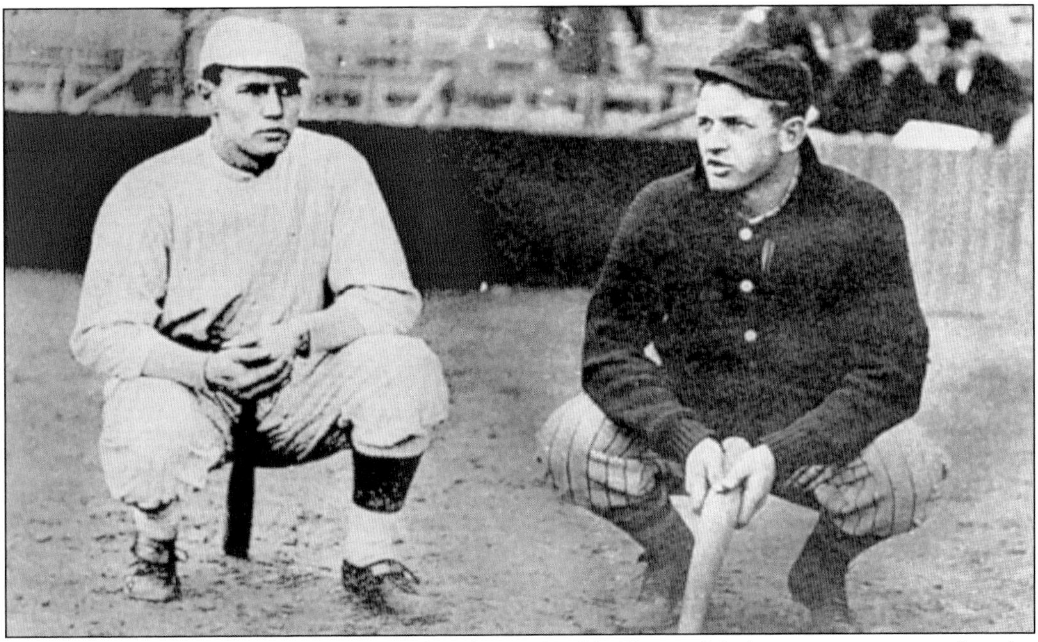

Two Aces. Boston's Smoky Joe Wood and New York's Christy Mathewson are pictured at the 1912 World Series. The series went eight games (there was one tie) with Wood, a 34-game winner during the season, winning three times. Mathewson lost to Wood, 3-2, in the deciding game when the Red Sox scored two unearned runs in the bottom of the tenth inning.

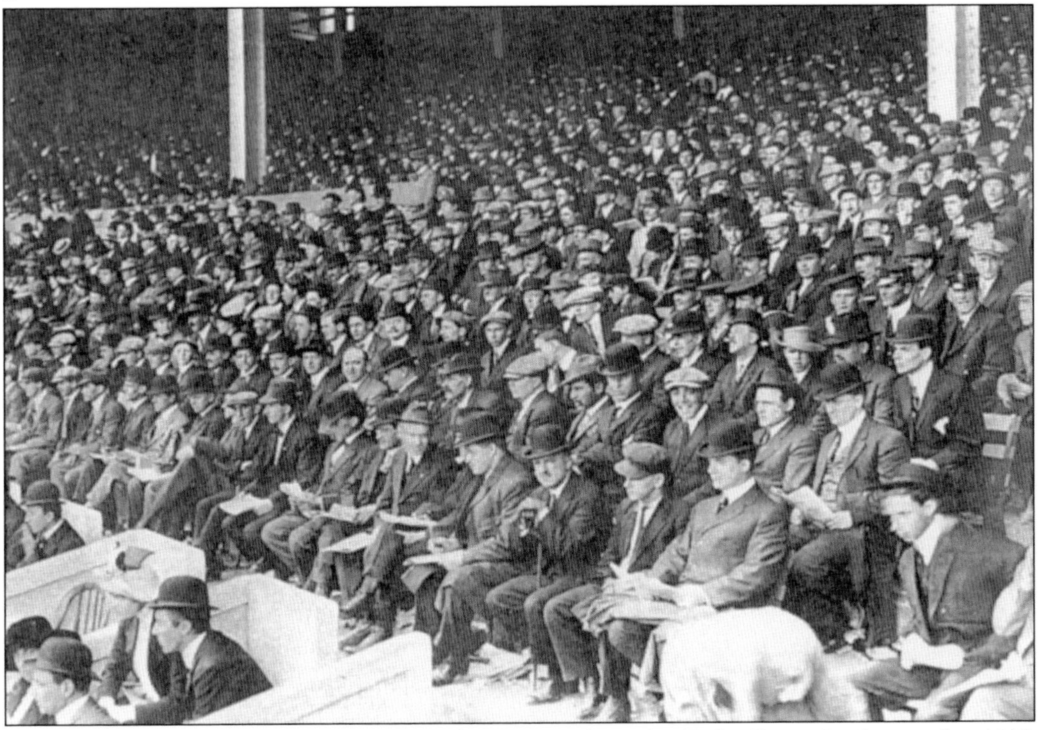

Packed House. A crowded grandstand is pictured at the Polo Grounds during the 1912 fall classic.

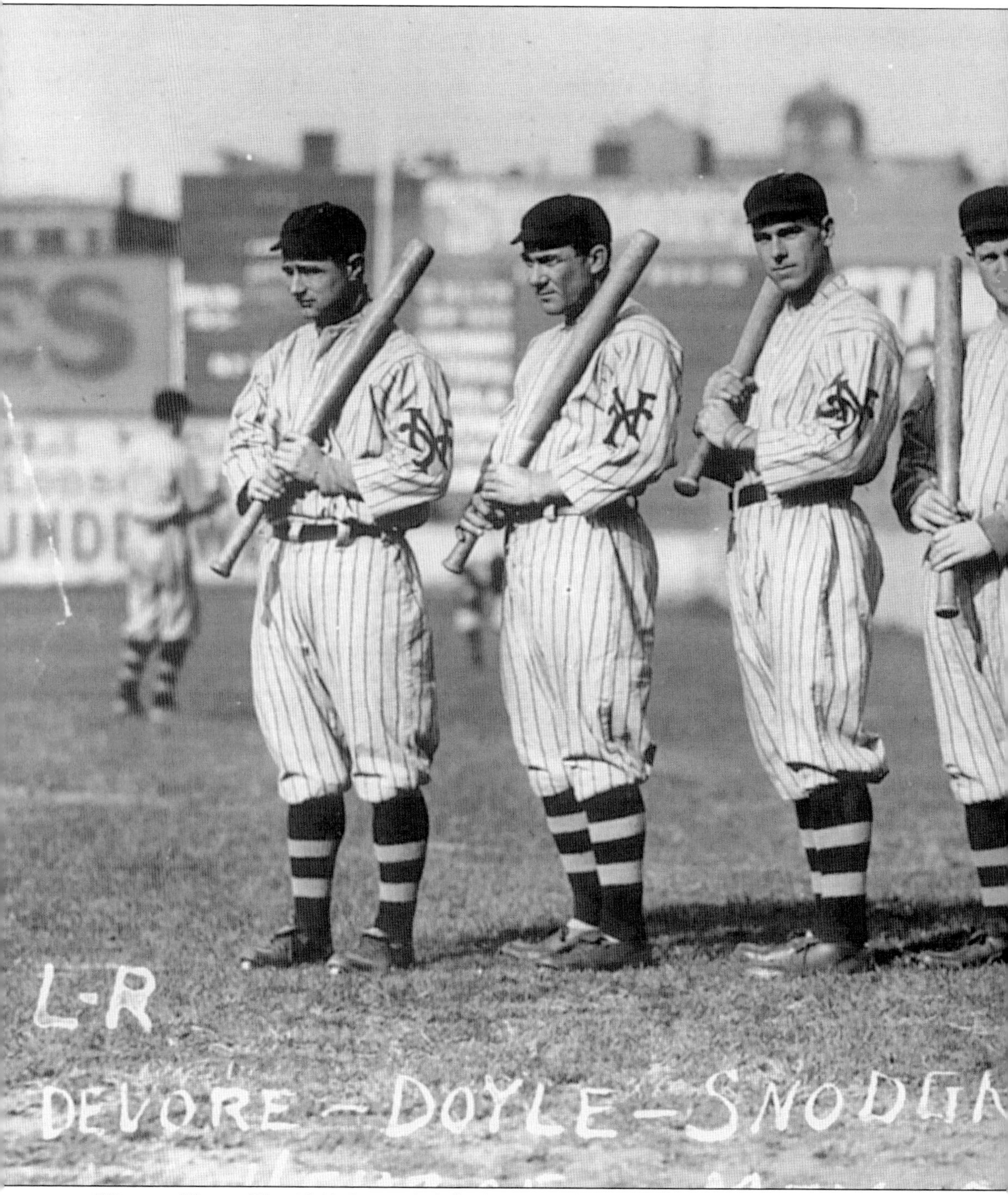

WHAT A TEAM. The 1912 Giants led the league in batting, runs, home runs, stolen bases, and ERA. The lineup featured, from left to right, left fielder Josh Devore, second baseman Larry Doyle, center fielder Fred Snodgrass, right fielder Red Murray, first baseman Fred Merkle, third baseman Buck Herzog, catcher Chief Meyers, and shortstop Art Fletcher. "McGraw allowed initiative to his men," Snodgrass told author Larry Ritter a half-century later. "We stole when

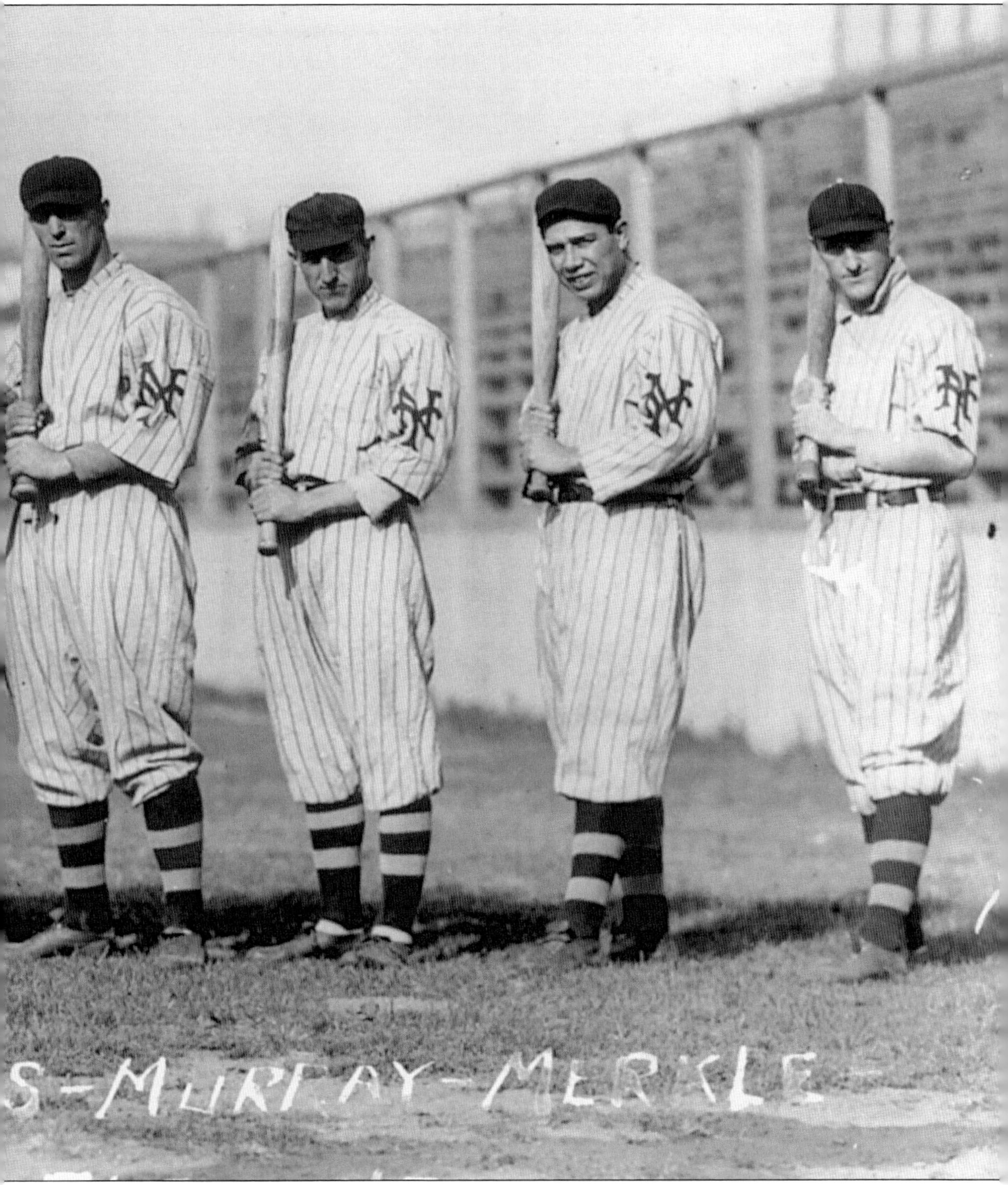

we thought we had the jump and when the situation demanded it. We played hit-and-run when we felt that was what was called for. We bunted when we thought it was appropriate. Every player on the team was expected to know how to play baseball, and that was the kind of a game baseball was in those days . . . There was a lot of strategy in baseball then, and there isn't very much today. We played a game in which the two key words were 'think' and 'anticipate'."

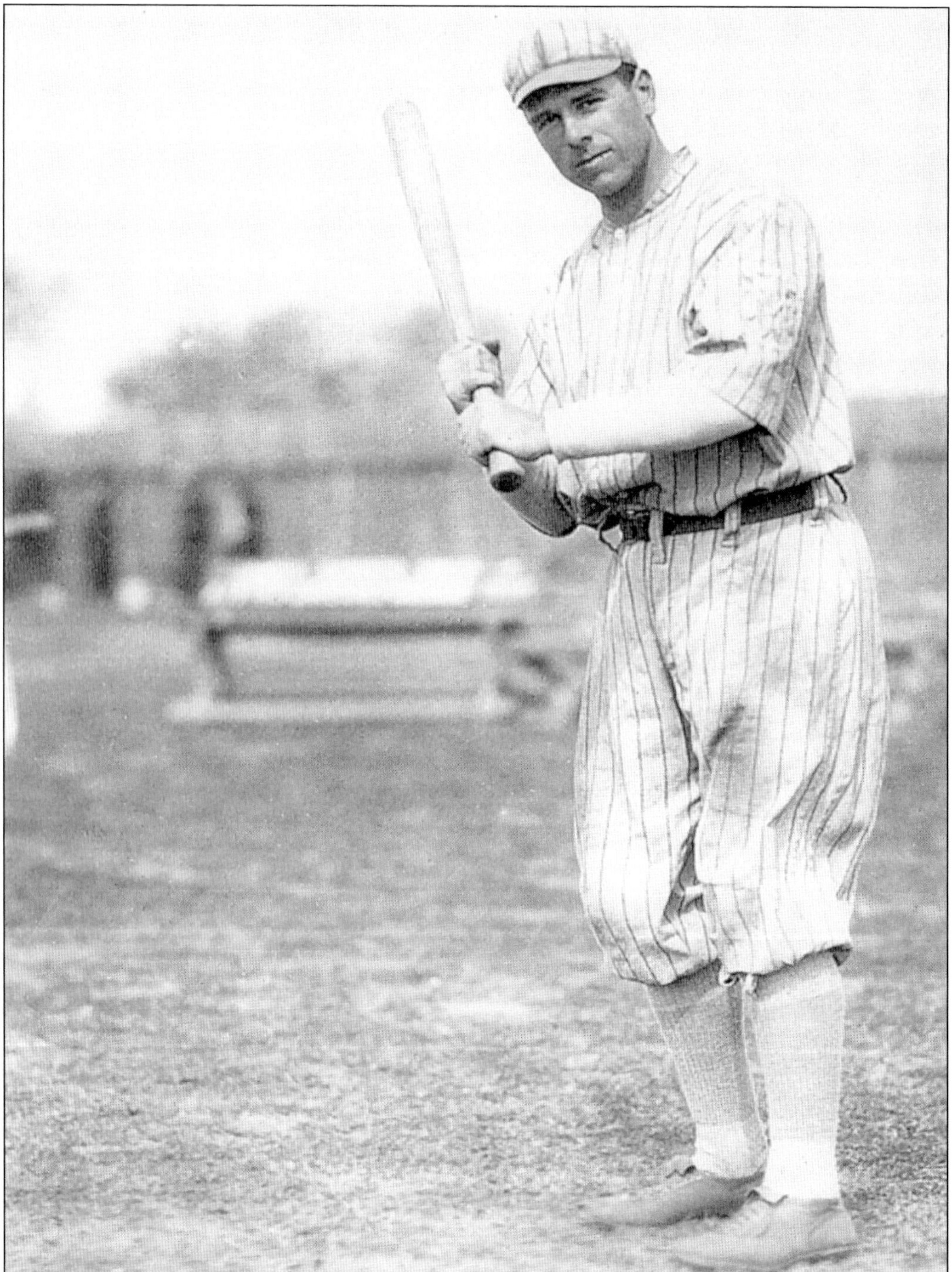

THE $30,000 MUFF. Fred Snodgrass was a solid performer during his eight seasons in New York, but he is best remembered for dropping an easy fly ball in center field in the last inning of the 1912 World Series. The "$30,000 muff," as reporters called the error (the amount was based on the difference between the winning and losing teams' shares), opened the gates for Boston to score two unearned runs off Christy Mathewson to win the championship.

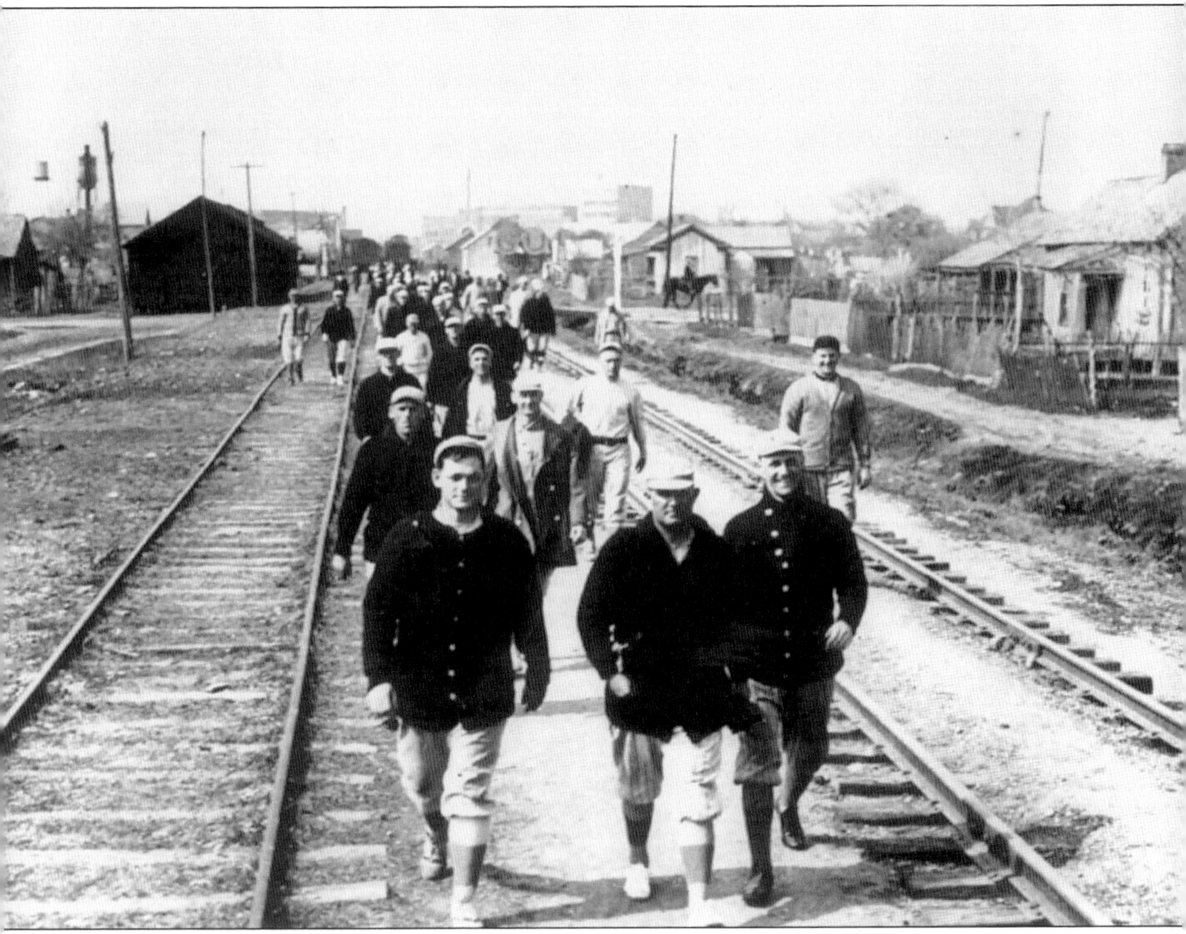

SPRING TRAINING, 1913. The Giants trained at Marlin, Texas, for many years. The club "thought that in a little town like that they could keep the fellows under control better," recalled Fred Snodgrass. "The ball park was about two miles from our hotel, and every day twice a day, morning and afternoon, we walked from the hotel to the ball park along some railroad tracks that ran close by." This photograph was taken in 1913 by Christy Mathewson.

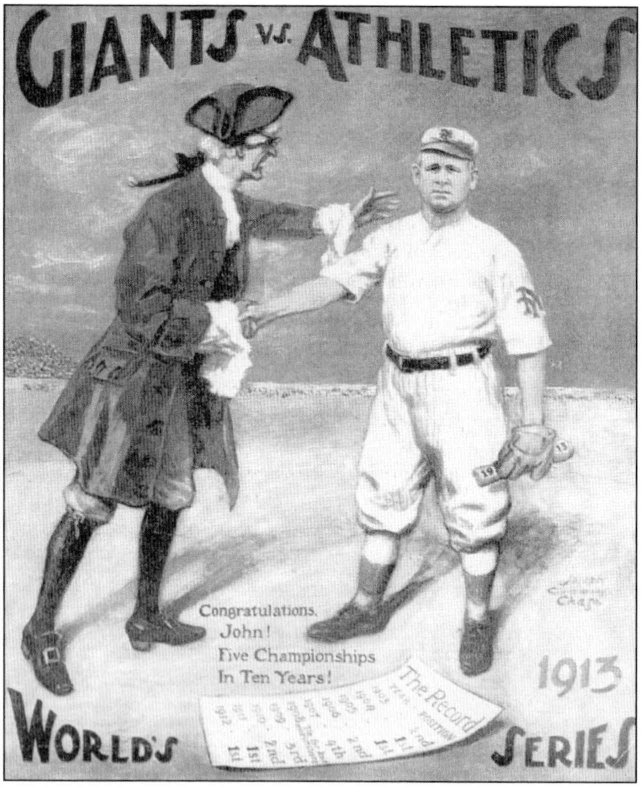

WORLD SERIES PROGRAM, 1913. McGraw's Giants waltzed to a third consecutive pennant in 1913 with a record of 101-51, then faced Connie Mack's Athletics in the World Series in a rematch of their 1911 meeting.

OCTOBER 7, 1913. The Giants' old nemesis, Home Run Baker, is tagged out at third base in the opening game of the 1913 World Series. Baker hit a two-run homer to help the Athletics past New York, 6-4, before 36,291 fans at the Polo Grounds.

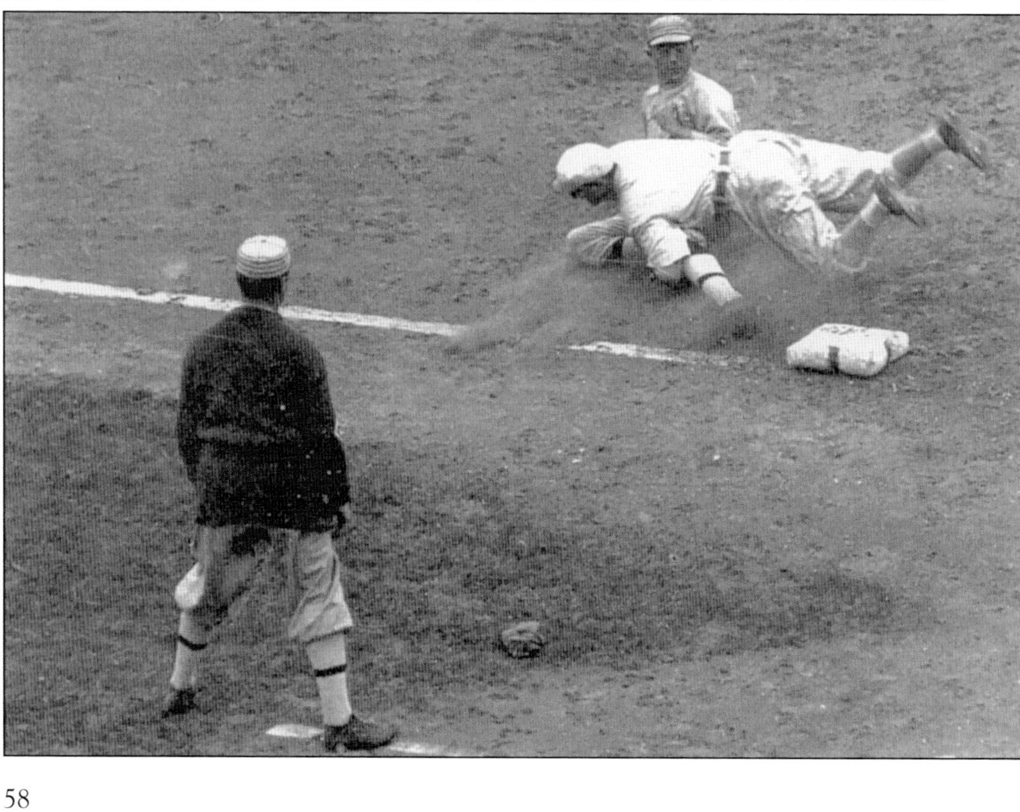

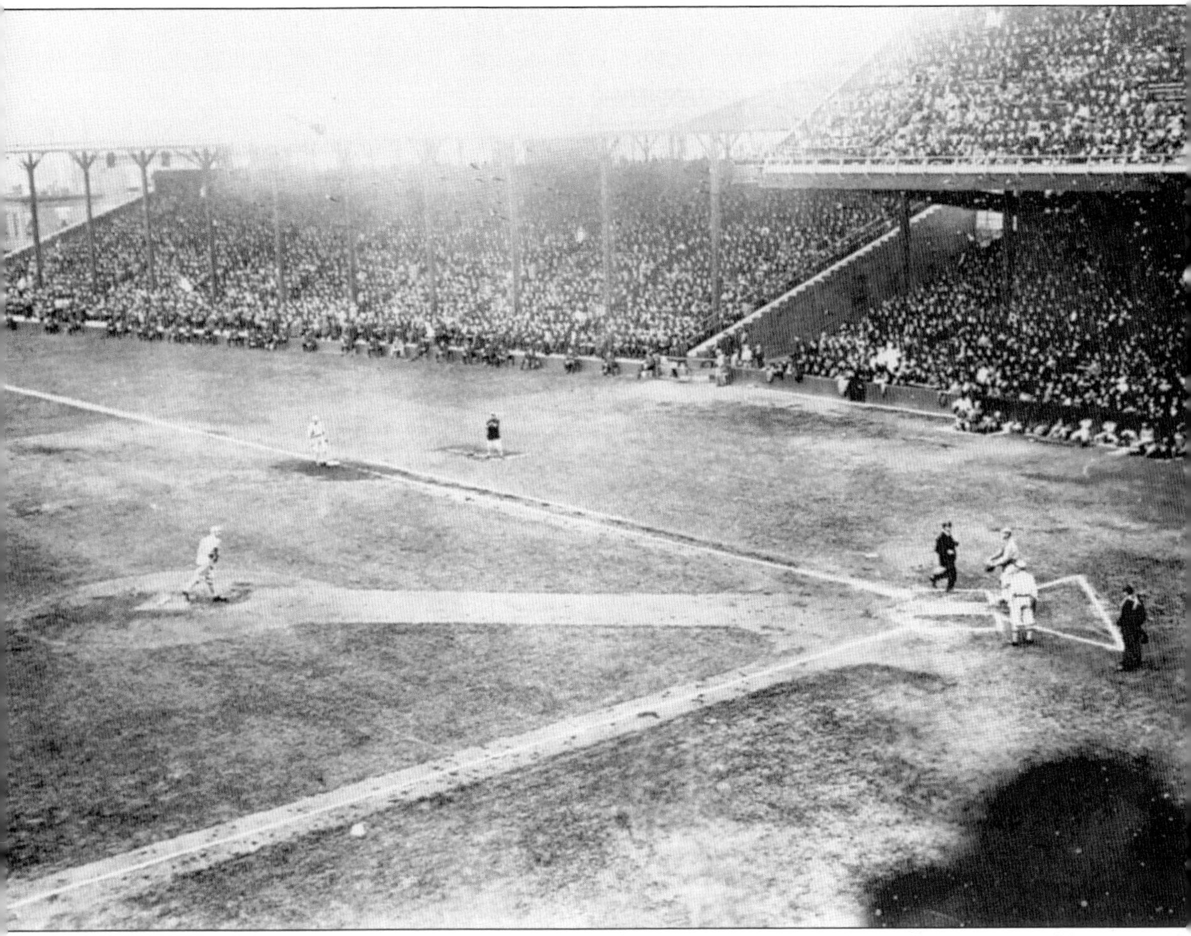

CHRISTY COMES THROUGH. Christy Mathewson warms up during game two of the 1913 World Series. Mathewson blanked the Athletics, 3-0, in ten innings for the Giants' only victory of the series. Mathewson singled in the winning run off Eddie Plank.

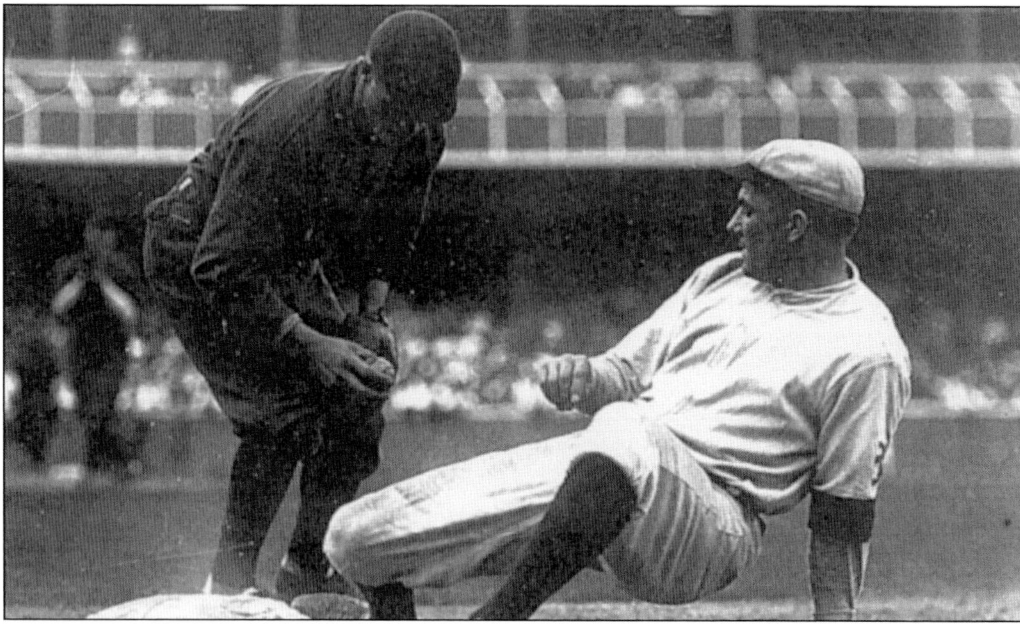

HAPPY TO BE A GIANT. Giants second baseman "Laughing Larry" Doyle was a fresh-faced, trusting 20 year old from Illinois when he first arrived at the Polo Grounds in 1907. When an opposing catcher asked the rookie what kind of pitches he liked to hit, Doyle innocently replied, "Fastballs, high and inside, sir." He saw nothing but curveballs the rest of the game. Doyle, one of McGraw's favorites, spent 13 of his 14 big-league seasons in a Giants uniform, winning a batting championship in 1915. It was Doyle who once exclaimed, "It's great to be young and a Giant."

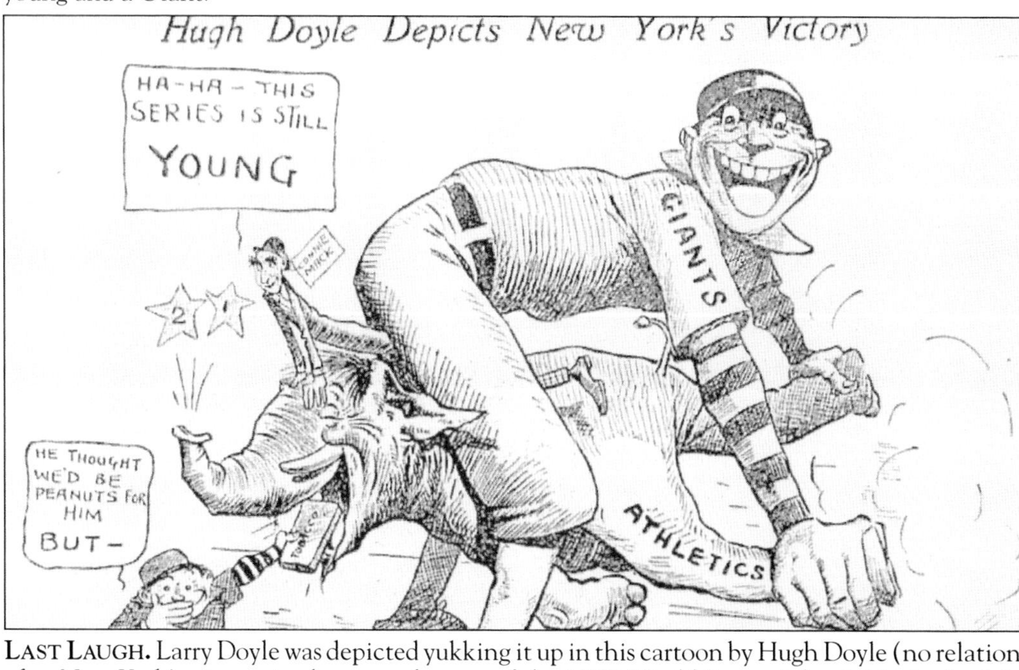

LAST LAUGH. Larry Doyle was depicted yukking it up in this cartoon by Hugh Doyle (no relation) after New York's victory in the second game of the 1913 World Series. The Athletics had the last laugh, however, sweeping the next three contests to win the world's championship.

JIM THORPE. Jim Thorpe dominated the 1912 Olympics in Stockholm, but "the world's greatest athlete" was a bust as a baseball player. John McGraw signed Thorpe in 1913 and put him in the outfield. Thorpe batted .143 in 19 games as a rookie, his fabled speed producing only two stolen bases. During his six years as a big-league gate attraction, which included stints in Cincinnati and Boston, Thorpe hit an aggregate .252 in 289 games with 7 home runs and 29 steals.

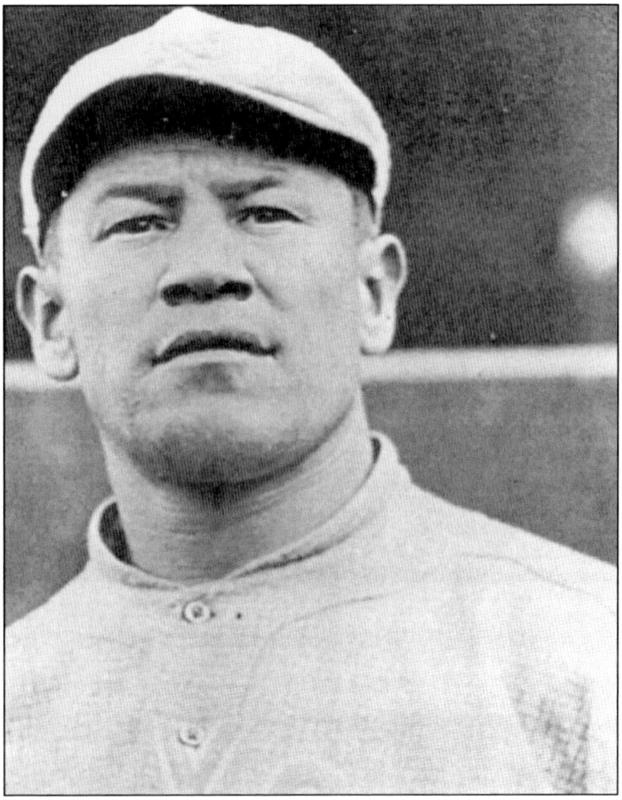

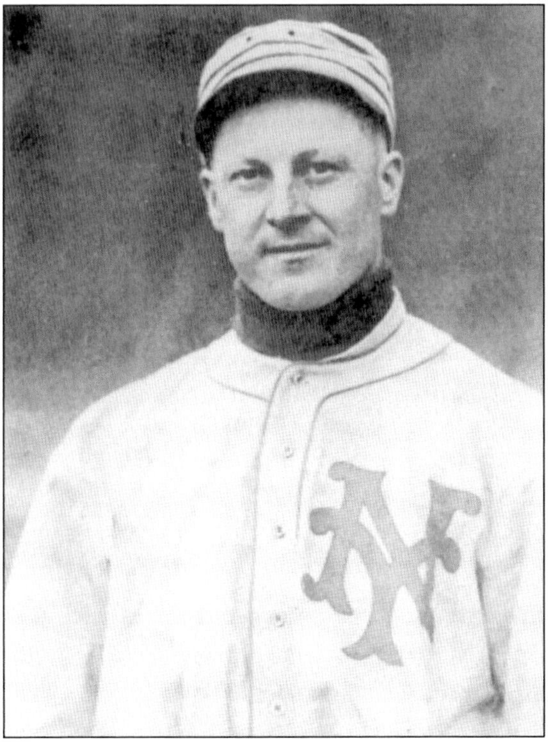

BENNY KAUFF. The collapse of the Federal League, an unsuccessful attempt to create a third major league circuit, allowed New York to pick up center fielder Benny Kauff. Kauff, who'd led the rival league in batting in each of its two seasons, vowed that he would "make Ty Cobb look like a bush leaguer." The colorful Kauff never made good on his boast, though he played regularly from 1916 to 1920 for McGraw.

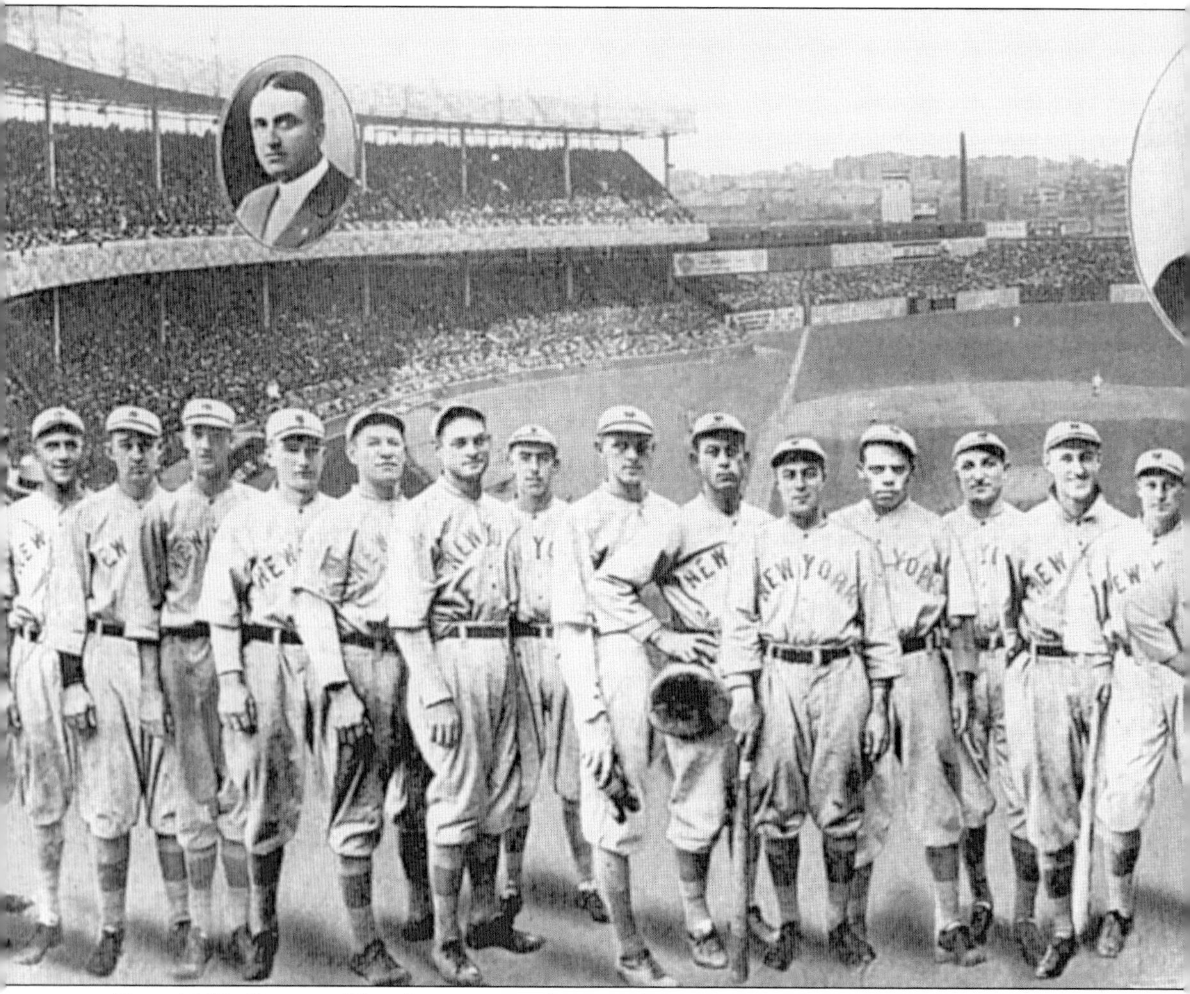

THE 1917 GIANTS. The Giants won their sixth pennant under McGraw in 1917, finishing an easy ten games in front of Philadelphia. The team was rebuilt almost completely since finishing last two years earlier. The outfield boasted a pair of .300 hitters in Benny Kauff and George Burns and a home run champion in Dave Robertson. The pitching staff was anchored by three southpaws: Ferdie Shupp, Slim Sallee, and Rube Benton. After beginning his career in

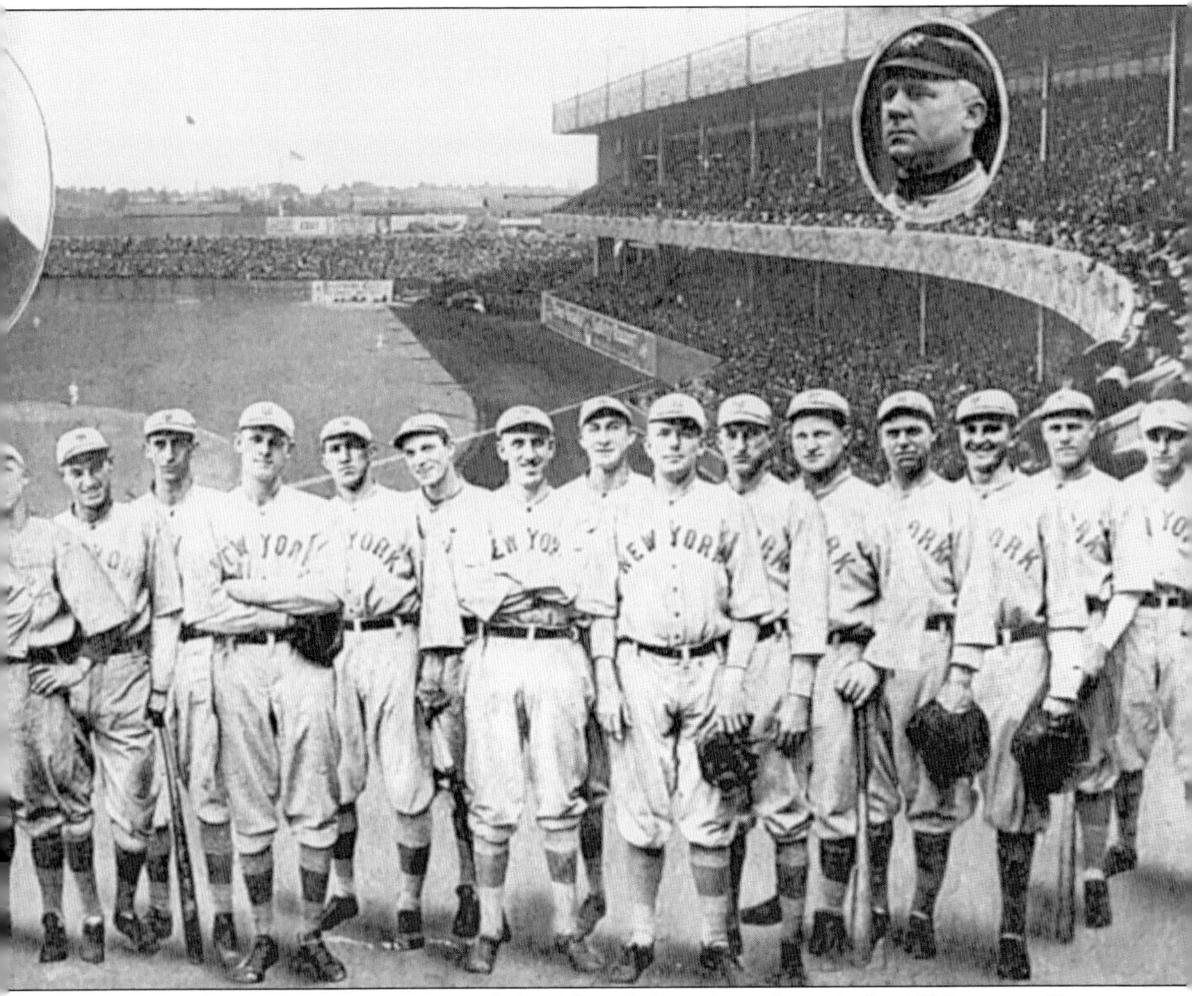

Cincinnati, John "Rube" Benton was traded to New York midway through the 1915 season. He enjoyed records of 16-8 in 1916, 15-9 in 1917, and 17-11 in 1919. Benton blanked the White Sox, 2-0, in the third game of the 1917 World Series but was saddled with the loss in the decisive sixth game when some burlesque fielding allowed three unearned runs to cross the plate.

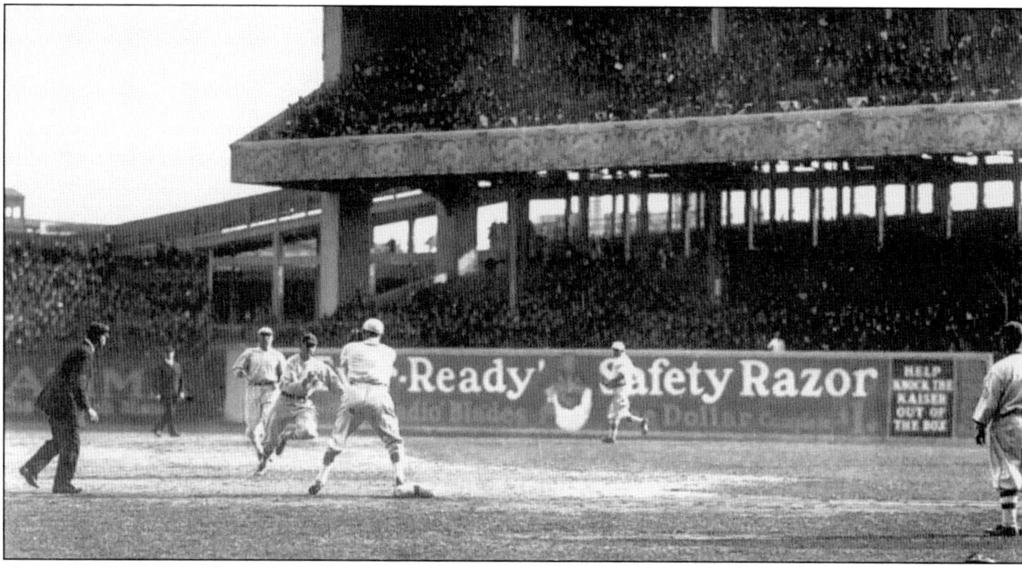

OUT AT THIRD. Chicago's Eddie Collins is about to be tagged out by Giants third baseman Heinie Zimmerman in the fourth game of the 1917 World Series. The Giants won, 5-0, behind Benny Kauff's two home runs and Ferdie Schupp's 7-hit pitching.

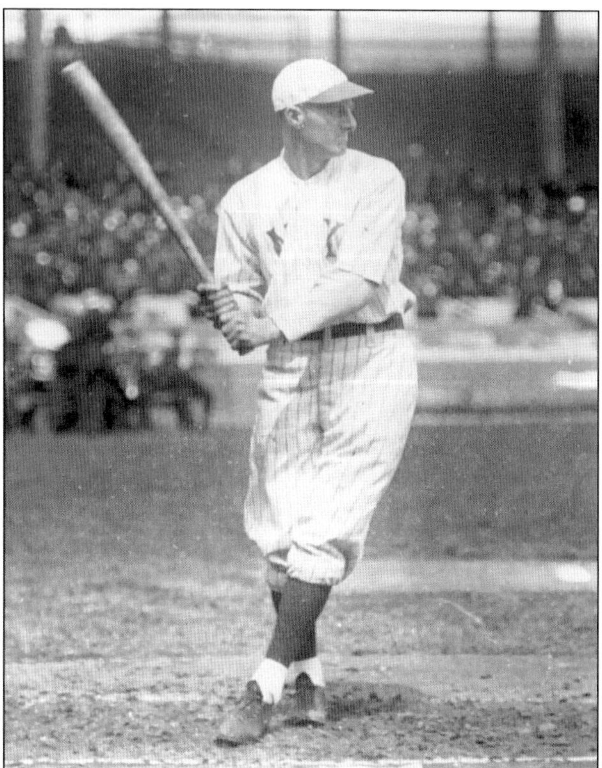

HEINIE THE GOAT. Third baseman Heinie Zimmerman led the league in RBIs in 1916 and 1917, but he is unjustly remembered as being the goat of the 1917 World Series. During a rundown in the fourth inning of the finale, he comically chased Eddie Collins across an unguarded home plate with the go-ahead run. The fielders who failed to back up the play were to blame, but Zimmerman got the criticism. "What was I supposed to do?" he asked. "Throw it to the umpire?"

BATTLING BUCK. Charles "Buck" Herzog was drafted out of the Pennsylvania League in 1908. John McGraw personally disliked the scrappy infielder, who nonetheless had three separate tours of duty with the Giants. Herzog's major claim to fame was a bloody brawl with Ty Cobb inside a hotel room during spring training in 1917. Herzog reportedly floored the Detroit star with the first punch, but by the time the fight was broken up Cobb had pummeled his antagonist unmercifully.

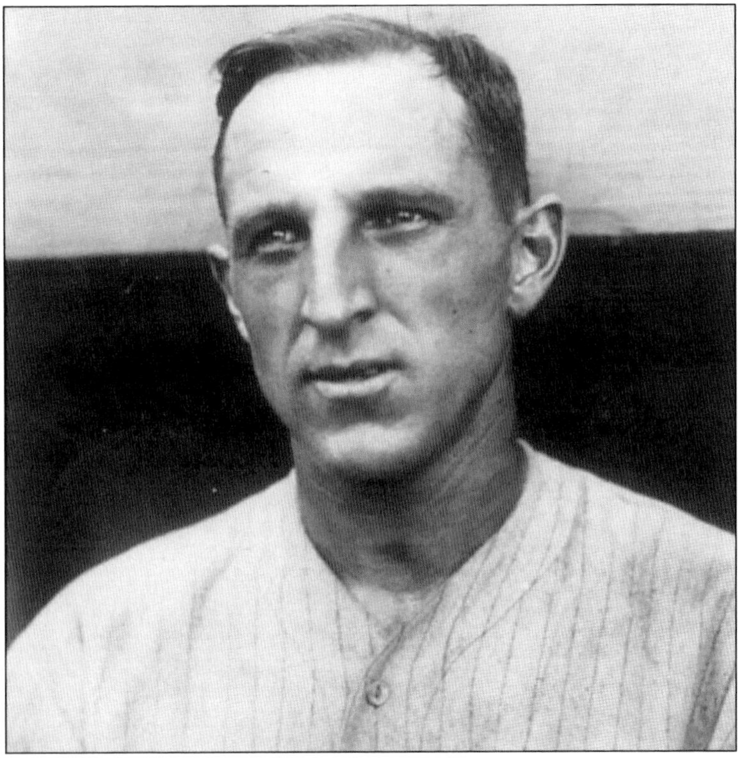

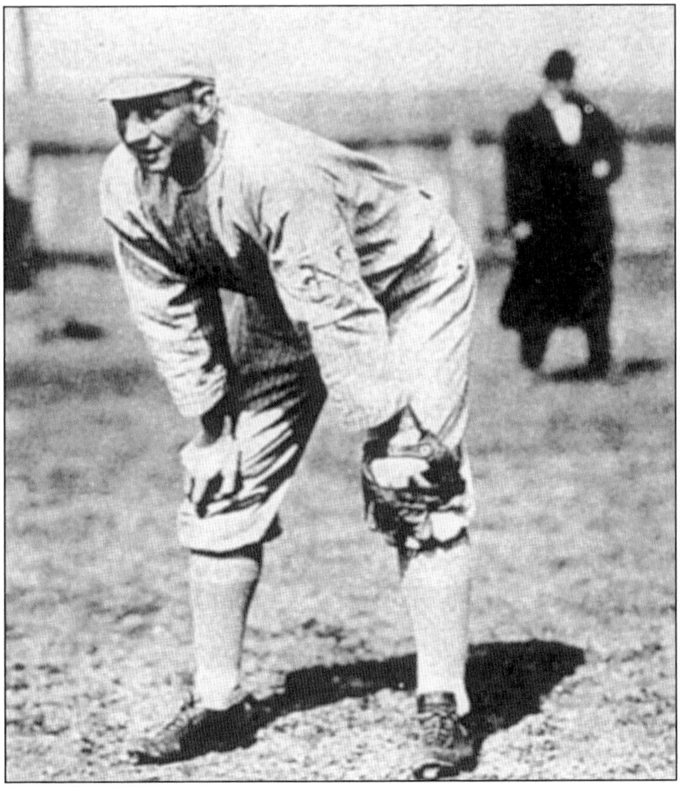

HARVARD EDDIE. The First World War resulted in shortened seasons and depleted rosters as major leaguers were called into service. Eddie Grant, the Giants' Harvard-educated third baseman of 1913–15, became an infantry major. On October 5, 1918, Grant was killed in the Argonne Forest. His body was never found, though the Giants honored his memory with a centerfield monument at the Polo Grounds.

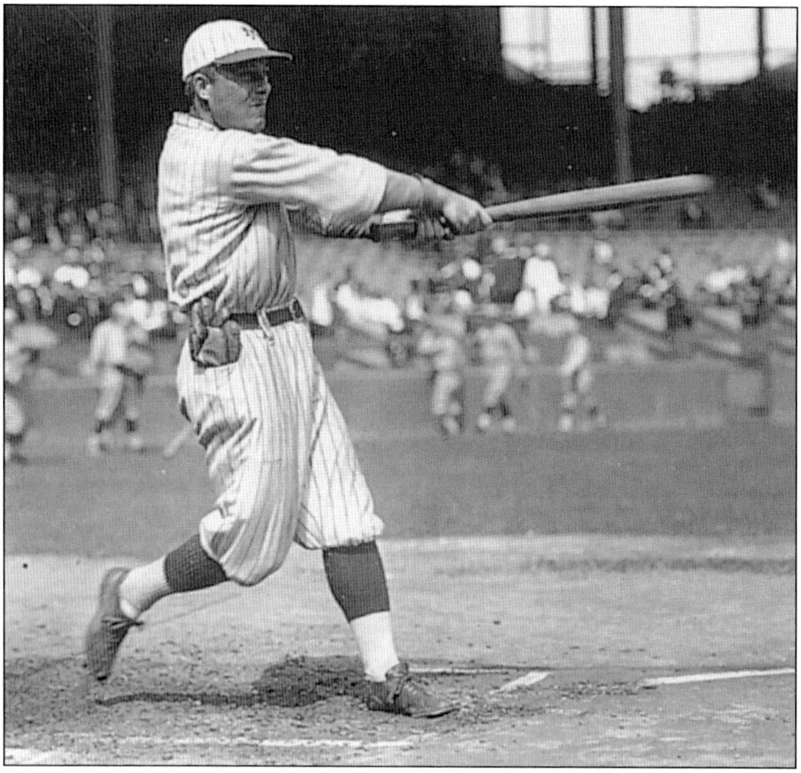

ON THE FLY. Speedy George Burns, a product of the New York State League, played 11 seasons (1911–21) in the Giants' outfield, leading the loop in stolen bases twice and in runs five times. An advertising sign at the Polo Grounds alluded to Burns' ballhawking ability: "Last year George Burns caught 198 flies, but Ajax Flypaper caught 19 billion, 865 million flies . . ."

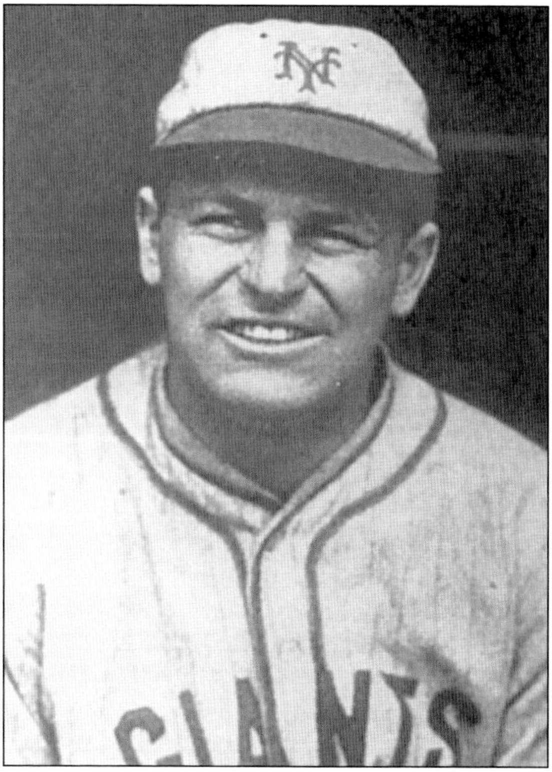

DYING YOUNG. Of all the players he managed, John McGraw kept pictures of only two in his office: Christy Mathewson and Ross "Pep" Youngs, both of whom died young. Youngs came to New York in 1917 as a gifted 20-year-old outfielder from Texas and batted .322 over a ten-year career. In 1926, Youngs fell seriously ill with Bright's disease, an incurable kidney disorder, and died the following fall. He was only 30. Despite having his life and career cut short, Youngs later was voted into the Hall of Fame.

Three

Four Flags in a Row

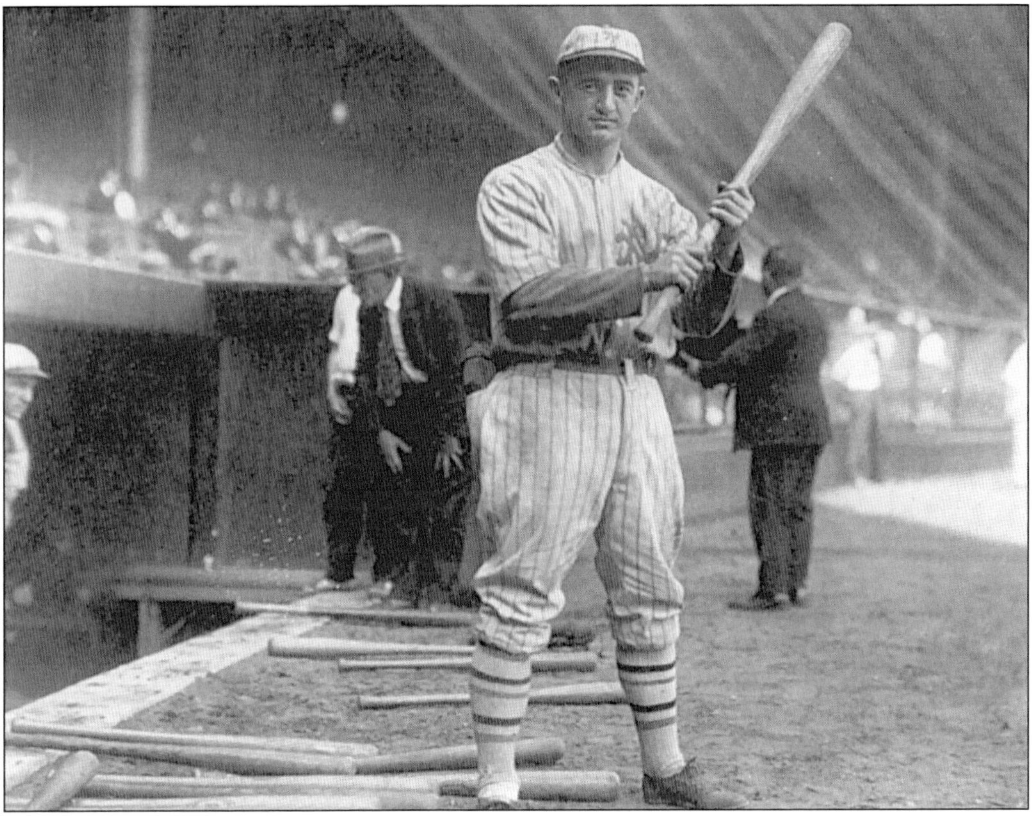

The Fordham Flash. Frankie Frisch was born in the Bronx and graduated from Fordham before joining the Giants in 1919. The quick, aggressive second baseman became the Giants' field leader and sparkled in October, hitting a collective .363 in his four World Series with New York. But Frisch represented a new kind of player, one that wouldn't stand for John McGraw's tongue-lashings.

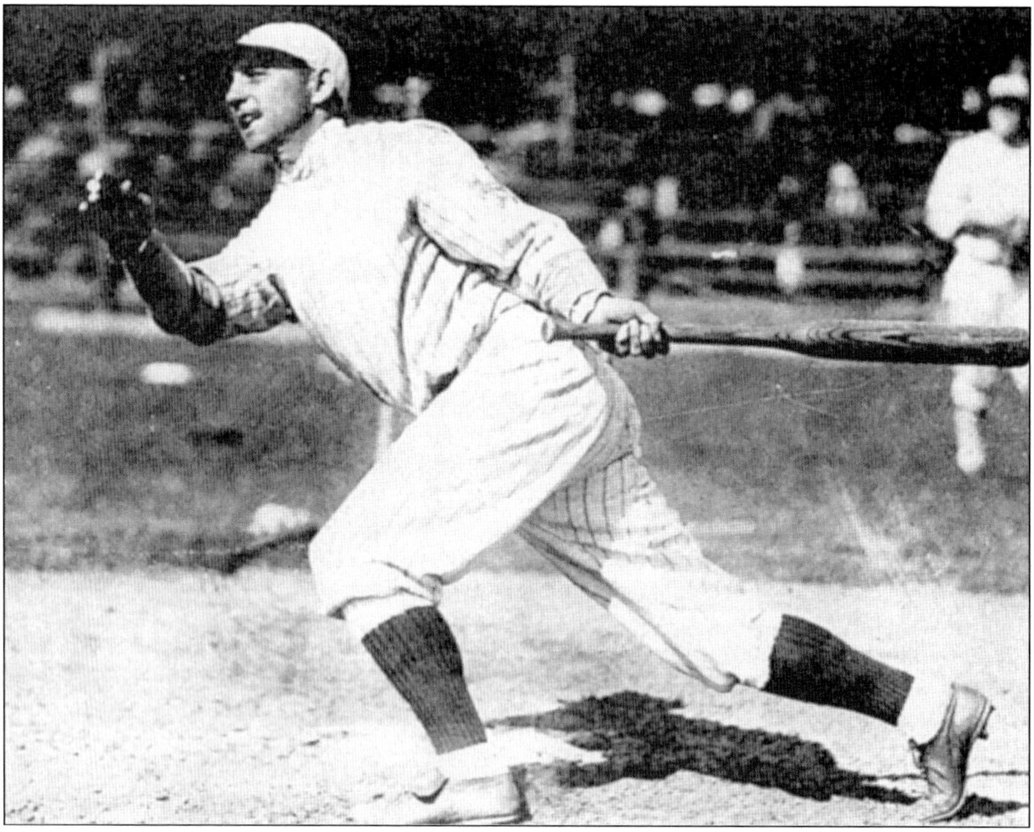

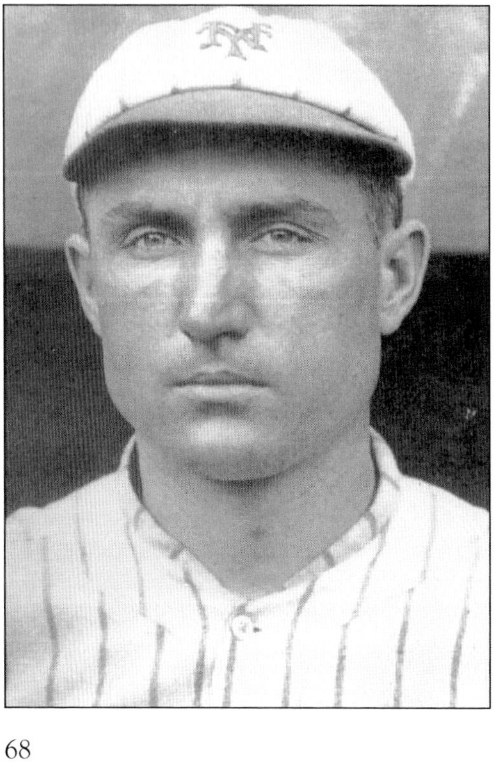

HEINIE GROH. Heinie Groh was originally signed by the Giants and spent the 1912 World Series on the bench. John McGraw suggested Groh's trademark bottle-shaped bat, a thin-handled, heavy-barreled weapon that was perfect for the little third baseman. In 1913, Groh was traded to Cincinnati, where he helped the Reds to a world's championship. Groh returned to the Giants in 1922, just in time to participate in another three World Series. Groh hit .474 in the 1922 World Series. For the rest of his life he carried 474 as his license plate number.

BEAUTY BANCROFT. Midway through the 1920 season John McGraw traded his regular shortstop of nine seasons, Art Fletcher, for Philadelphia's Dave "Beauty" Bancroft. Between 1921 and 1923 the switch-hitting Iowa native had batting marks of .318, .321, and .304 as the Giants grabbed the pennant each year. After spending six seasons in Brooklyn and Boston, Bancroft wrapped up his Hall-of-Fame career as a Giant in 1930.

HIGHPOCKETS KELLY, 1921. At 6-foot-4, George Kelly was nicknamed "Highpockets" for obvious reason. Debuting as a 19 year old in 1915, the gangly San Francisco native was sent to Pittsburgh two years later but was soon reacquired by John McGraw. Kelly became the regular first baseman in 1920, claiming his first of two RBI crowns, then followed up with a league-high 23 homers in 1921. Kelly left New York after the 1926 season, wrapping up his Hall-of-Fame career with Brooklyn in 1932.

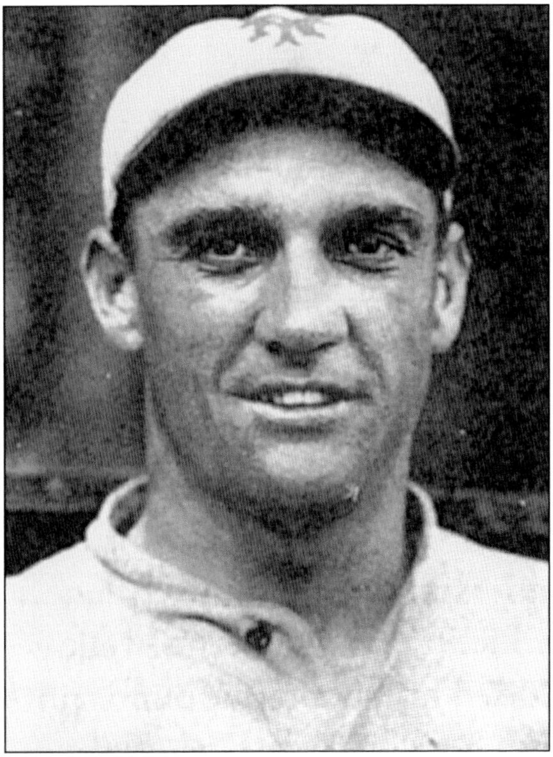

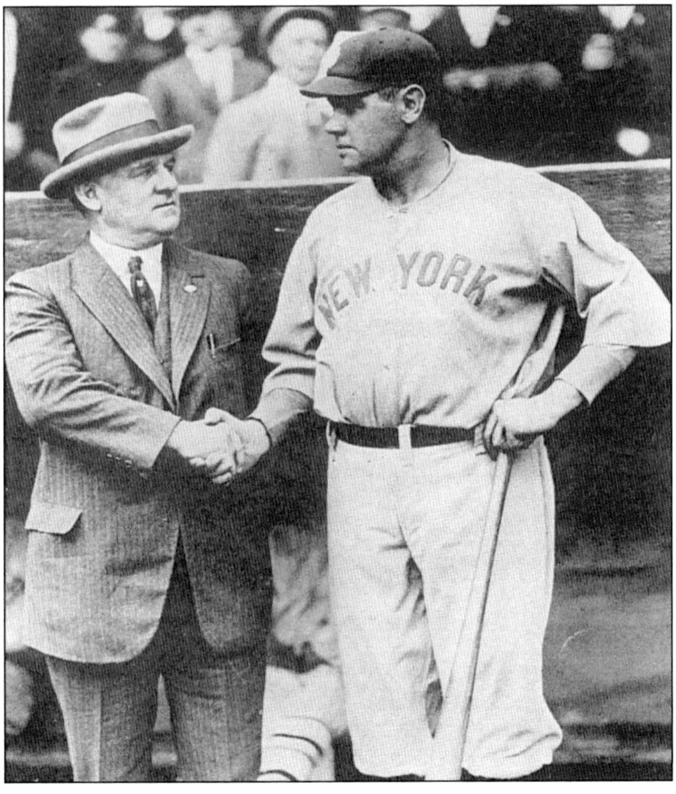

NO LOVE LOST. John McGraw and Babe Ruth size each other up prior to the beginning of one of the three straight World Series the Giants and Yankees played against each other between 1921 and 1923. McGraw despised the Yankees' slugger, who had hit a mind-boggling 59 homers in 1921, blaming him for the seismic shift in baseball strategy, from one of bunts and stolen bases to that of swinging from the heels.

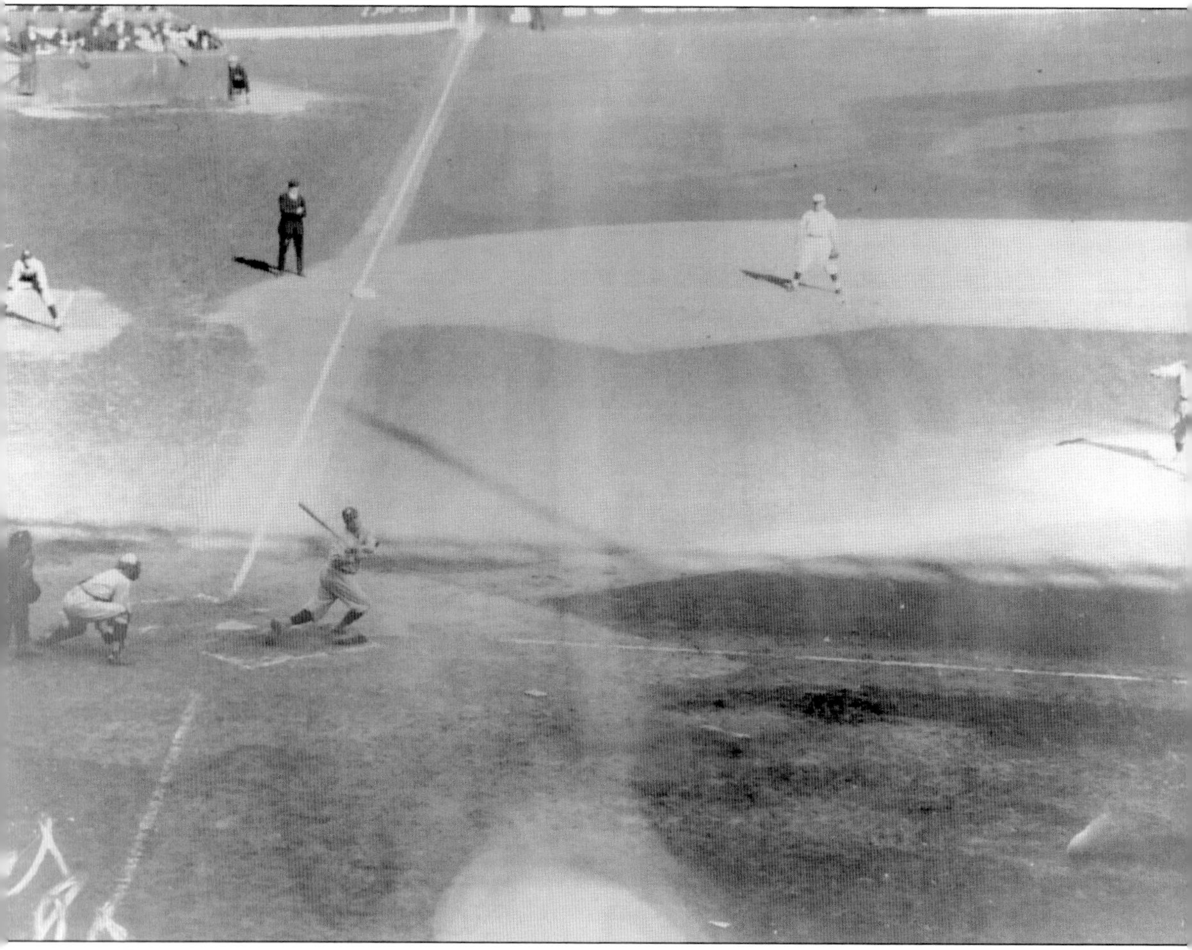

TWO IN A ROW FOR THE GIANTS. Babe Ruth swings and misses during the 1922 World Series. For two Octobers in a row, Ruth and the Yankees had a hard time of it against their rivals. When the teams met in a best-of-nine format in the 1921 World Series, the Giants stormed back to whip the Yankees, five games to three, after dropping the first two contests by identical 3-0 scores. The leagues returned to a best-of-seven format in 1922. This time the Giants swept the Yankees four straight (there was one tie game). While the first two all-New York World Series were expected to be a showcase for Ruth's mighty slugging, McGraw's staff held the Babe to a single home run in the '21 series and a paltry .118 average with no home runs the following autumn. Ruth and the Bronx Bombers would rebound with a vengeance in the 1923 World Series, but for now McGraw felt vindicated by his style of inside baseball.

MONEY PITCHER. Art Nehf was the only pitcher to win a game in each of the four World Series the Giants played between 1921 and 1924. Nehf, acquired from the Braves in August 1919, averaged 20 wins during his first three full seasons with the Giants. The good-natured southpaw pitched the clincher in the 1921 and 1922 World Series, outdueling Schoolboy Hoyt, 1-0, in the former and besting Joe Bush in the latter, 5-3. He tossed a 1-0 shutout in the 1923 fall classic, and beat Walter Johnson in the opener of the 1924 World Series.

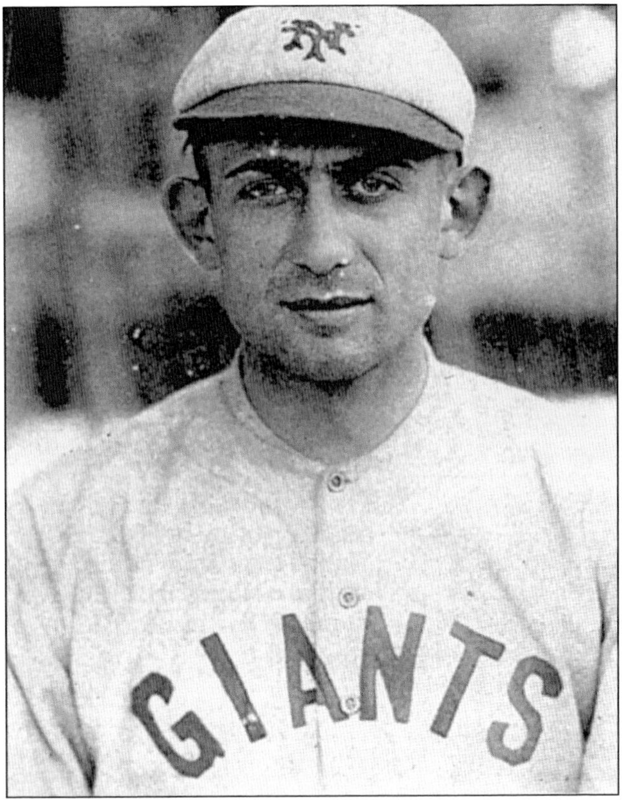

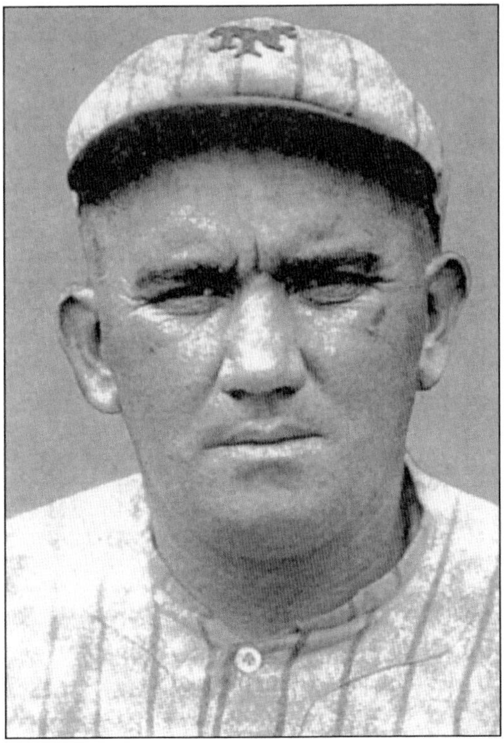

BANNED FOR LIFE. Spitball specialist "Shufflin' Phil" Douglas was one of the heroes of the 1921 World Series, beating the Yankees twice. By the middle of the following summer he was 11-4 with a 2.62 ERA when, upset over one of John McGraw's tongue-lashings, he drunkenly wrote a letter to a St. Louis player suggesting that, for the right price, he would sit out the rest of the year. The offer was reported to Commissioner Kenesaw Mountain Landis, who banned Douglas from baseball for life.

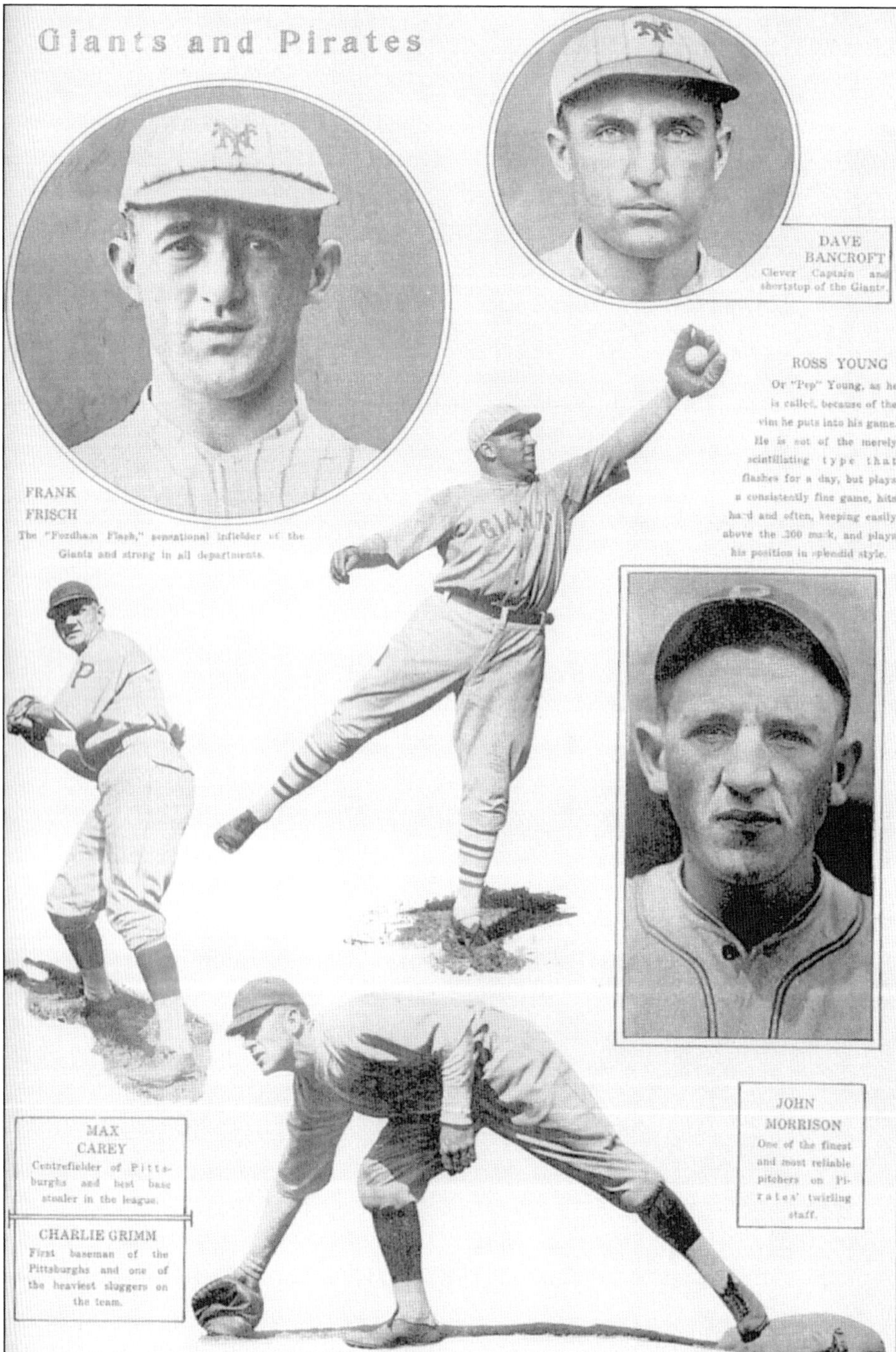

THE BEST EVER. The 1922 Giants were the third and last of John McGraw's world champions and one of the finest aggregations of talent ever seen. They won 93 games in a tough league, batted .304 as a team, and swept the mighty Yankees in the World Series. In addition to McGraw and coach Hughie Jennings, five players from the team have plaques at Cooperstown, including the three Giant stars seen on this rotogravure page from 1922.

WAKE UP, MUSCLES. Future Yankees manager Casey Stengel learned the fine art of platooning players from the master, John McGraw, who expertly moved role players like Stengel in and out of the lineup. The colorful, clutch-hitting outfielder was traded from the Phillies to New York during the 1921 season and responded with a pair of .300 seasons as a Giant. When Casey took his first look around the Polo Grounds, he said, "Wake up, muscles. We're in New York now."

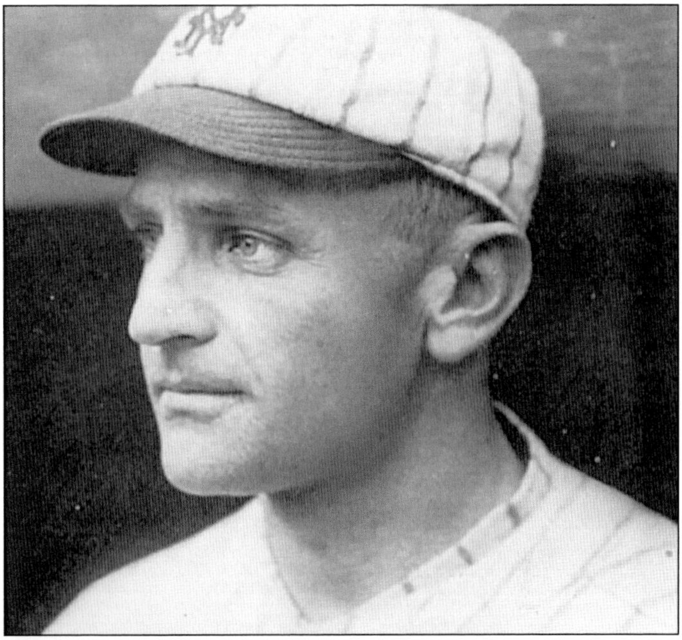

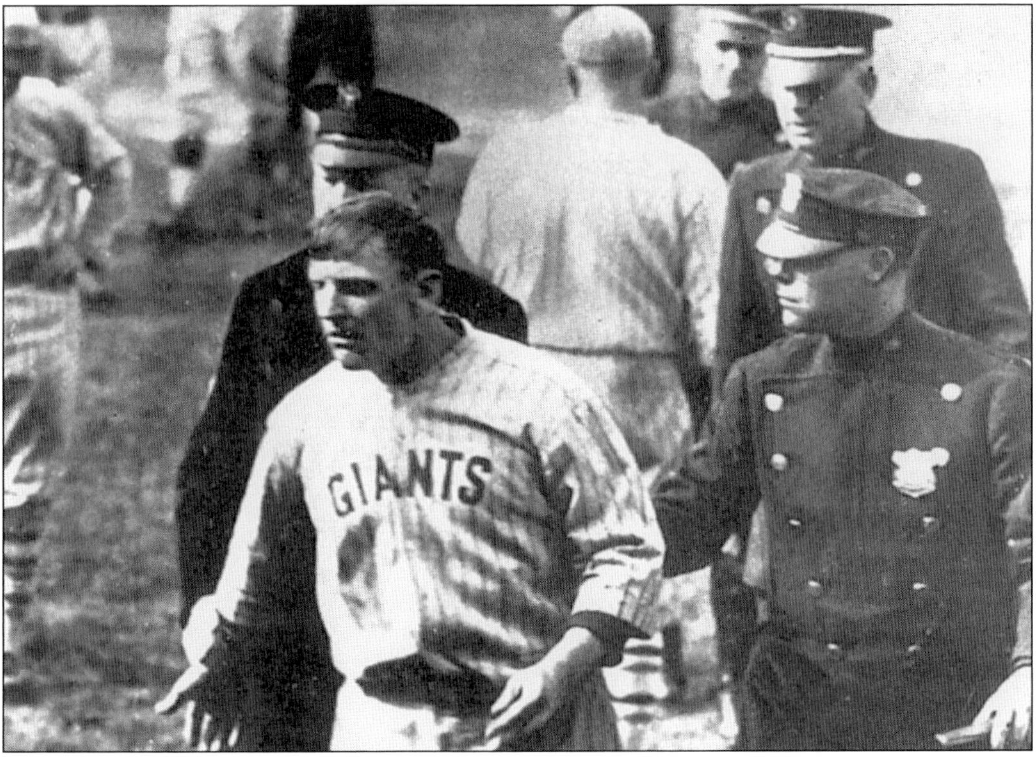

FIGHTING MAD. On May 7, 1923, Casey Stengel got into a brawl with Lefty Weinert when the big Philadelphia pitcher aimed a fastball at his head. Casey, who had been hit by a pitch his previous time up, threw his bat and charged the mound. It took several policemen to break up the ruckus, which resulted in a ten-day suspension for Stengel. Casey hit .339 that summer to help the Giants win a third consecutive pennant.

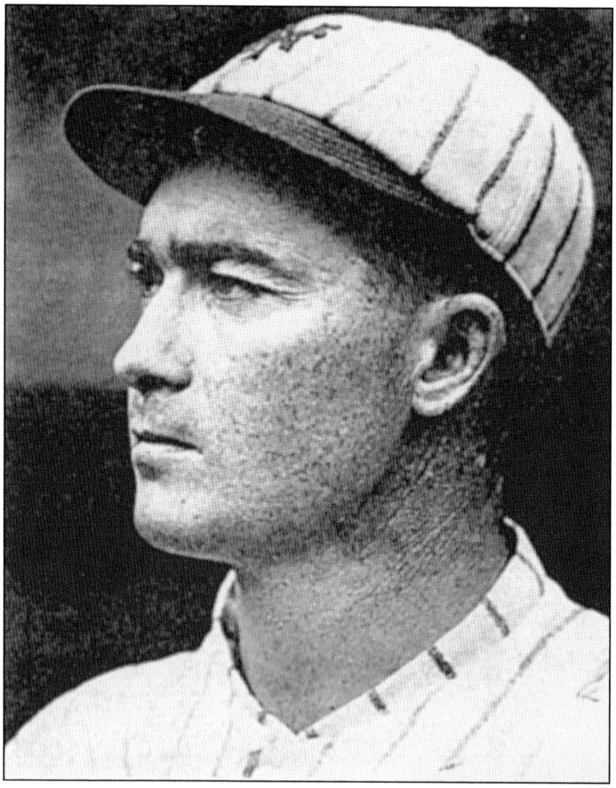

JESSE BARNES. The first Giant to wear a uniform during World War I was pitcher Jesse Barnes, who had just been acquired from the Braves. The right-hander from Oklahoma returned to win 25 games for the second-place Giants in 1919, best in the National League, and added 20 more in 1920. Equally effective as a starter or reliever, Barnes made three relief appearances in the 1921 World Series and got credit for two wins.

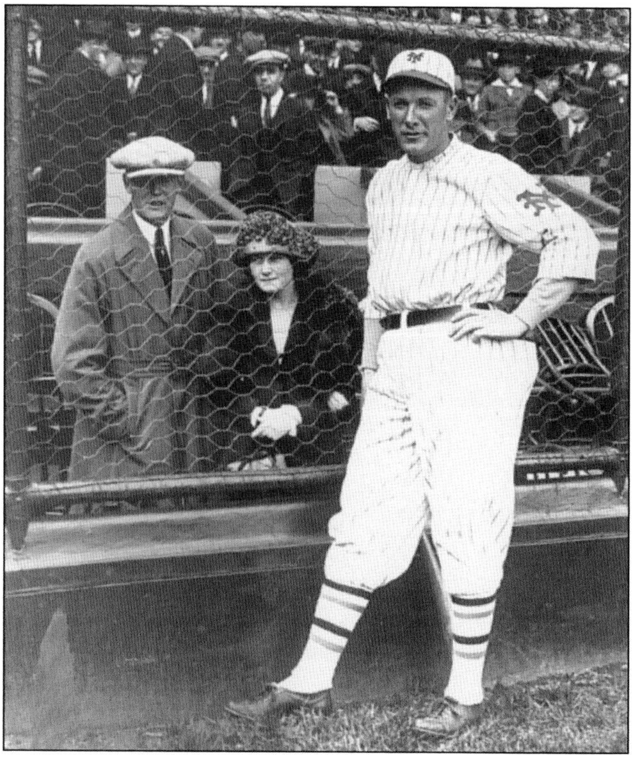

GOOD IN THE CLUTCH. Emil "Irish" Meusel is pictured with his brother Bob (an outfielder with the Yankees) and his sister-in-law. Irish spent 6 of his 11 big-league seasons in the Giants' outfield, leading the league with 125 RBIs in 1925. "I would say he was as reliable a man as I ever saw for driving in the winning run," said Fred Snodgrass. "Put that winning run on second base with two outs and, boy, was he tough."

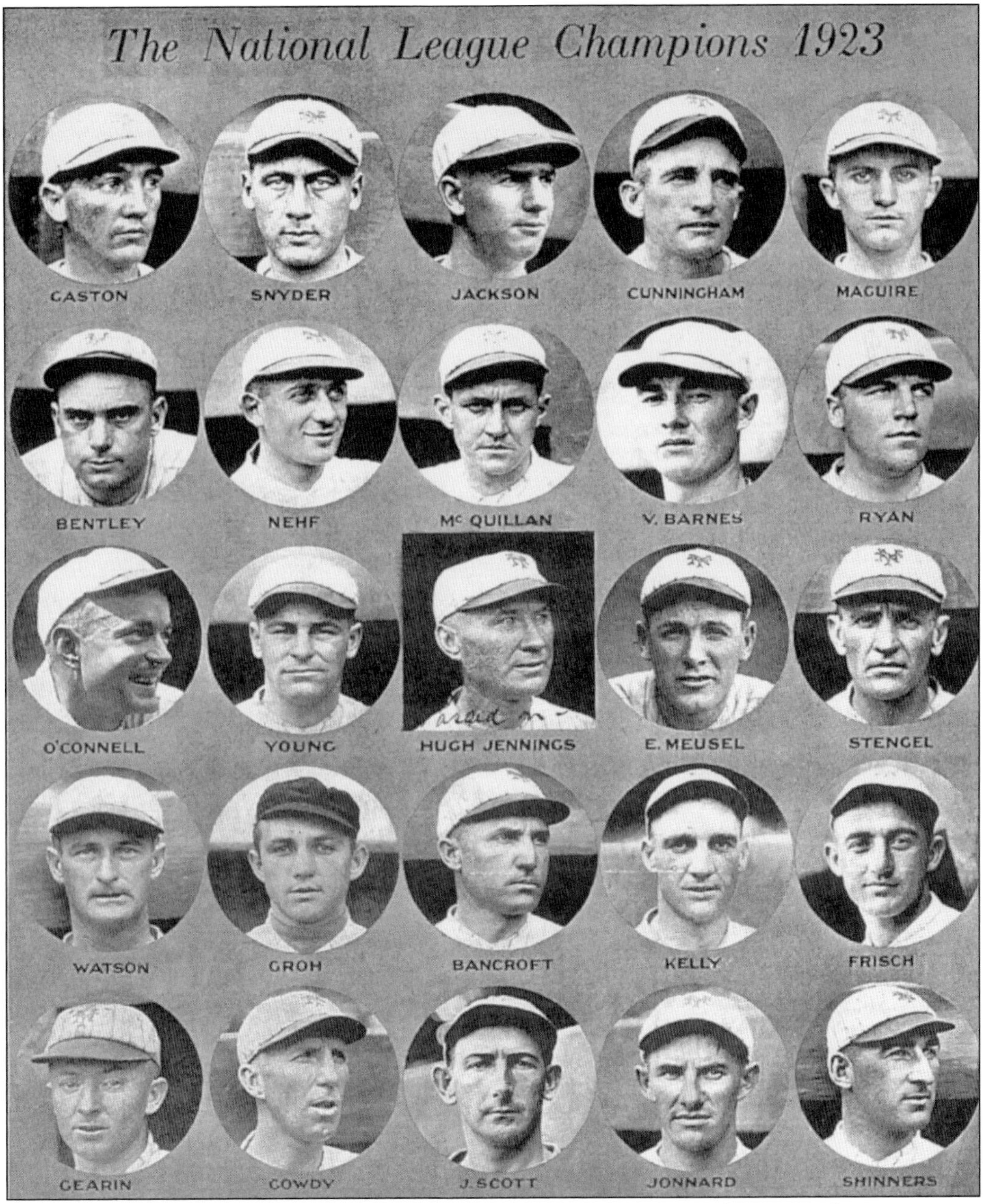

THE 1923 PENNANT WINNERS. The Giants won 95 games in 1923, four more than runner-up Cincinnati. Notable contributors to McGraw's third straight pennant were Rosy Ryan, who won a team-best 16 games as a starter and reliever; Jack Bentley, who won 13 games and batted a sizzling .427, including .500 as a pinch-hitter; and Irish Meusel, George Kelly, and Frankie Frisch, each of whom drove more than 100 teammates across the plate.

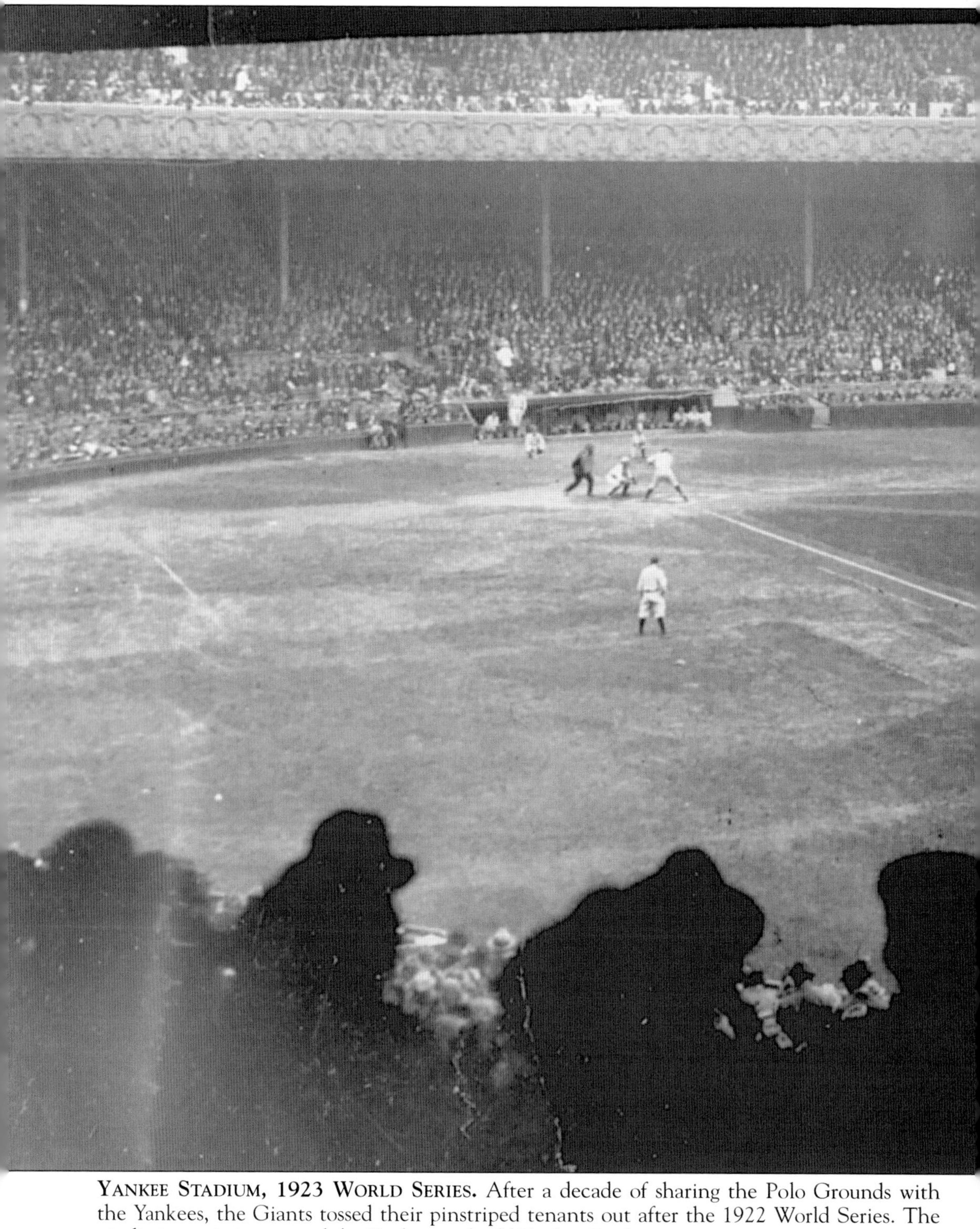

YANKEE STADIUM, 1923 WORLD SERIES. After a decade of sharing the Polo Grounds with the Yankees, the Giants tossed their pinstriped tenants out after the 1922 World Series. The vindictive eviction caused the Yankees to build Yankee Stadium just a quarter-mile away across the Harlem River. The magnificent 62,000-seat stadium truly was "the house that Ruth built."

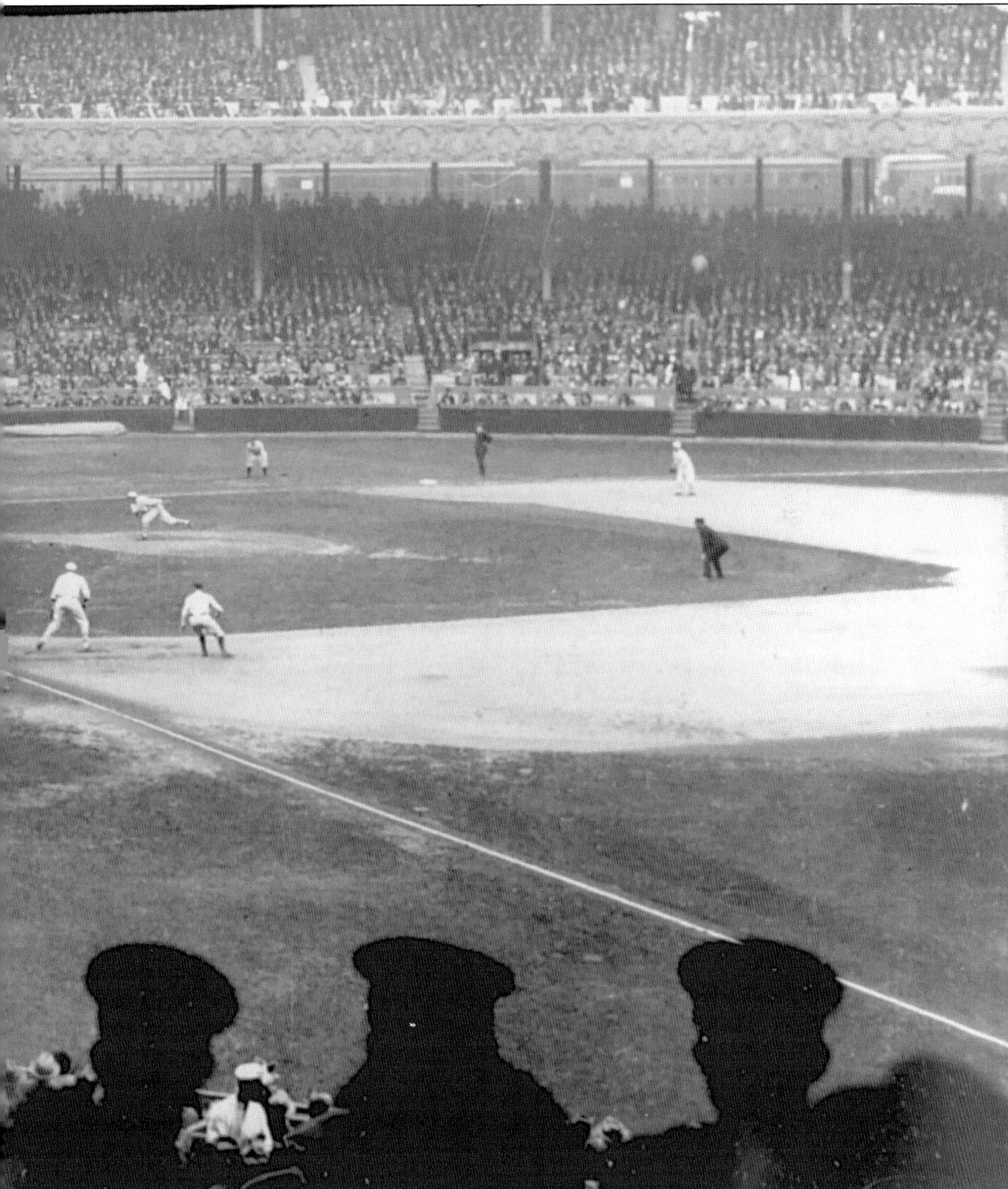

During the 1923 World Series, Babe Ruth finally broke out of his post-season slump, belting three home runs as the Yankees beat the Giants in six games, foiling the Giants' bid for an unprecedented third straight world's championship.

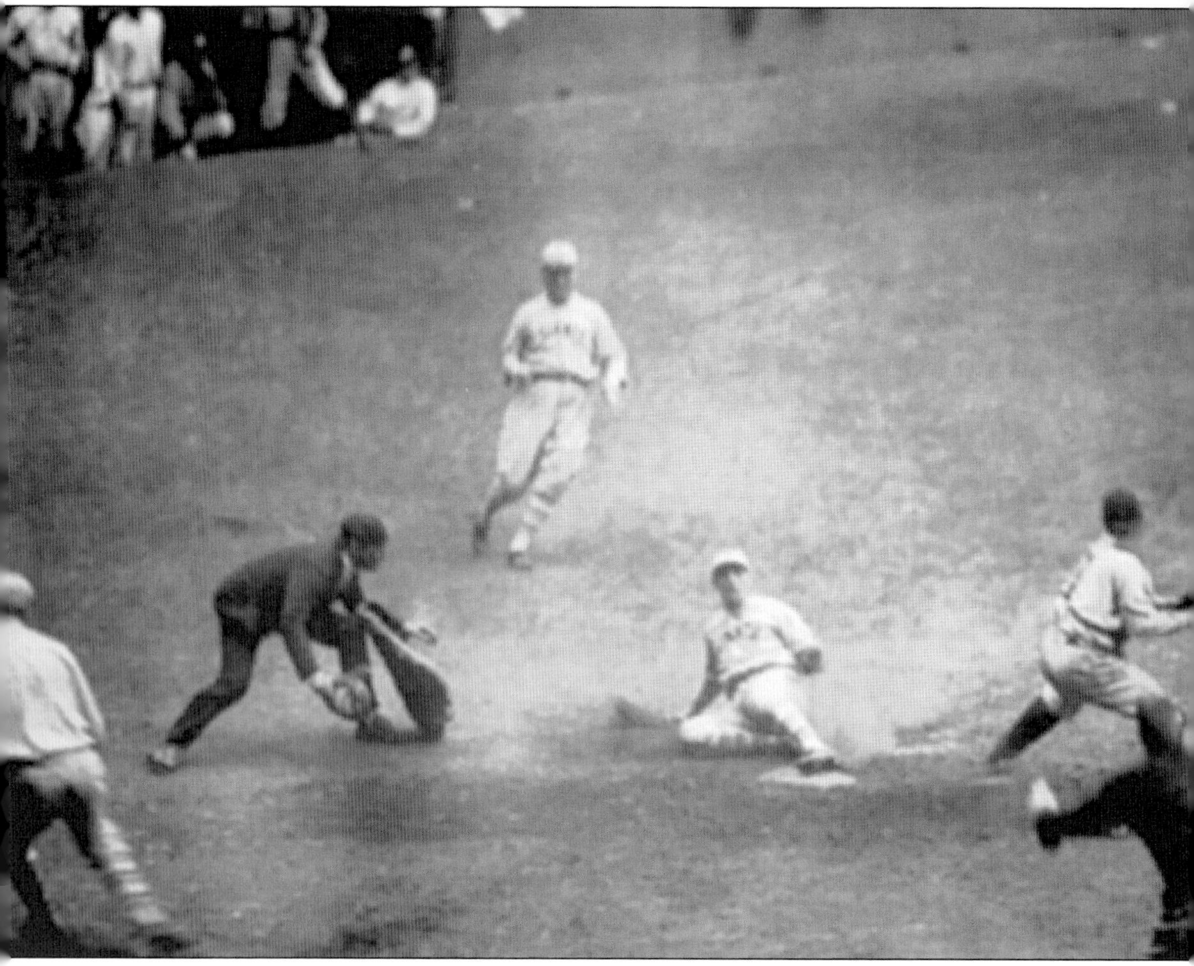

CASEY THE HERO. A pair of dramatic home runs by Casey Stengel provided the only victories for the Giants in the 1923 World Series. In the opener, he legged out an inside-the-park home run in the ninth inning to beat the Yankees, 5-4. Casey's improbable dash ended with a slide across home plate (pictured here) and made the 34 year old a national sensation. Two afternoons later, Stengel won the third game, 1-0, with a solo home run in the seventh inning. This time the ball landed in the seats, allowing Stengel to leisurely circumnavigate the bases while thumbing his nose at the Yankees' bench. To Stengel's chagrin, his heroics didn't keep him from being traded to the lowly Boston Braves a month after the series ended.

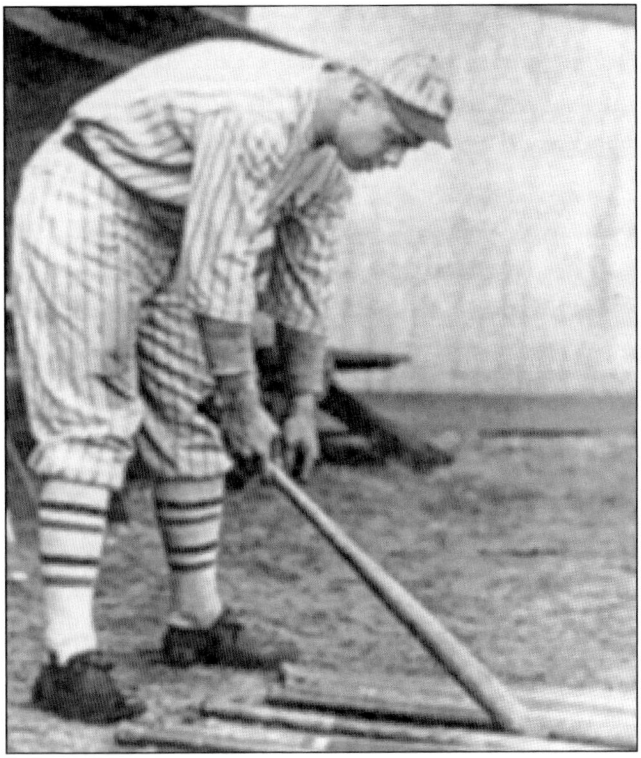

BILL TERRY CHOOSES A BAT, 1924. In 1924, McGraw's Giants became the first team to string together four straight pennants. A valuable part-time player was first baseman Bill Terry, who had signed with New York after tearing up the Southern Association as a pitcher and hitter with Memphis. Terry hit only .239 his first full season in New York, but over the next dozen summers his average would dip under .300 just once.

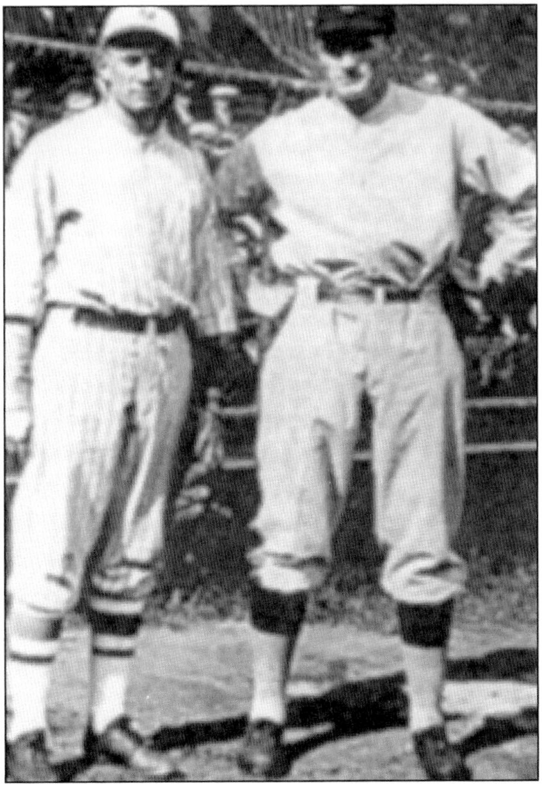

NEHF VS. JOHNSON. Art Nehf (left) was McGraw's pick to open the 1924 World Series against Washington's legendary Walter Johnson, who was making his first post-season start after 18 big-league seasons. Ignoring the widescale public sentiment for the popular Johnson, the Giants eked out a 4-3 win in 12 innings, as both starting pitchers went the distance.

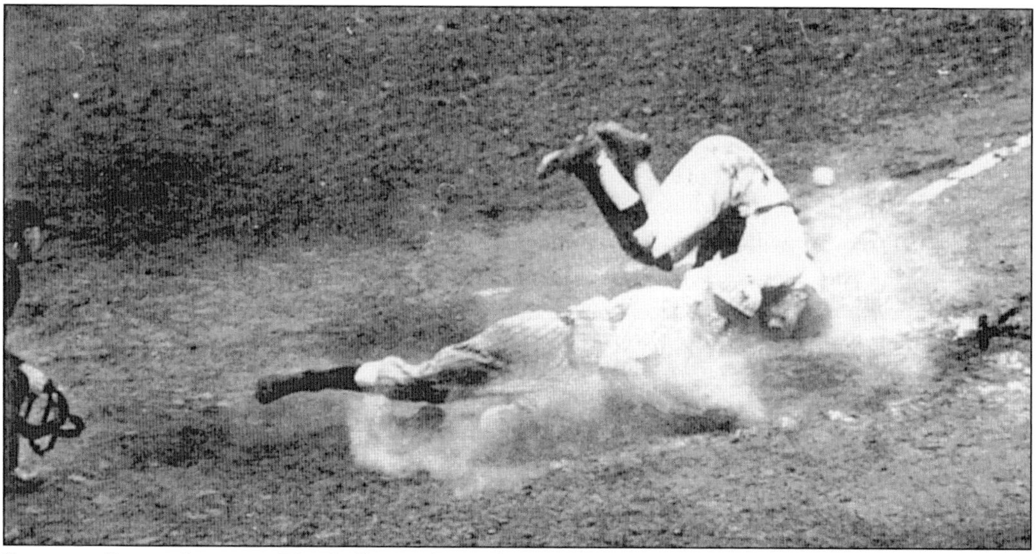

SECOND GAME ACTION. The ball gets loose from Washington catcher Muddy Ruel as George Kelly scores the tying run in the ninth inning of the second game of the 1924 World Series. But the Giants lost when the Senators came back to score a run off Jack Bentley in the bottom of the ninth.

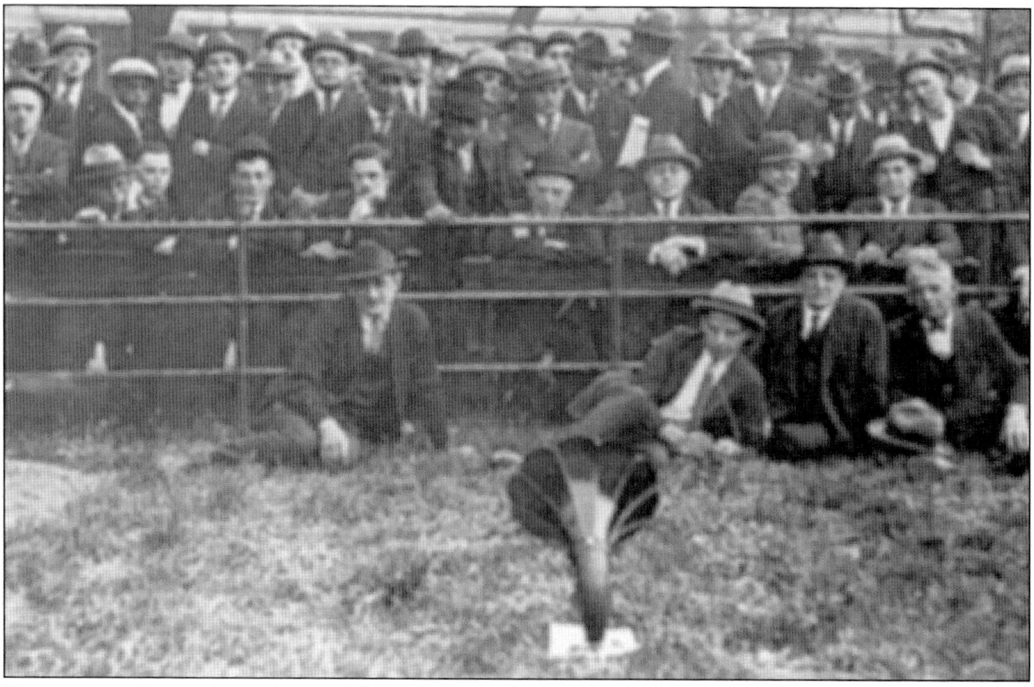

TUNED IN. Giants fans who couldn't score a ticket to the fifth game of the 1924 World Series at the Polo Grounds had to depend on the radio. Here a crowd listens in at City Hall Park as the Giants beat Washington, 5-2. New York lost the series, however, when a bad-hop single over the head of rookie third baseman Fred Lindstrom allowed the Senators to score the winning run in the 12th inning of the final game.

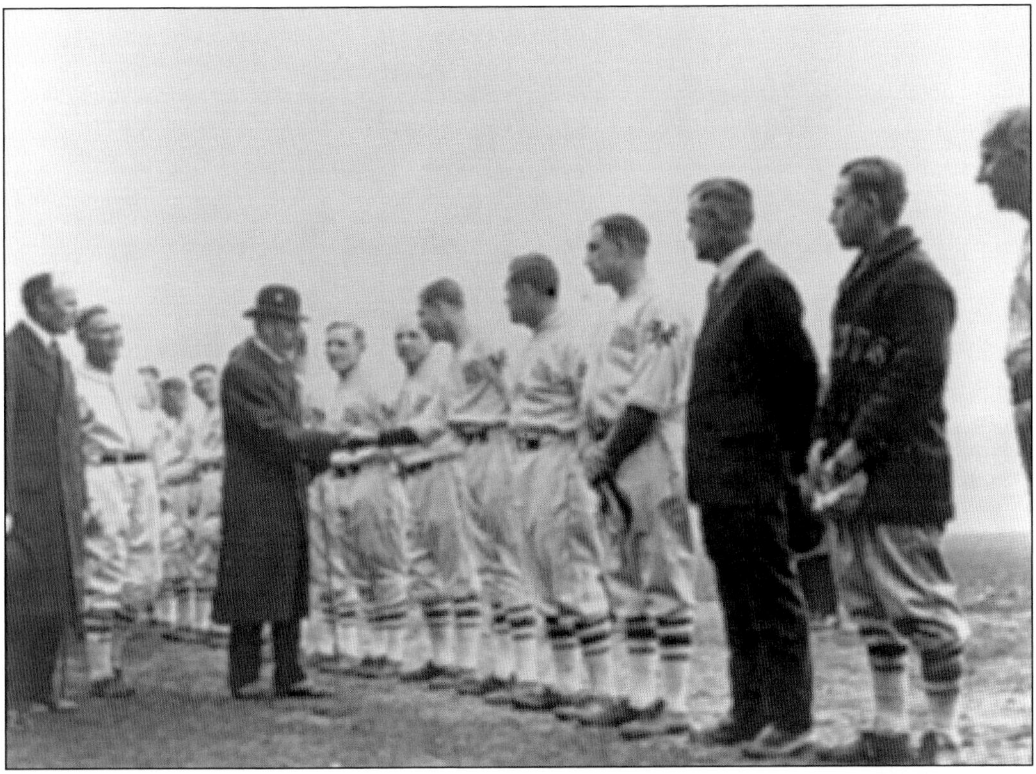

THE GIANTS ON TOUR. In 1924, the Giants joined the Chicago White Sox on a post-season tour of Canada, England, France, and Ireland. Here, Travis Jackson shakes hands with King George V of England. Arthur Conan Doyle, the creator of Sherlock Holmes, was impressed with John McGraw and predicted America's game would "sweep England." To this day, Englishmen much prefer cricket.

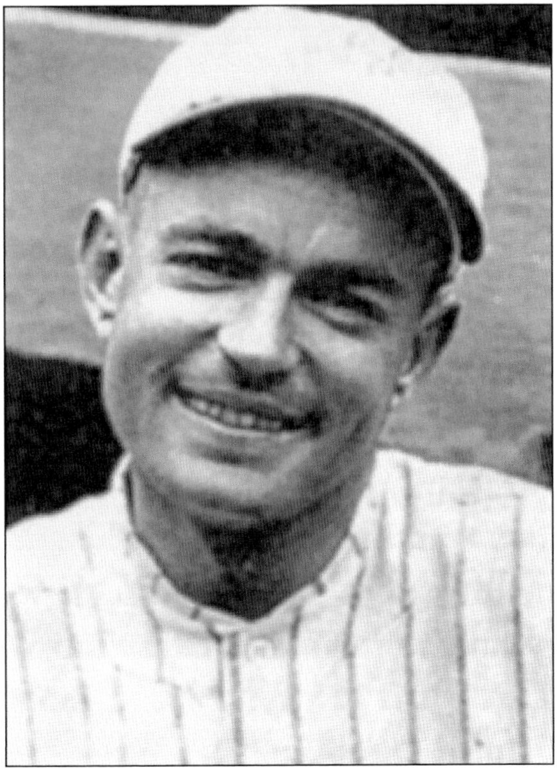

CROOKED O'CONNELL. In 1922, the Giants shelled out $75,000 to buy Jimmy O'Connell, a record amount for a minor leaguer. In the final days of the 1924 pennant race, O'Connell offered Philadelphia shortstop Heinie Sand $500 if he "wouldn't bear down too hard" that afternoon against the Giants. When Sand reported the attempted bribe to the commissioner's office, O'Connell not only admitted his guilt, he added that coach Cozy Dolan had put him up to it. Both men were booted out of organized ball for life.

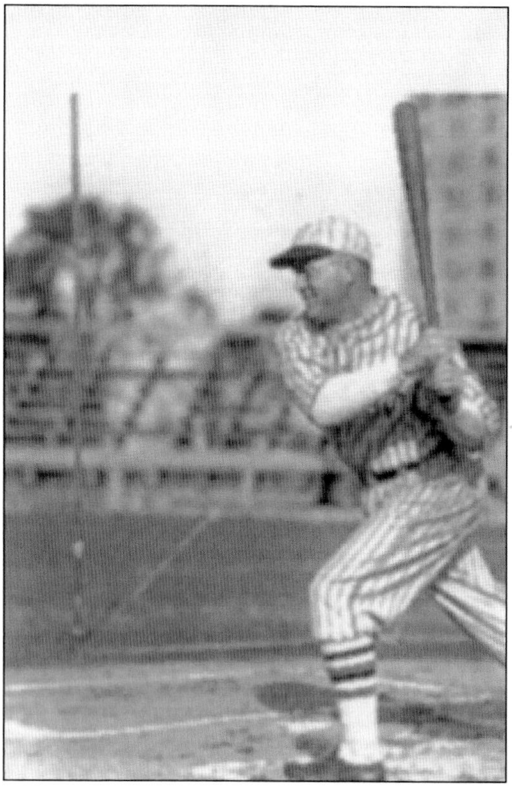

Problem Child. As his .358 career batting average and seven batting titles illustrate, Rogers Hornsby was probably the greatest right-handed batter of all time. He was also unapologetically brusque and dictatorial. Nonetheless, John McGraw took a chance, acquiring Hornsby shortly after the moody second baseman had player-managed the Cardinals to a World Series win in 1926. Hornsby batted .361 in his only year in New York, then was sent packing to the Boston Braves.

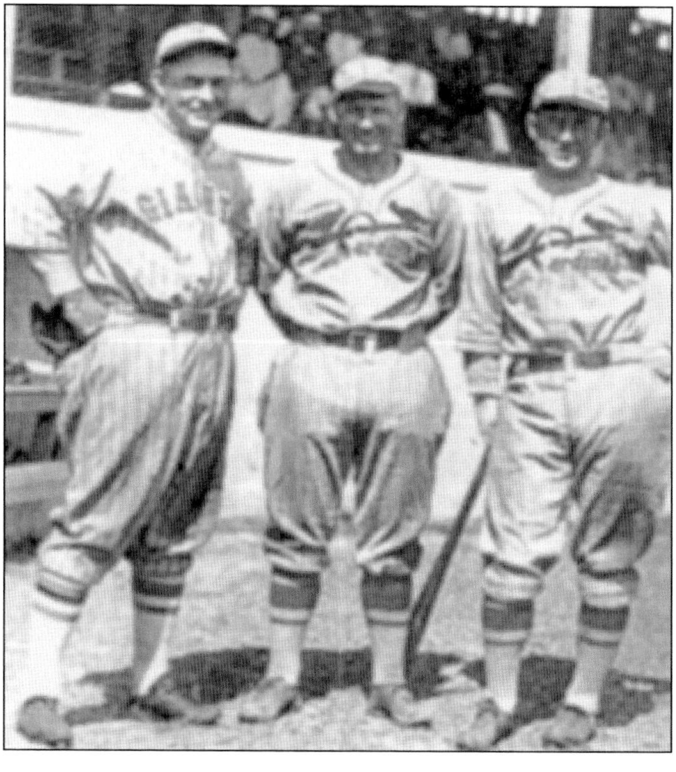

Goodbye, Frankie. By the end of the 1926 season, Frankie Frisch and his manager could barely tolerate each other's presence. So, in one of the most spectacular one-for-one trades in baseball history, John McGraw sent Frisch (who he berated as "Krauthead") to St. Louis for Rogers Hornsby. St. Louis manager Bob O'Farrell posed with Hornsby (left) and Frisch during the 1927 season. While Hornsby quickly wore out his welcome in New York, Frisch helped guide the Cardinals to four pennants and two world championships over the next 11 years.

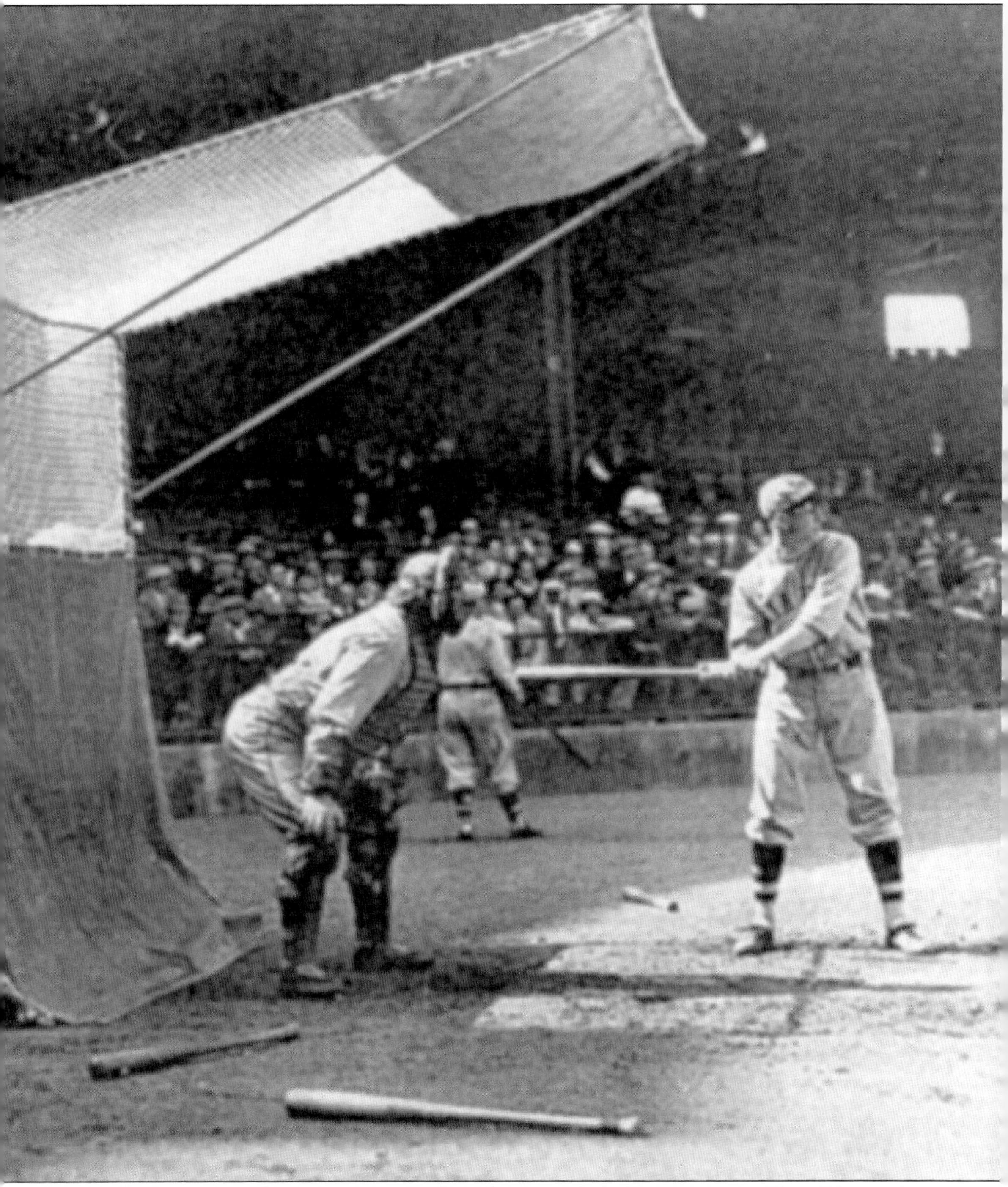

SWING TIME. Travis Jackson is pictured taking his cuts in the batting cage. The 155-pound shortstop from Arkansas was lethal with a bat in his hand, hitting .291 during his 15 seasons (1922–36) at the Polo Grounds. But he also excelled in the things that didn't show up in boxscores: bunting, hitting behind the runner, and taking the extra base. Steady and consistent, Jackson was voted into the Hall of Fame in 1982.

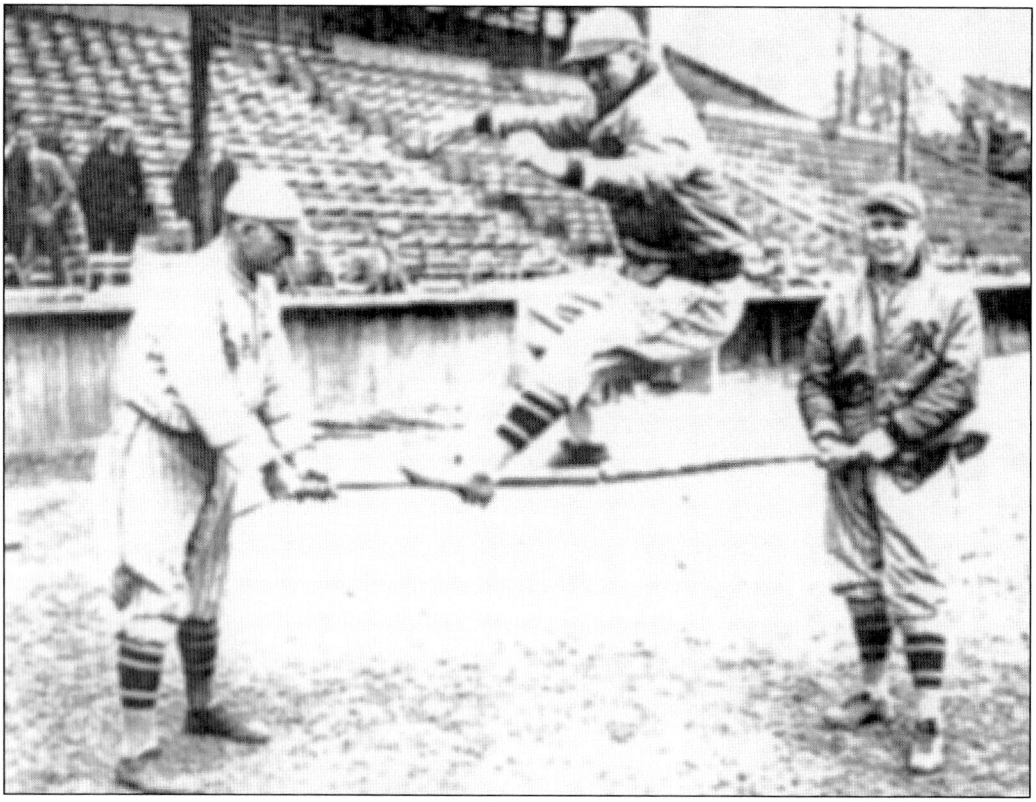

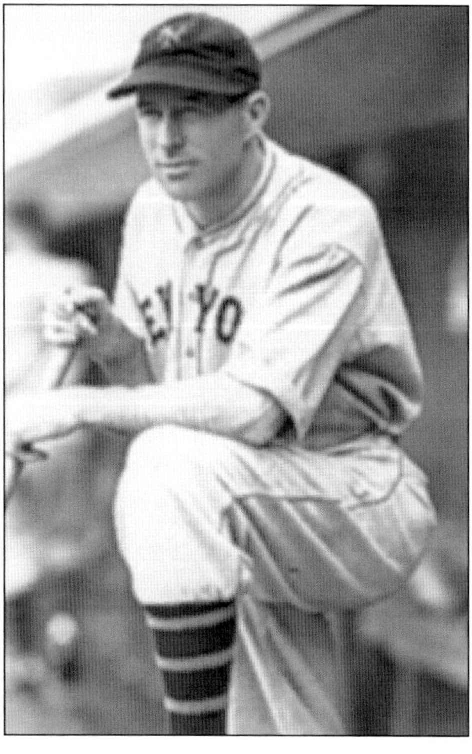

SOME TOMFOOLERY, 1932. Travis Jackson jumps over bats held by coach Tommy Clarke (left) and outfielder Chick Fullis in 1932. In the years immediately following his last pennant winner in 1924, McGraw was not exactly jumping for joy. Despite fielding strong teams, St. Louis, Chicago, and Pittsburgh passed New York in the standings.

LEFTY O'DOUL, 1928. Only Ty Cobb, Rogers Hornsby, and Shoeless Joe Jackson hit for a higher lifetime average than Francis "Lefty" O'Doul, whose 11-year career included two stints as a Giant. "When I was playing ball in the big leagues my bats would be jumping up and down in the trunk," recalled the amiable .349 career hitter. "Couldn't wait to get to the ball park and grab that bat. Big crowd, sock a triple, nothing like it! Maybe I was a ham. What's the use of doing something when nobody's looking?"

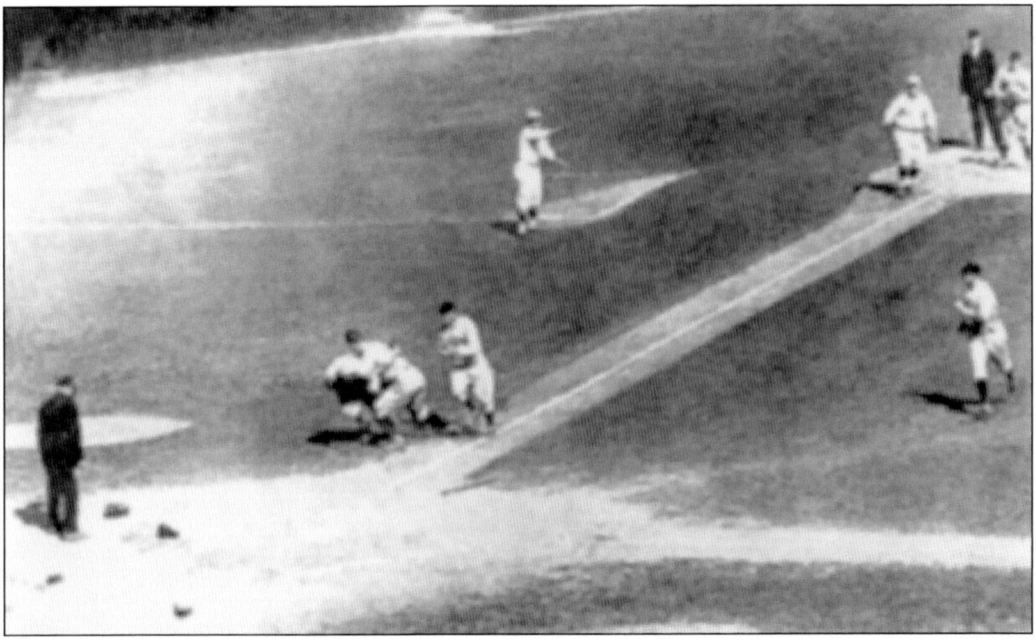

HELD UP: SEPTEMBER 27, 1928. The Giants finished in second place by two games in 1928 and this play was a big reason why. In a late-season game against the Cubs, Chicago catcher Gabby Hartnett tackled Andy Reese as the Giants' baserunner attempted to score. Hartnett, who didn't have the ball and thus should have been called for interference, held Reese long enough to be tagged out by Cubs third baseman Clyde Beck.

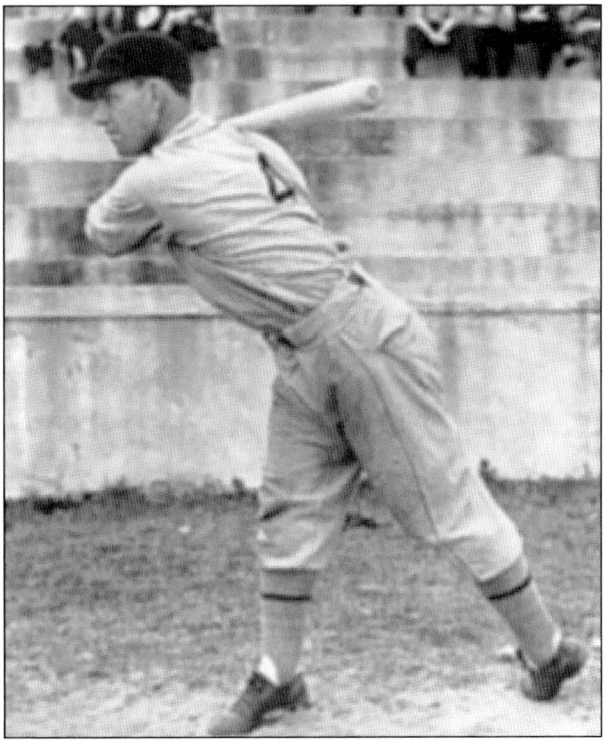

HOME RUN KING. Mel Ott of Gretna, Louisiana, was one of the few players to jump from a high school team to the majors, breaking into the Giants' outfield when he was only 17 years old. Between 1926 and 1942 he led the league in home runs six times. On the last day of the 1929 season Philadelphia pitchers intentionally walked him five times—once with the bases loaded—to prevent him from tying Chuck Klein for the home run title.

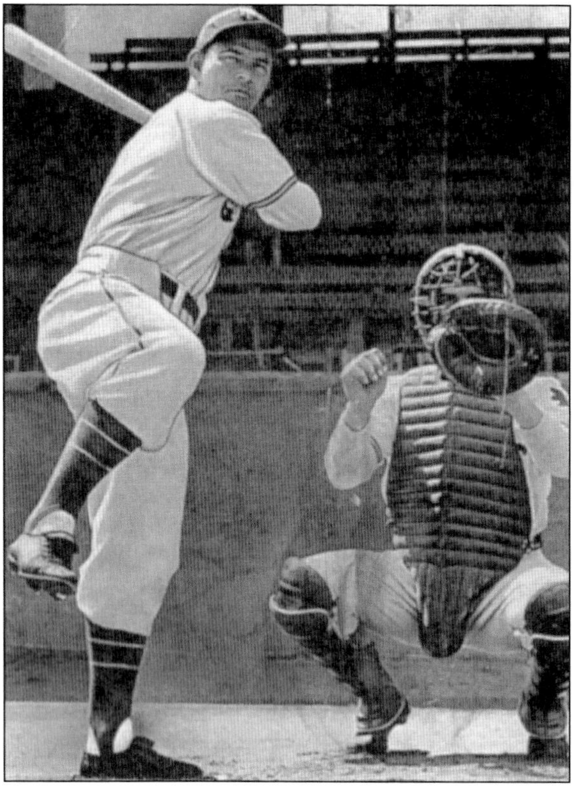

THE MIGHTY OTT. Weighing only 165 pounds, Mel Ott utilized a distinctive leg kick to loft two-thirds of his 511 career home runs over the Polo Grounds' 256-foot fence. "The kid's the most natural hitter I've ever seen," said John McGraw. "He's got a perfect swing." As to the question of changing Ott's unusual stance, McGraw responded, "Why change anybody if they can do well what they're doing?"

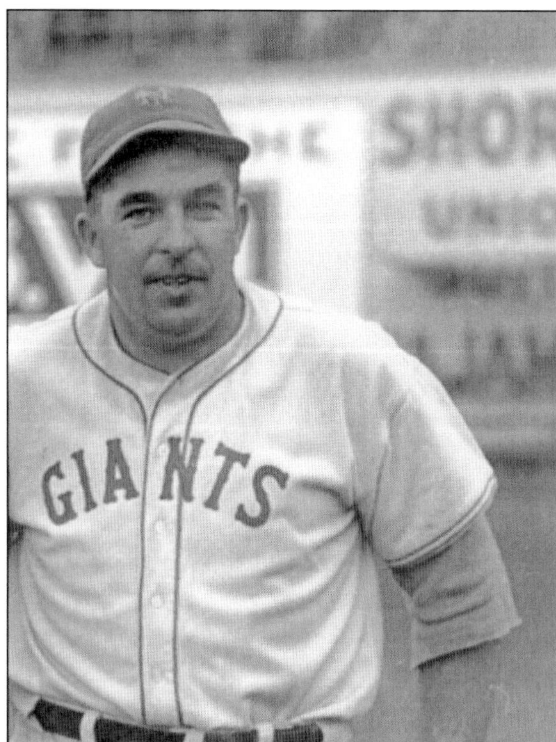

FAT FREDDIE. Fred Fitzsimmons, a broad-shouldered knuckleballer, joined the Giants in 1925. "They called him 'Fat Freddie' but there wasn't an ounce of fat on him," recalled a teammate. "He just had a round body. It just burned him up to be called fat and he was ready to tear somebody apart." Fitzsimmons' unorthodox "turntable" delivery produced 170 victories before he was shipped to Brooklyn during the 1937 season.

A CHANGING OF THE GUARD. On June 3, 1932, John McGraw called Bill Terry into his office and turned the club over to him. Thus ended McGraw's 30-year run as the Giants' manager, during which time his teams won 10 pennants and finished second 11 times. McGraw's unexpected retirement shocked the baseball world and knocked news of Lou Gehrig's record four home runs that afternoon in a game at Philadelphia off the front page of every paper.

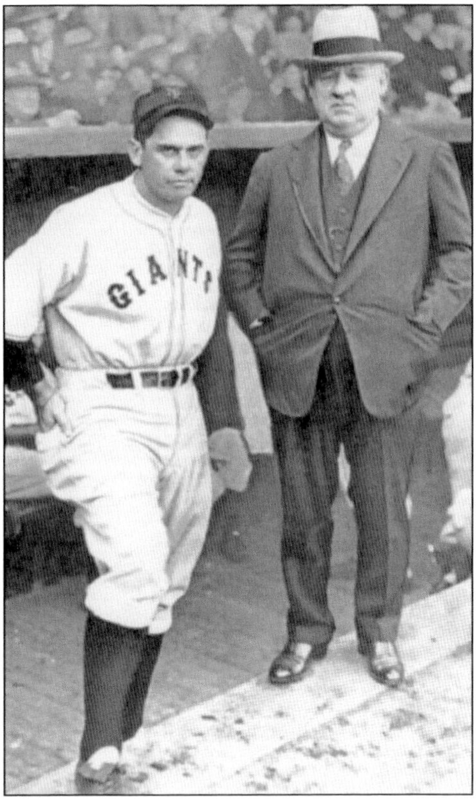

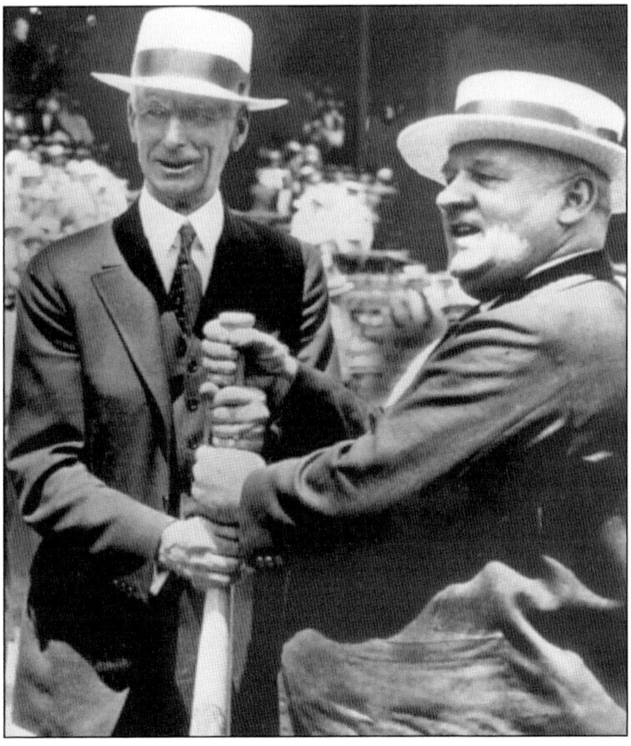

MAC AND MACK. The two winningest managers in major league history, John McGraw and Connie Mack, meet at the inaugural All-Star Game in 1933 in Chicago. Once rivals, in retirement they now formed a mutual admiration society. "There has been only one manager," Connie Mack insisted, "and his name is John McGraw." Eight months later, on February 25, 1934, McGraw died of intestinal cancer. A front-page obituary in the *New York Times* called him "baseball's greatest figure."

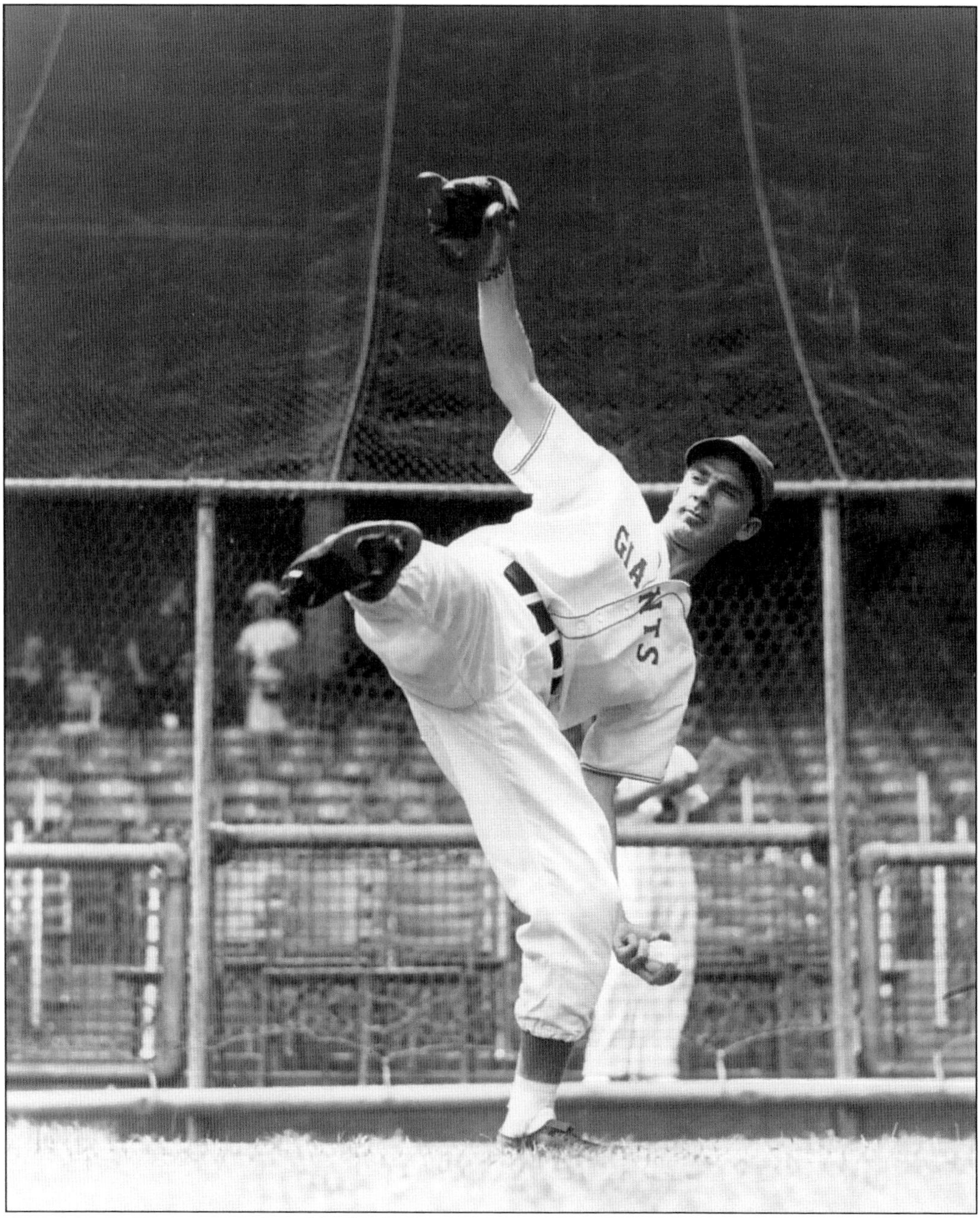

THE MEAL TICKET. Carl Hubbell's high leg kick and practically untouchable screwball were the calling cards of his 16-year (1928–43) Hall-of-Fame career in New York. Dubbed "The Meal Ticket" because of his ability to deliver in the clutch, Hubbell led the loop in victories with 23 in 1933, 26 in 1936, and 22 in 1937; not coincidentally, the Giants won the pennant each year. Hubbell won 253 games overall, including five straight 20-win seasons, and had the league's lowest ERA three times. He was a two-time Most Valuable Player and won a record 24 straight games over two seasons. "The source of his skill is his matchless control in using his curveball to set up his screwball," observed fellow pitcher Waite Hoyt. "Emotions, if he has any, never affect him."

Four

Terry, Ott, and Leo the Lip

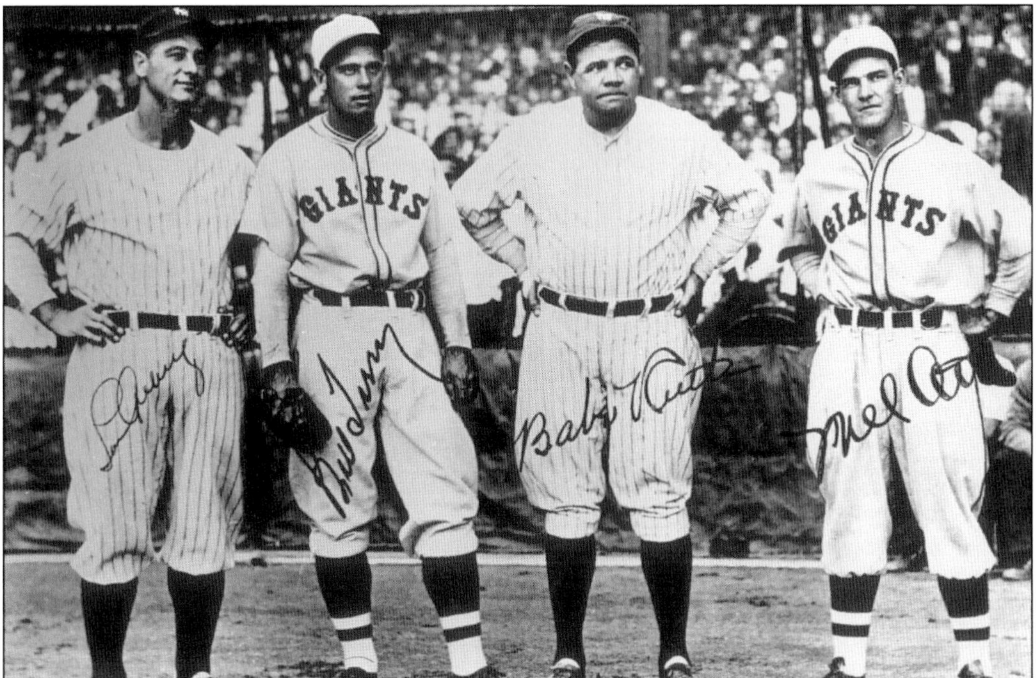

Fantastic Foursome. New Yorkers considered themselves blessed to be able to watch four of the game's greatest figures during the 1920s and 30s. Pictured, from left to right, are Lou Gehrig, Bill Terry, Babe Ruth, and Mel Ott. In 1930, Terry was the chief executioner in one of the most murderous offenses ever assembled. That summer Terry batted .401 while the third-place Giants hit .319 as a team! No National Leaguer since then has batted over .400, and no team ever has bettered New York's lofty average.

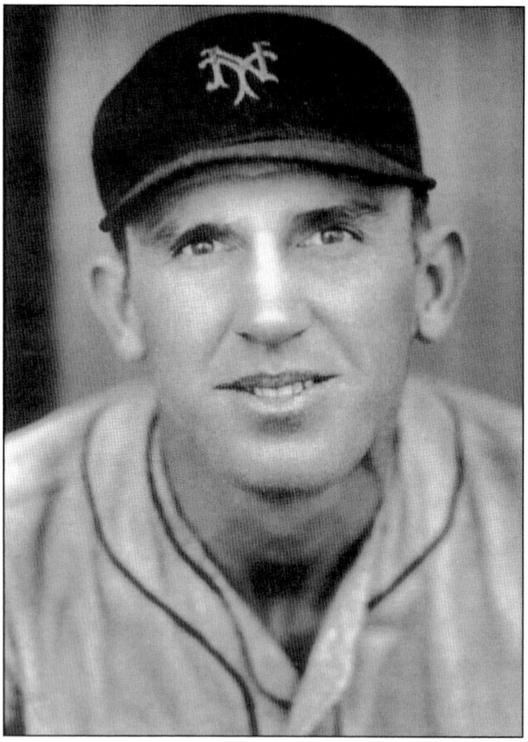

Jo-Jo Moore. Left fielder and lead-off man Jo-Jo Moore batted .298 during his 12 years with New York, including four .300 seasons. The thin Texan, a member of several All-Star teams in the 1930s, had a 23-game hitting streak in 1934, falling short of the club record of 27 set in 1900 by Charles Hickman. Moore "was a ballplayer's ballplayer," said Carl Hubbell. "Now, I don't know just exactly what that means, but I know what I mean by it and I'm just glad he played on my team."

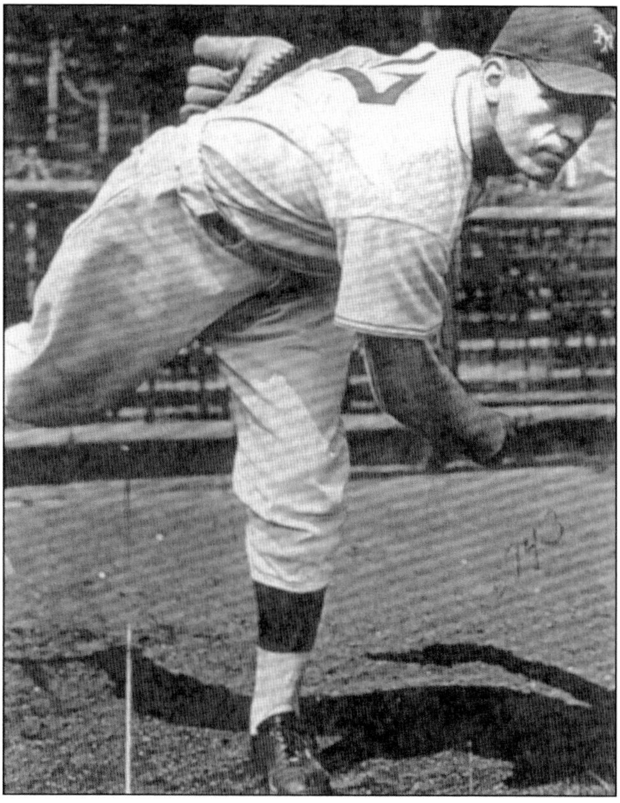

Prince Hal. Hal Schumacher made his pitching debut for the Giants in 1931, when he was only 20 years old. Over the next 13 seasons, all of them in New York, the right-handed starter displayed a remarkable consistency. Relying principally on his fastball and sinker, he won 19 games twice, 13 games four years in a row, and 12 games twice. His best year was 1934 when he posted a 23-10 mark. He split four decisions in World Series play.

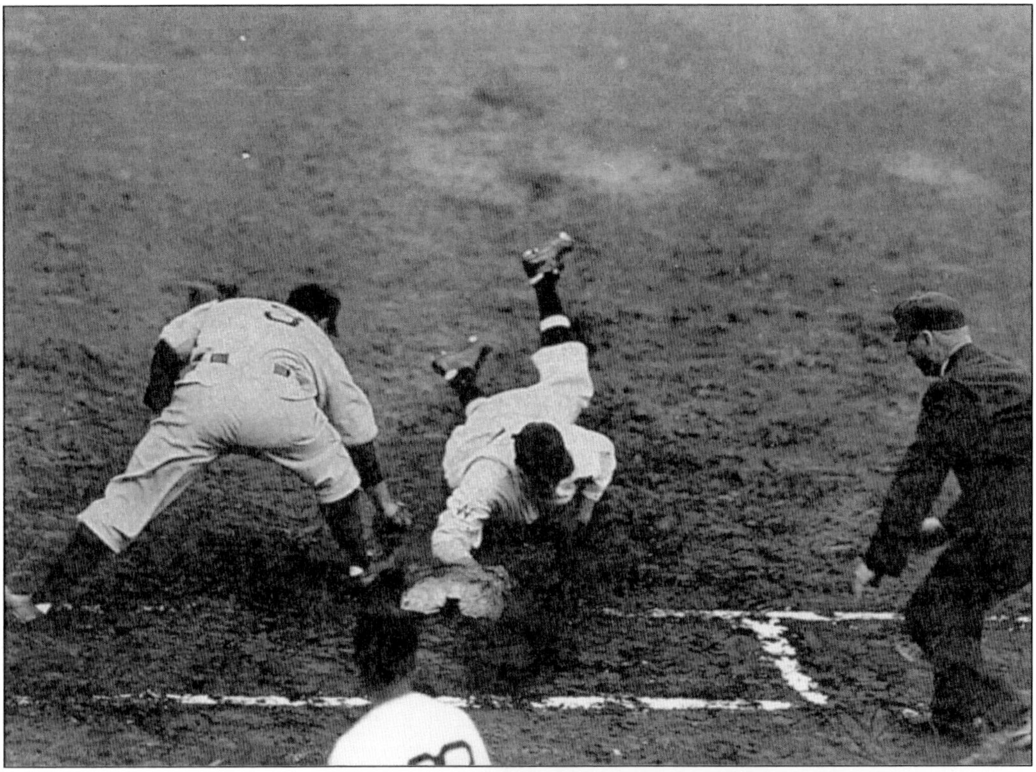

World Series Action, October 5, 1933. Washington's Joe Cronin evades the tag of Giants first baseman Bill Terry in the third game of the 1933 World Series. Washington won, 4-0, but New York beat the Senators in five games to claim its first championship since 1922.

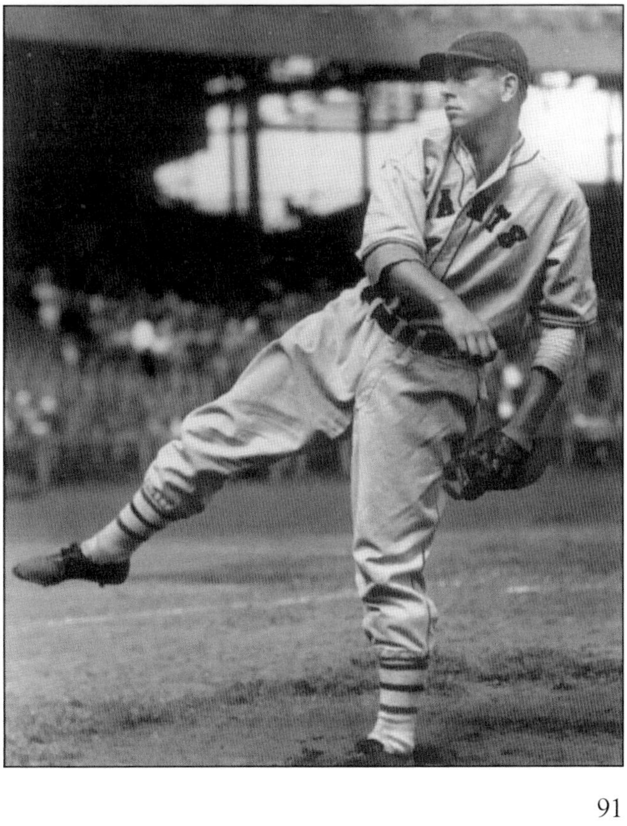

Tarzan on the Mound. Roy Parmelee was dubbed "Tarzan" because of his wildness on the mound, but by 1933 he had settled down enough to win 13 games for Bill Terry's world champions. He won a career-high 14 games in 1935, after which he was traded to the Cardinals.

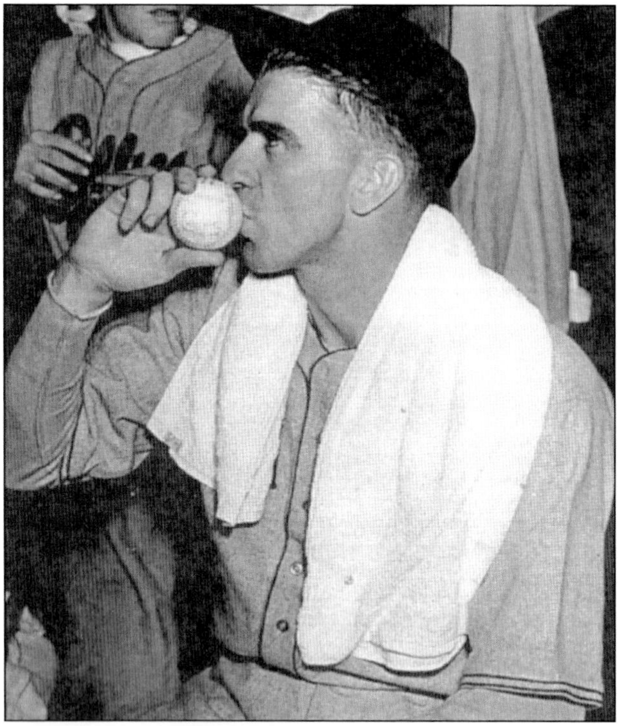

FIVE IN A ROW. Carl Hubbell gives the baseball a smooch after pulling off one of the most fabled feats in All-Star Game history. In the 1934 game, played July 10th at the Polo Grounds, Hubbell struck out five future Hall of Famers in a row: Babe Ruth, Lou Gehrig, Jimmy Foxx, Al Simmons, and Joe Cronin.

JUBILANT GIANTS. A clubhouse full of happy Giants celebrate one of the back-to-back pennants they won in 1936–37. Sitting second from left is shortstop Dick Bartell, otherwise known as "Rowdy Richard," who Carl Hubbell described as "a little bantam rooster." Despite the feisty Bartell's .381 batting, the Giants lost the 1936 World Series to the Yankees in six games.

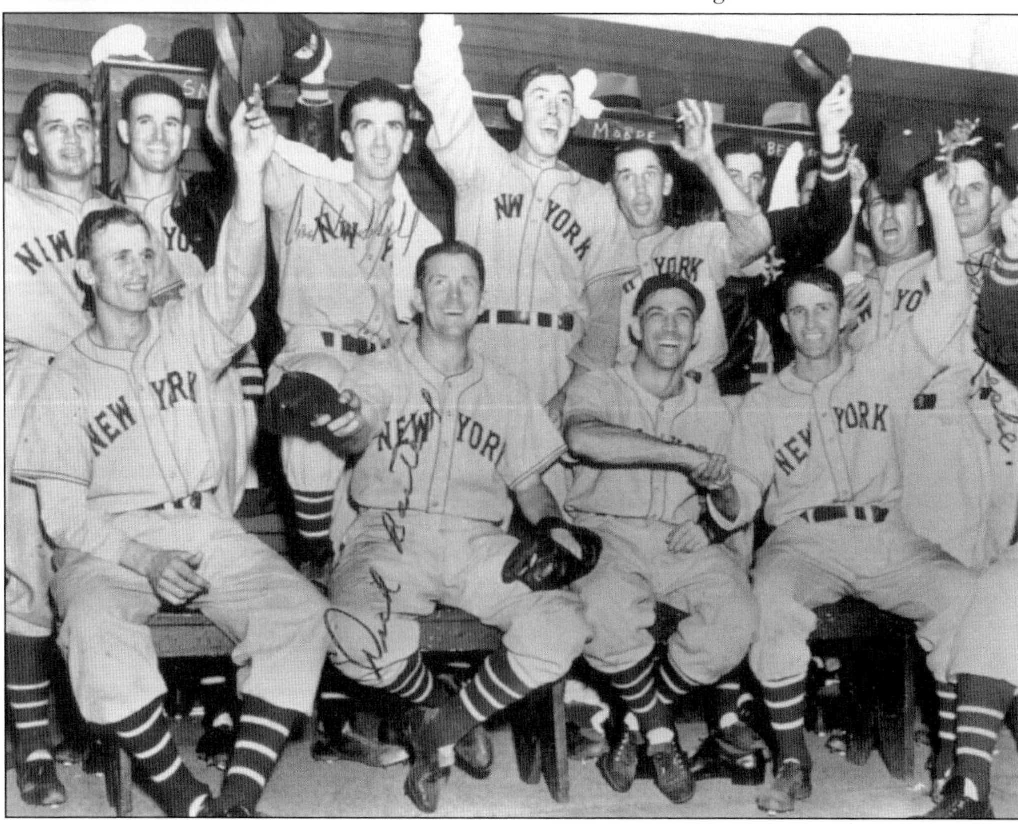

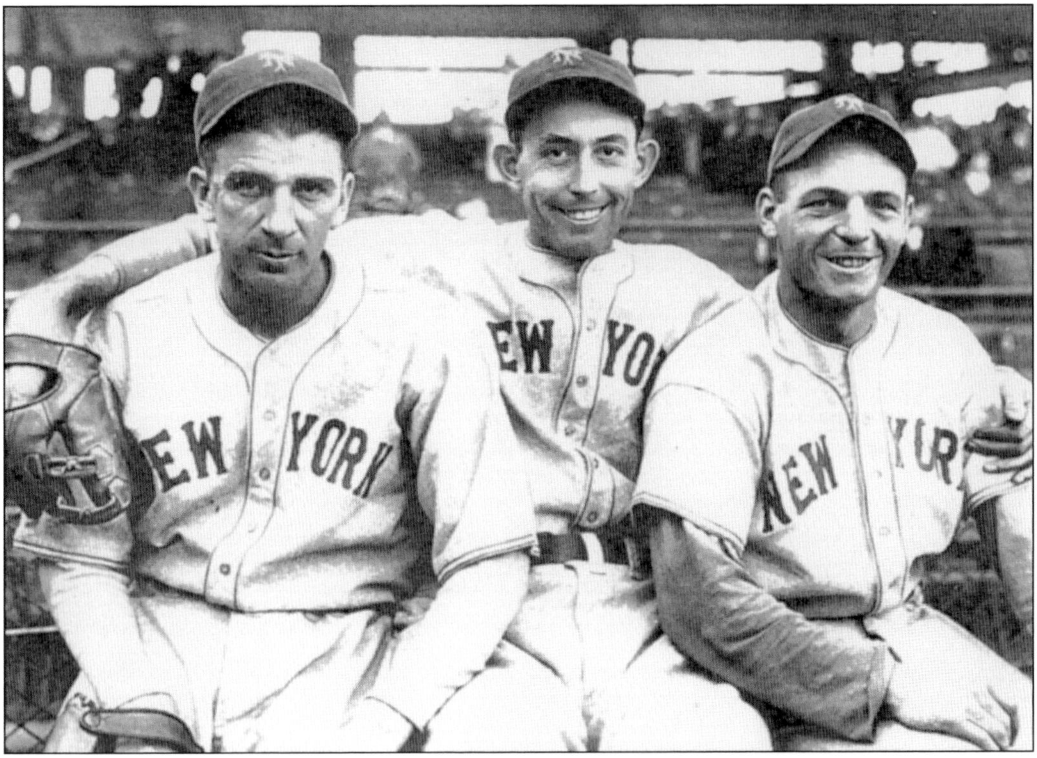

SWEET MUSIC. Cliff "Mountain Music" Melton is flanked by Carl Hubbell and Hal Schumacher in 1937, the year the rookie southpaw from North Carolina won 20 games for Bill Terry's third and last pennant winner. Melton "was a good pitcher," remembered Jo-Jo Moore, "but he just lacked that one pitch. He was a fastball pitcher and you got to have something else to go with it." Failing to develop a decent changeup or curve, Melton compiled a mediocre 66-71 record over the next seven seasons with the Giants.

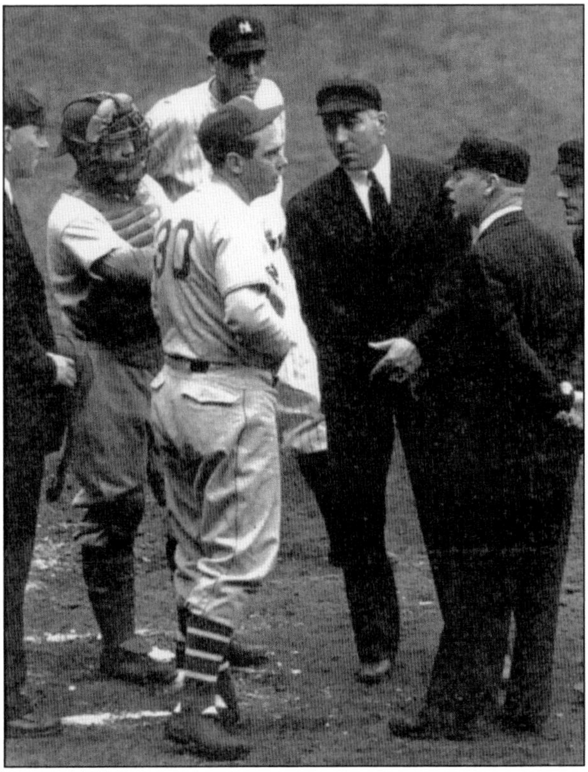

WORLD SERIES MIX-UP. Bill Terry presents his case to the umpires in the sixth inning of the 1937 World Series opener. At issue is which pitcher is going to relieve starter Carl Hubbell. Listening in is Giants catcher Gus Mancuso, who gave the umpire Harry Gumbert's name while Terry called for Dick Coffman. In the end it didn't matter, as the Yankees scored seven times en route to an 8-1 victory.

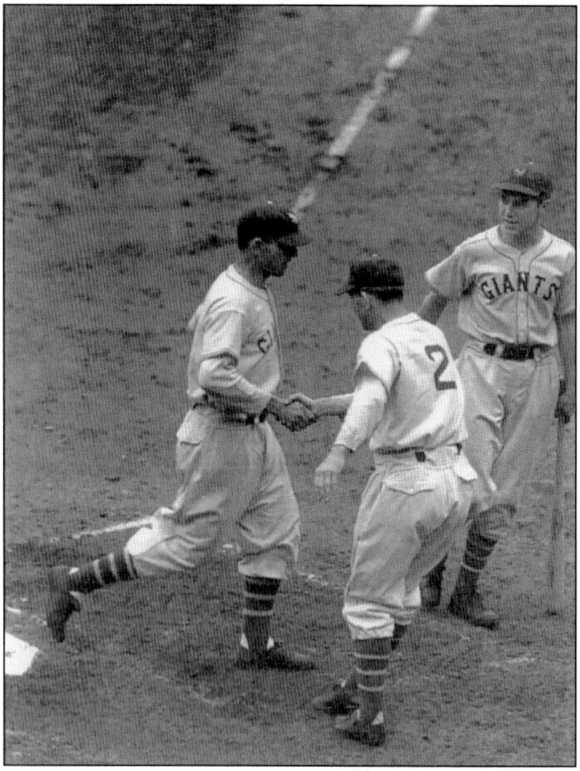

FIGHTING BACK. Dick Bartell greets Mel Ott at the plate after Ott's two-run home run tied game five of the 1937 World Series at two runs apiece. The Yankees went on to score a pair of runs in the fifth, however, to win the game and clinch the series. It would be another 14 years before the Giants appeared in another fall classic.

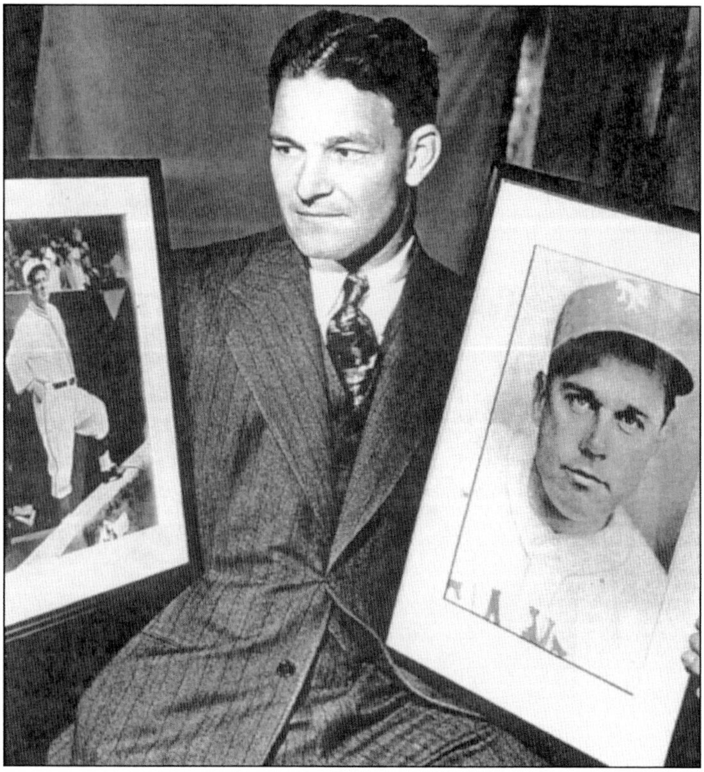

OTT TAKES OVER. After another second-division finish in 1941, Mel Ott replaced Bill Terry as manager. Terry's teams had won three pennants and finished second twice, but once he was named general manager his effectiveness diminished. Ott, pictured here holding photographs of his predecessors, Terry and John McGraw, skippered the Giants to just one first-division finish in seven years before being replaced by Leo Durocher during the 1948 season.

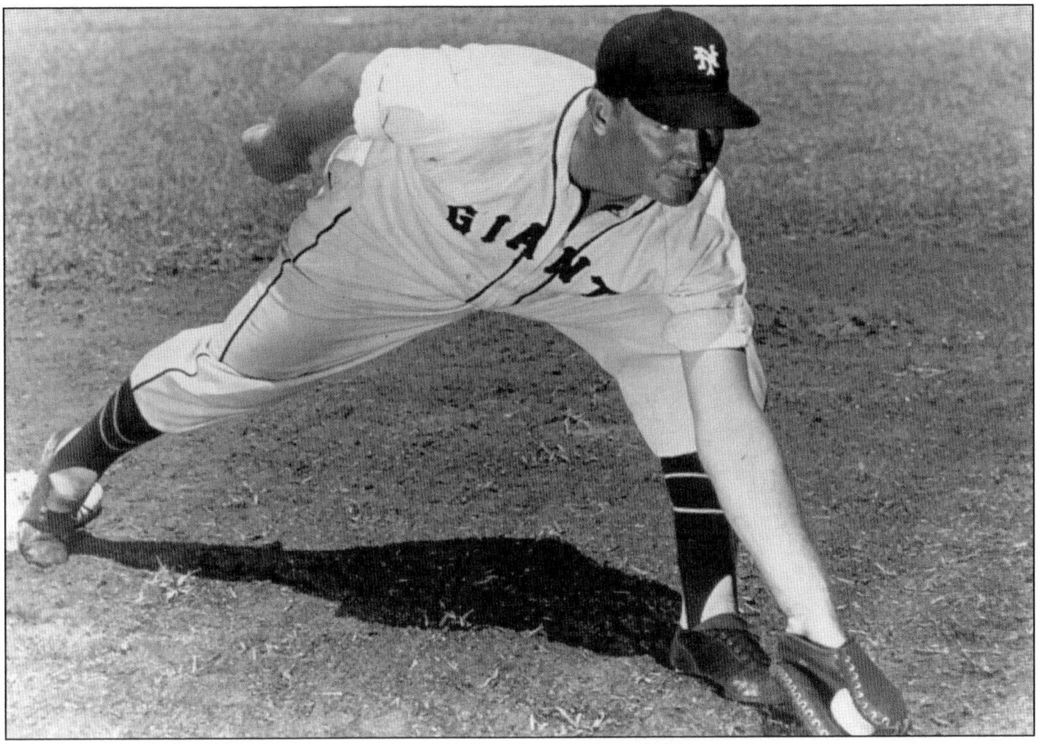

THE BIG CAT. Johnny Mize disliked reporters and pitchers equally, though he hit only the latter. The strong, taciturn Georgian had already won two home run titles with the Cardinals when he was dealt to New York in 1942. "I wasn't too crazy about playing in the Polo Grounds because I wasn't that much of a pull hitter," recalled the Hall-of-Fame first baseman. Nonetheless, Mize added two more home run championships as a Giant, blasting 51 in 1947 and 40 the following season. He ended his days with the Yankees, playing on five straight world championship teams between 1949 and 1953.

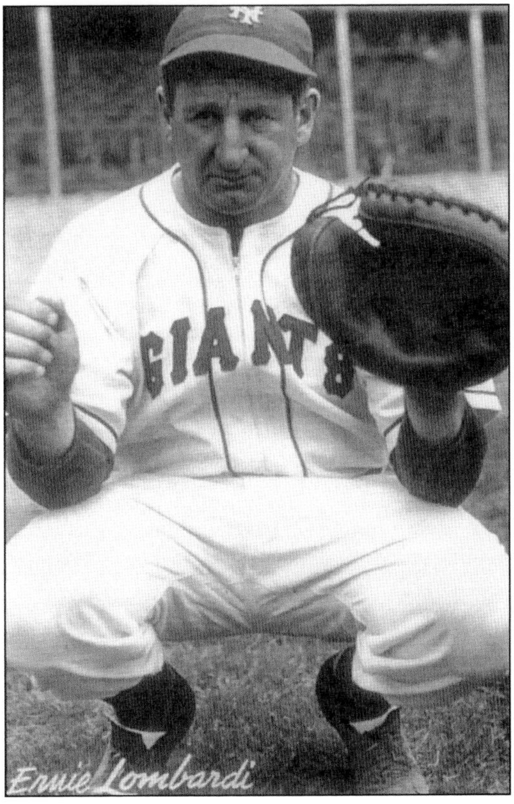

THE SCHNOZZ. Ernie Lombardi came to the Giants in 1943 after winning his second batting championship the previous year with the Braves. The lumbering, banana-nosed catcher, unavoidably nicknamed "Schnozz," was the Giants' regular backstop for most of the next five years. Despite his .306 career average, Lombardi got little respect during his lifetime. He wound up working in a gas station after leaving the game and was dead nine years before being named to the Hall of Fame in 1986.

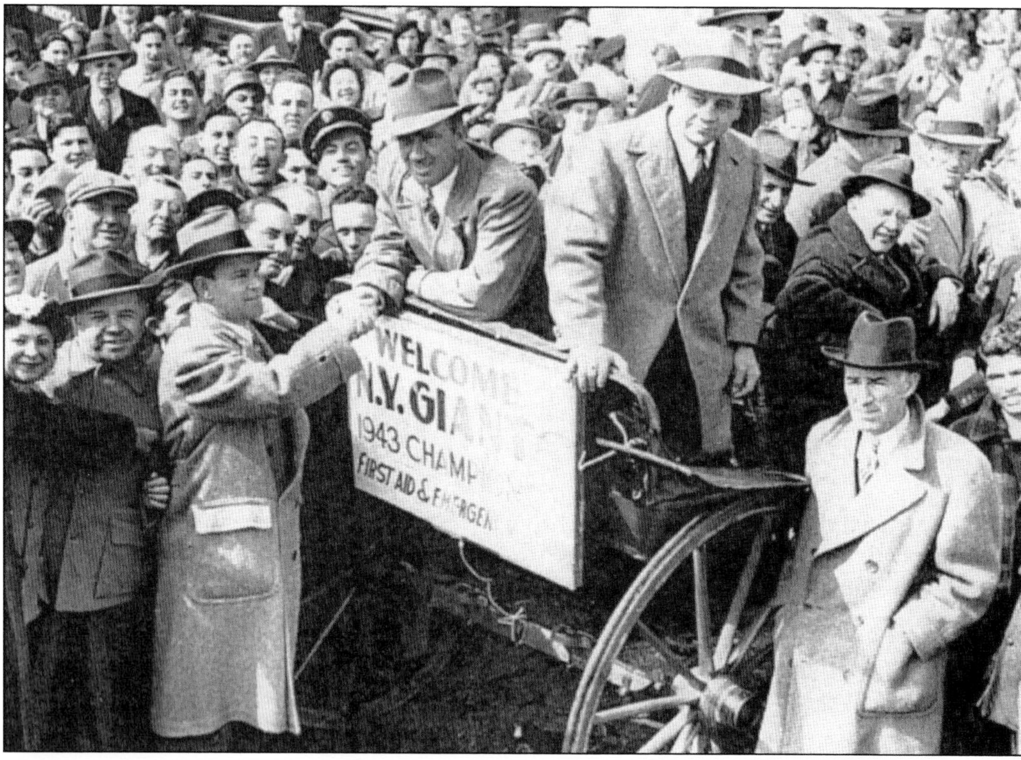

FIRST IN THEIR HEARTS. During World War II, baseball sacrificed along with the rest of the country. Among other inconveniences, travel restrictions forced teams like the Giants to hold spring training in the North. Here the optimistic citizens of Lakewood, New Jersey, greet manager Mel Ott (at left, shaking hands with Carl Hubbell) with a horse-drawn carriage bearing a sign, "Welcome N. Y. Giants 1943 Champions." Sufficiently jinxed, the Giants went on to finish dead last for the first time since 1915.

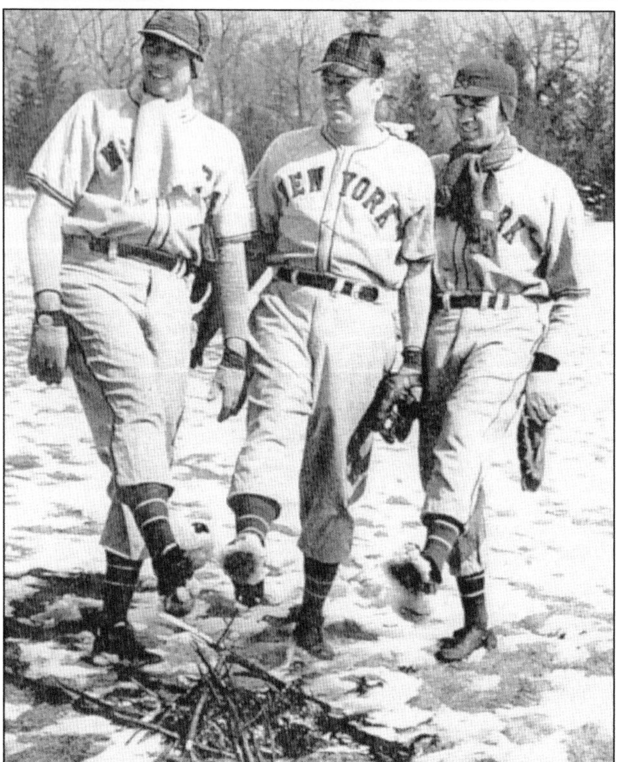

WARMING UP IN THE WAR YEARS. Pitchers Cliff Melton, Van Lingle Mungo, and Carl Hubbell toasted their tootsies over a fire during their first day of spring training in Lakewood in 1943.

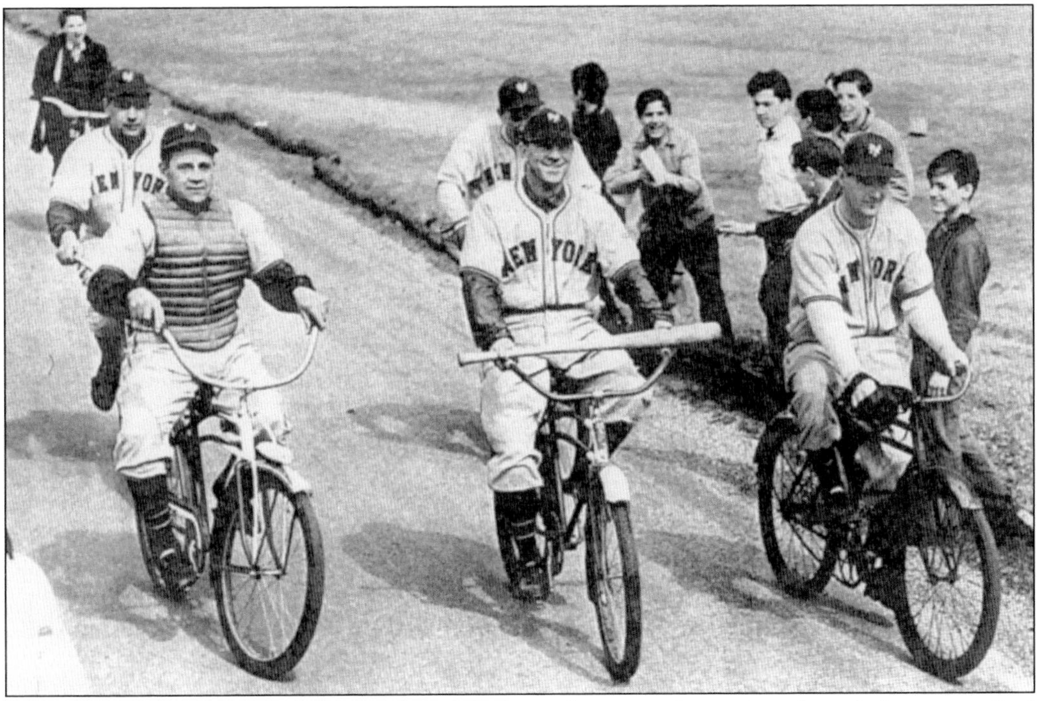

PEDDLING BALLPLAYERS, 1943. The rationing of tires and gasoline forced Giants to find alternative modes of transportation during their years of spring training in Lakewood. Peddling their way from the camp hotel to the practice diamond are, from left to right, Gus Mancuso, Dick Bartell, and Tom Sunkel. In the back are Babe Barna and Carl Hubbell.

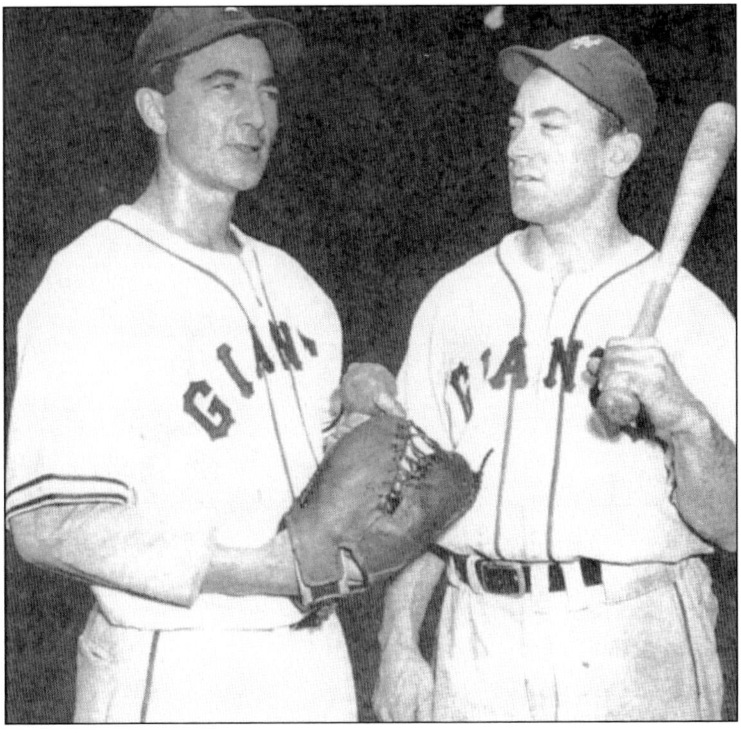

DANNY GARDELLA. Danny Gardella (right), seen here with his brother Al, was a happy-go-lucky native New Yorker and one of eight Giants to jump to the new Mexican League in 1946. The mass exodus caused New York to finish last and led to a blacklisting of the defectors when they tried to re-enter the major leagues. Gardella sued organized baseball for reinstatement and won a $60,000 out-of-court settlement, but the ostracized outfielder had only one more major-league at-bat, in 1950 for St. Louis.

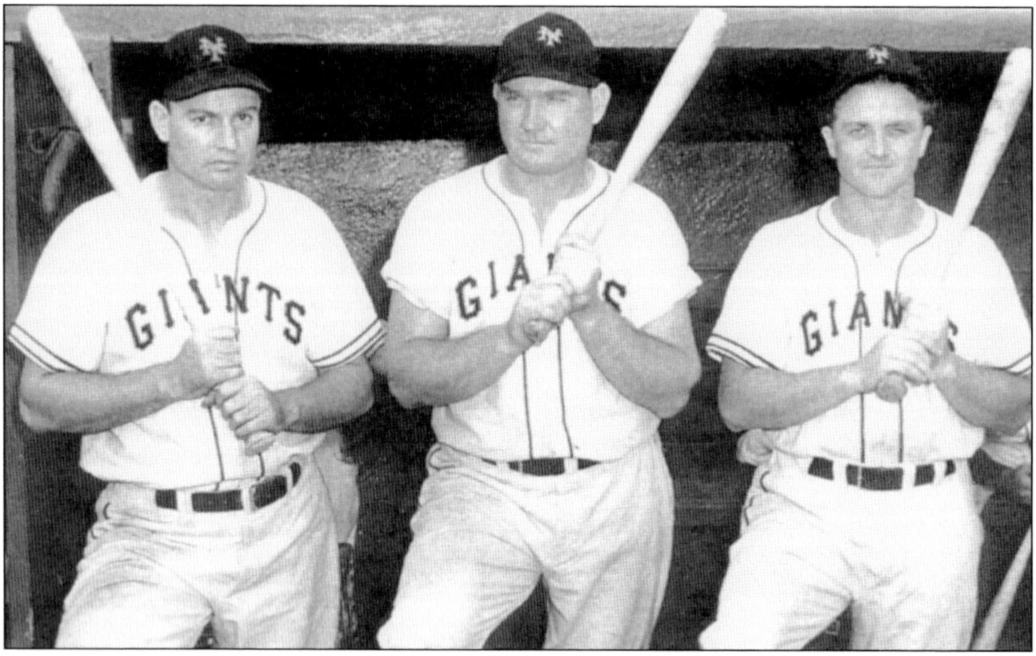

THE WINDOW BREAKERS. In 1947 the fourth-place Giants set a major-league record with 221 home runs. From left to right, catcher Walker Cooper, first baseman Johnny Mize, and left fielder Willard Marshall shook up the Polo Grounds to the tune of 122 home runs and 367 RBIs.

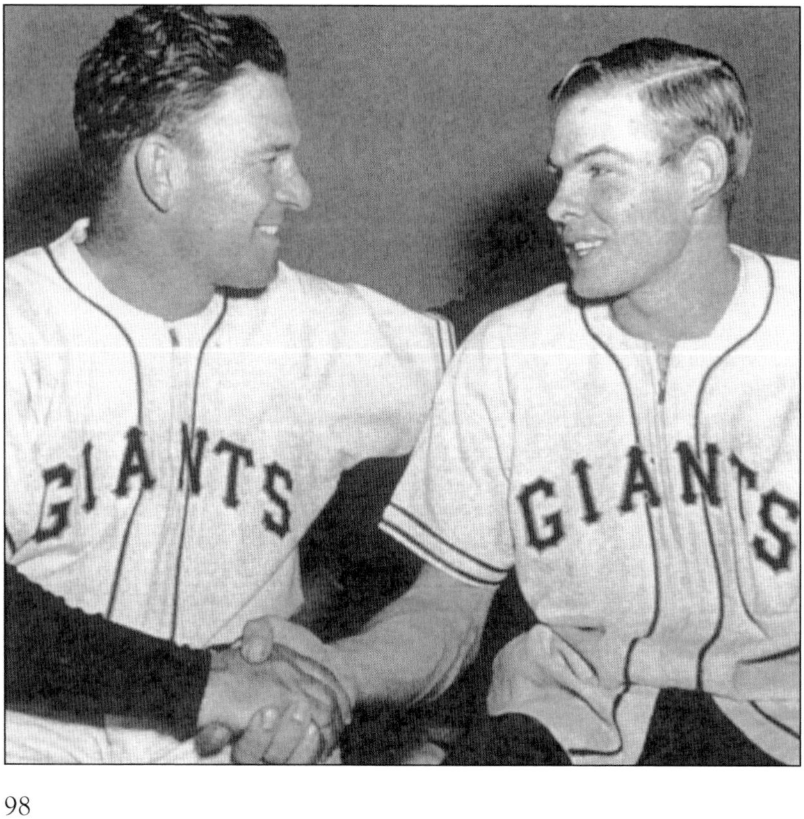

THE HONDO HURRICANE. Clint Hartung is greeted by manager Mel Ott, who like most observers expected great things from the highly touted pitcher-outfielder. Unfortunately for the Giants, the 6-foot-5 Texan was a failed phenom. During his six seasons in New York (1947–52), the "Hondo Hurricane" batted a mere .238 and won just 29 games with a 5.02 ERA.

WAY TO GO, SID! The Giants were always on the lookout for a Jewish star to take advantage of New York's large Jewish population. The closest they came was Sid Gordon, a power-hitting outfielder-third baseman who spent most of the 1940s at the Polo Grounds. Here Gordon, a Brooklyn native, enjoys a "day" at Ebbets Field in 1948. Among his gifts were a new car, golf clubs, and a set of luggage. The last item came in handy when Gordon was traded to Boston the following year.

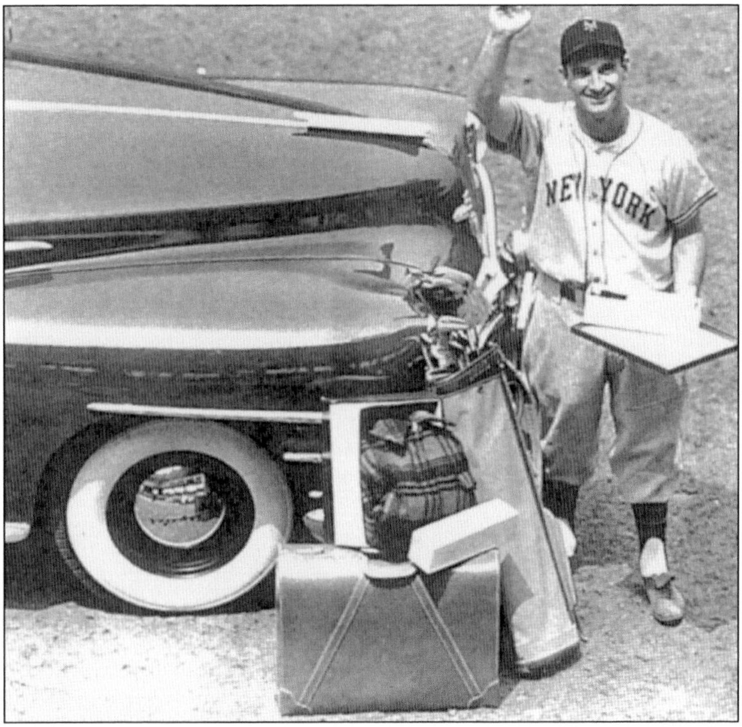

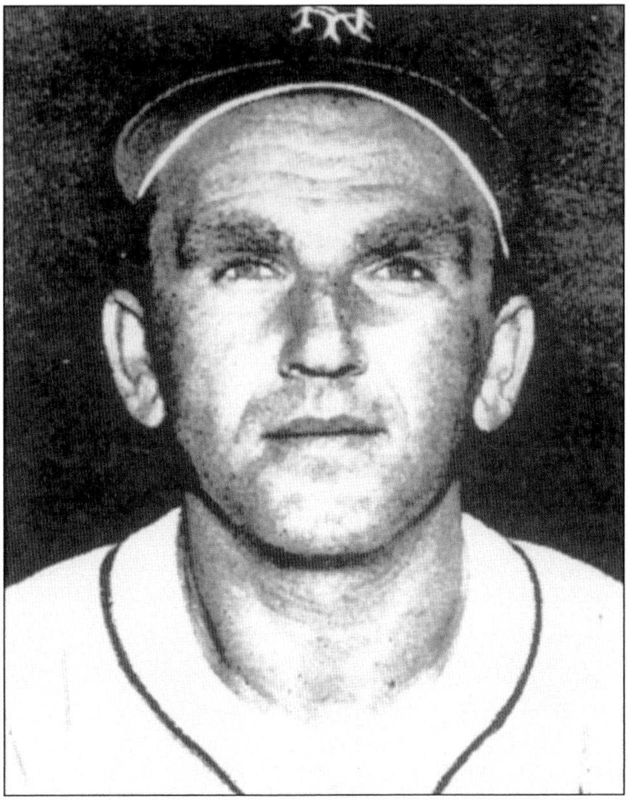

KOSLO'S CURVE. Dave Koslo, known as George Koslowski when he was growing up in Wisconsin, was a stylish curveballer who led all National League pitchers with a 2.50 ERA in 1949. Dividing his time between starting and the bullpen, Koslo reached double figures in victories a half dozen times for the Giants between 1941 and 1953.

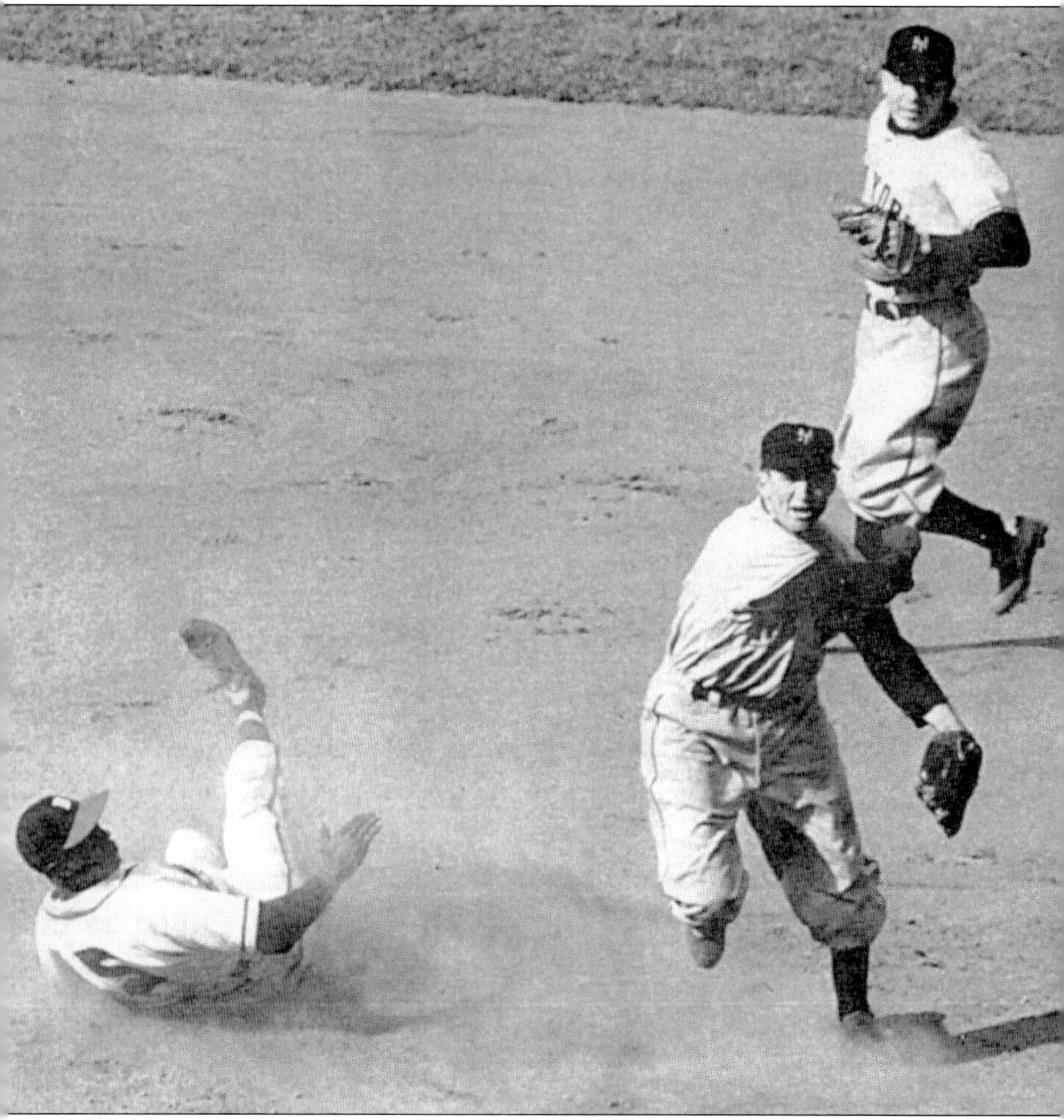

DARK AND STANKY. Shortstop Alvin Dark (foreground) and second baseman Eddie Stanky are seen here turning a double play as a former teammate, the Braves' Sam Jethroe, slides past. The double-play combo solidified New York's middle infield immediately upon their arrival from Boston in 1950. That summer both players hit .300 as the rejuvenated Giants finished just five games out of first place. The 23-year-old Dark and 34-year-old Stanky (known as "The Brat") were savvy, competitive players destined to enjoy long careers as coaches and managers after leaving the Polo Grounds.

LUCKY LOHRKE. Jack Lohrke played seven seasons in the majors, the first five with the Giants. The reserve infielder was better known for having missed a bus trip that killed his entire minor-league team in 1946. From that point on, he was known as "Lucky Lohrke."

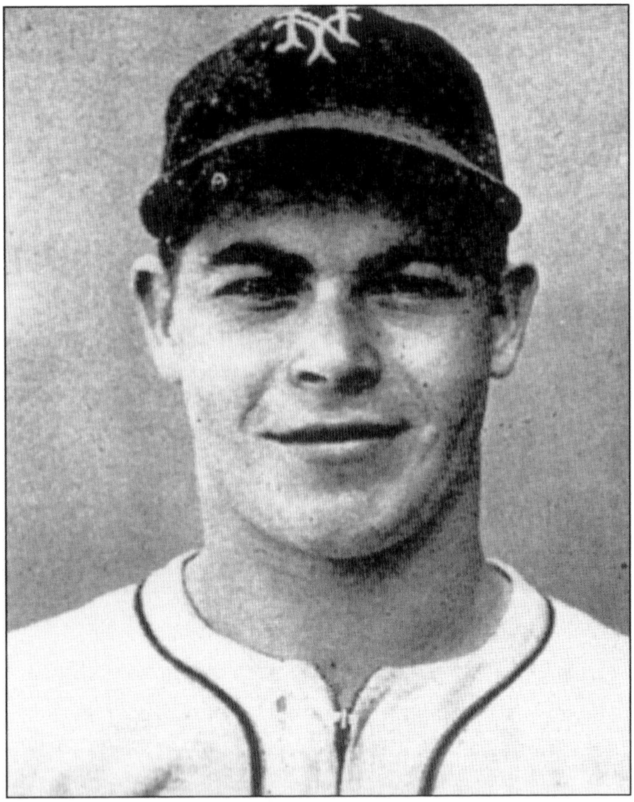

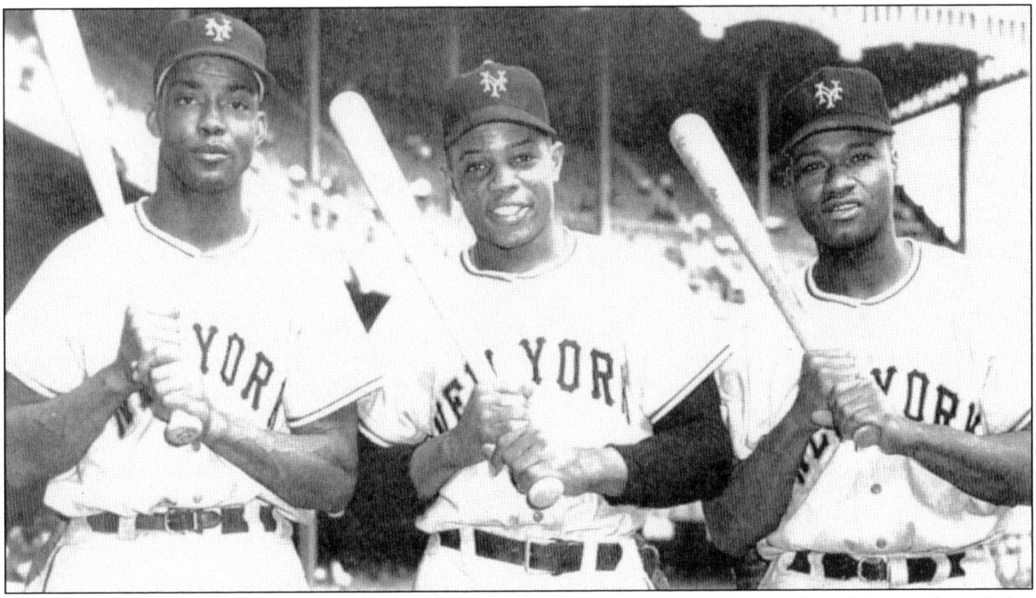

PIONEERING PLAYERS. Hank Thompson (right) played for the Kansas City Monarchs of the Negro National League before becoming, in 1947, one of the first African-American players in the American League. On July 5, 1949, he and Monte Irvin (left) became the first blacks to play for the Giants. Two years later Thompson, Irvin, and Willie Mays (center) formed the first all-black outfield in World Series history.

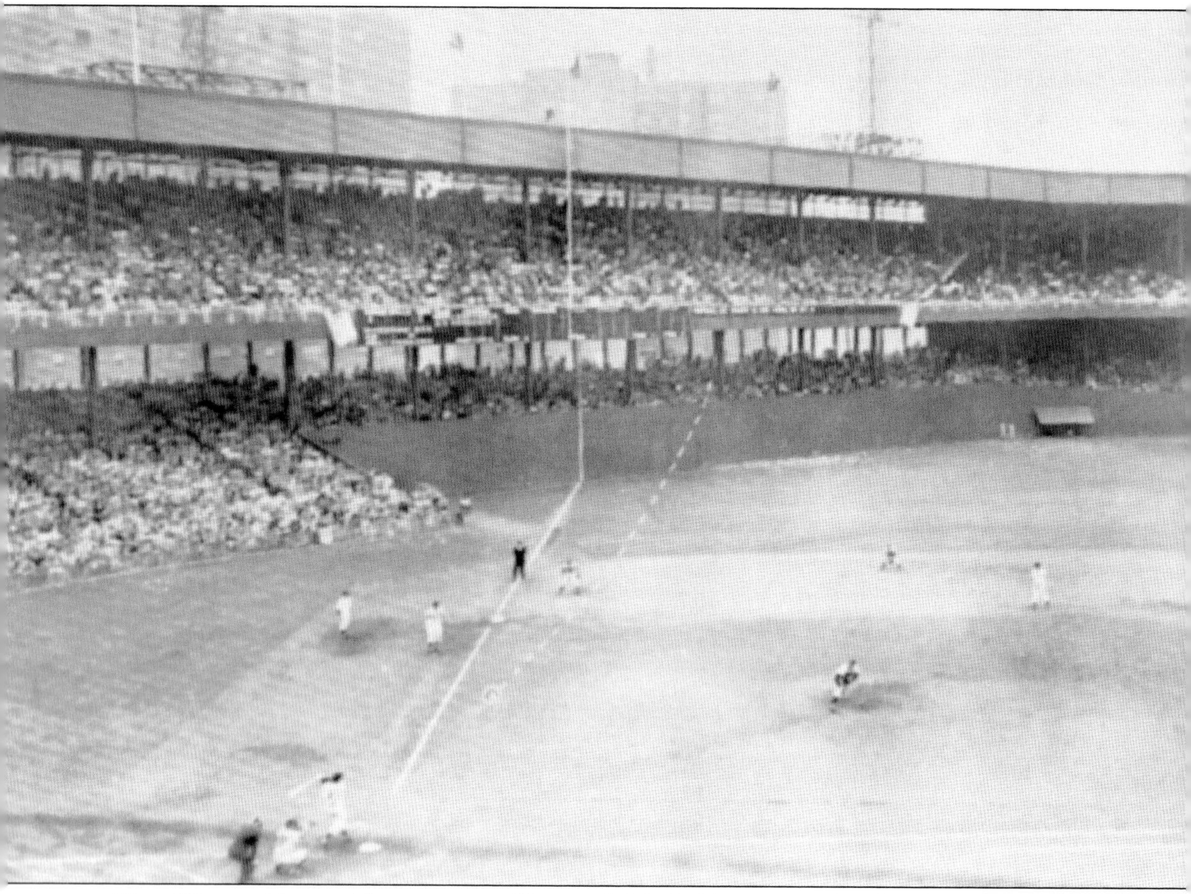

THE "SHOT HEARD 'ROUND THE WORLD." It's 3:47 p.m. on October 3, 1951, and Bobby Thomson has just hit the most famous home run in history, a three-run shot off Brooklyn's Ralph Branca that gave New York a 5-4 victory, the 1951 pennant, and capped an improbable Giants comeback. Trailing the Dodgers by 13 1/2 games on August 11th, Leo Durocher's outfit won 39 of their last 47 games to finish in a dead heat with Brooklyn. Thomson's home run came in the bottom of the ninth in the final game of a special three-game playoff. It was an unbelievable finish to an unbelievable season. "Now the story ends," wrote Red Smith. "And there is no way to tell it. The art of fiction is dead. Reality has strangled invention. Only the utterly impossible, the inexpressibly fantastic can ever be plausible again."

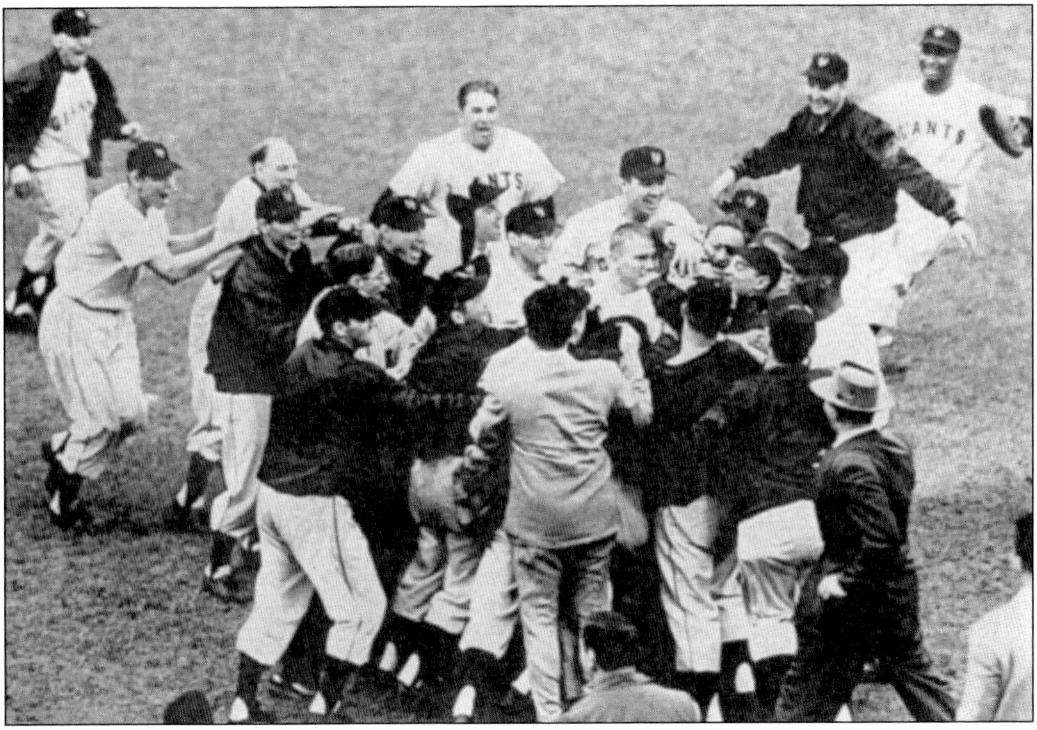

CELEBRATE! Bobby Thomson is swarmed by teammates as he crosses the plate and is then (bottom photo) joined by manager Leo Durocher and owner Horace Stoneham in the uproarious Giants locker room after his famous home run. Unfortunately for Giants fans, the celebrated third baseman's heroics didn't carry over to the World Series, which began the following day. Thomson hit just .238 with no home runs as the hated Yankees beat the Giants in six games.

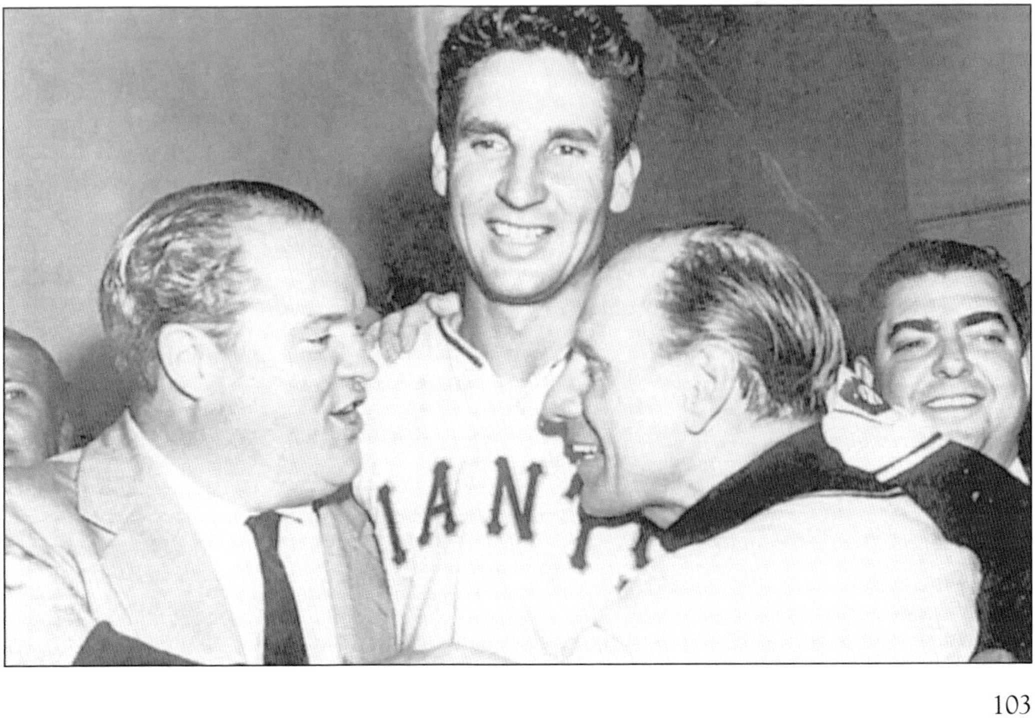

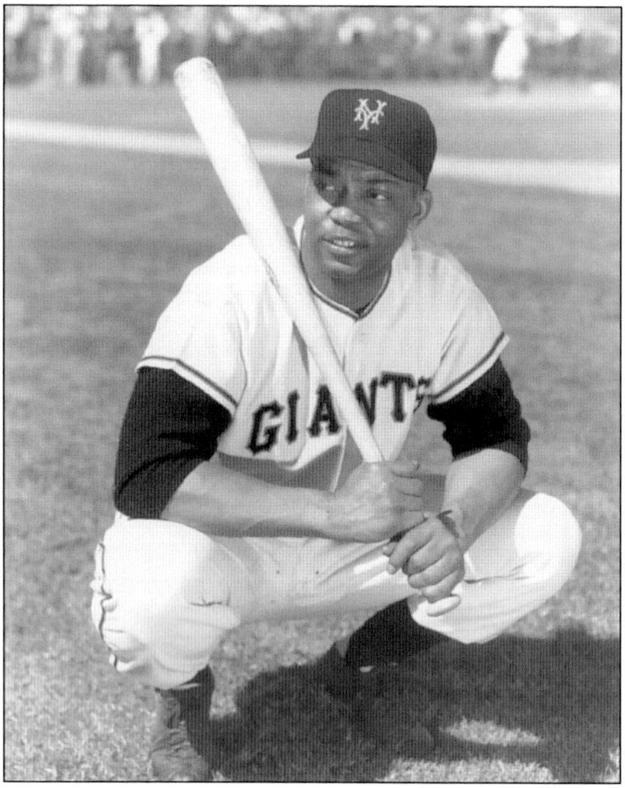

MONTE IRVIN. Baseball's color barrier prevented Hall of Famer Monte Irvin from playing in the majors until he was 30 years old, but he made the most of his opportunity. The Alabama native had three .300 seasons for the Giants, led the league with 121 RBIs in 1951, and batted .394 in two World Series.

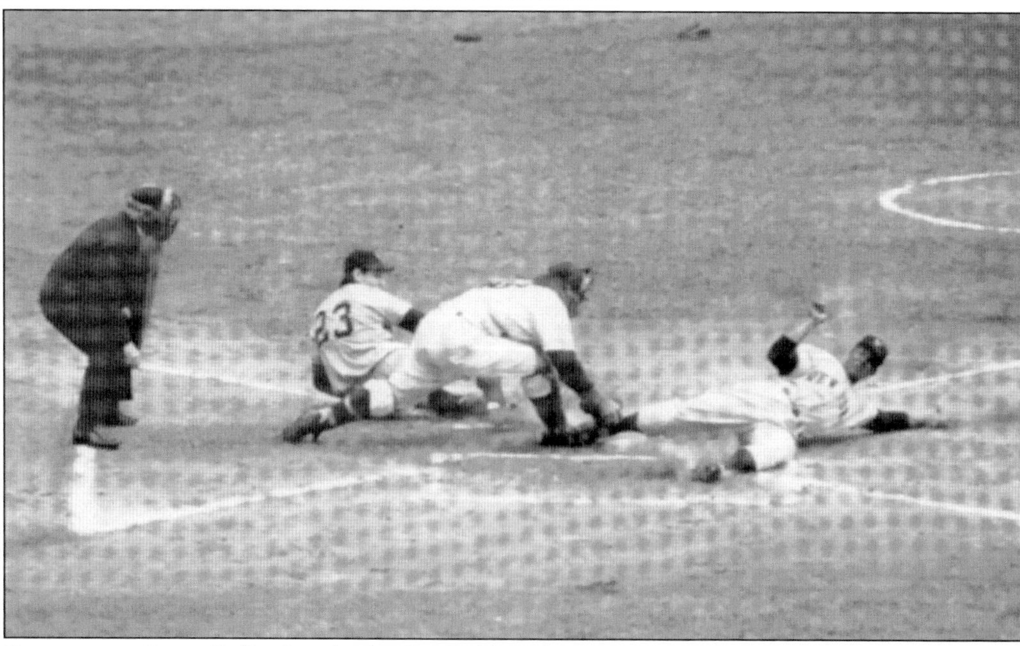

STEALING A RUN. Still riding high after Bobby Thomson's home run, the Giants surprised the Yankees with a 5-1 victory in the opener of the 1951 World Series. Monte Irvin had four hits and stole home. Thomson is the batter falling away as Irvin arrives at the plate a split second before the ball. Yogi Berra is the catcher.

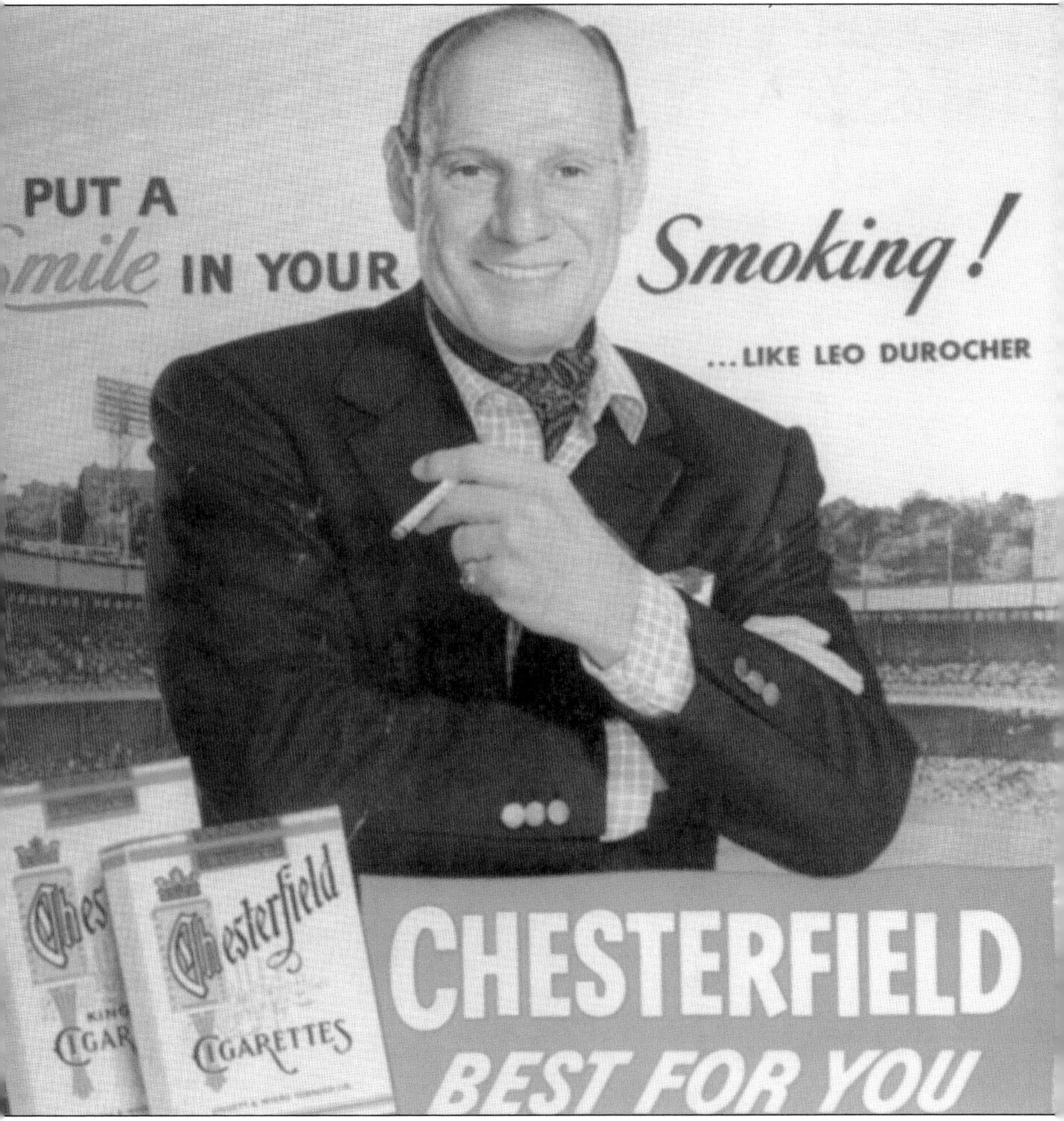

LEO THE LIP. Giants manager Leo "The Lip" Durocher looks typically dapper in this *c.* 1950 cigarette ad. The colorful, pugnacious Durocher broke in with Babe Ruth's Yankees in 1928 and was the shortstop on St. Louis's famous "Gas House Gang" of the 1930s before moving on to play and manage in Brooklyn. Durocher married Hollywood star Lorraine Day and coined the now-famous American credo "Nice guys finish last," a dig at Giants manager Mel Ott. Ironically, Durocher replaced Ott, skippering the Giants for 7 of his 23 managerial seasons. There he won a pair of pennants and the 1954 World Series. "He was the kind of manager who absolutely could not tolerate mediocrity," recalled one Giant. "He expected and demanded the most that you could give. If you didn't hustle you couldn't play for him." Durocher finished with a career managerial record of 2,010 wins and 1,710 losses.

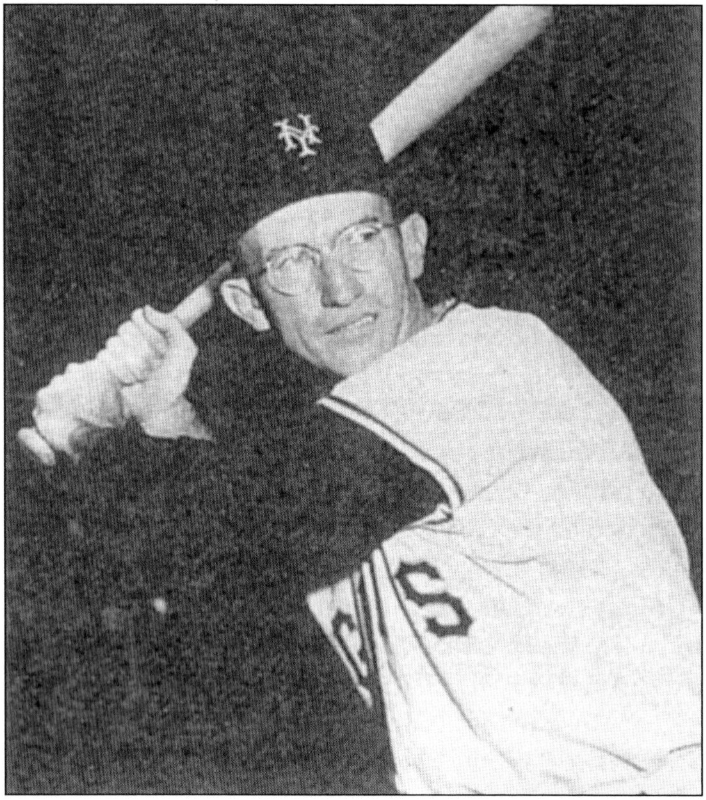

SPECS RIGNEY. Shortstop Bill Rigney was notable for his basket catches, years before Willie Mays made them famous. He also was one of the few big leaguers to wear glasses. The 1950 deal for Alvin Dark and Eddie Stanky ended Rigney's days as a regular. "I thought of asking to be moved because I knew I could still play," Rigney recalled, "but being a Giant was part of my life. I wanted to end up a Giant." Rigney replaced Durocher as manager after the 1955 season.

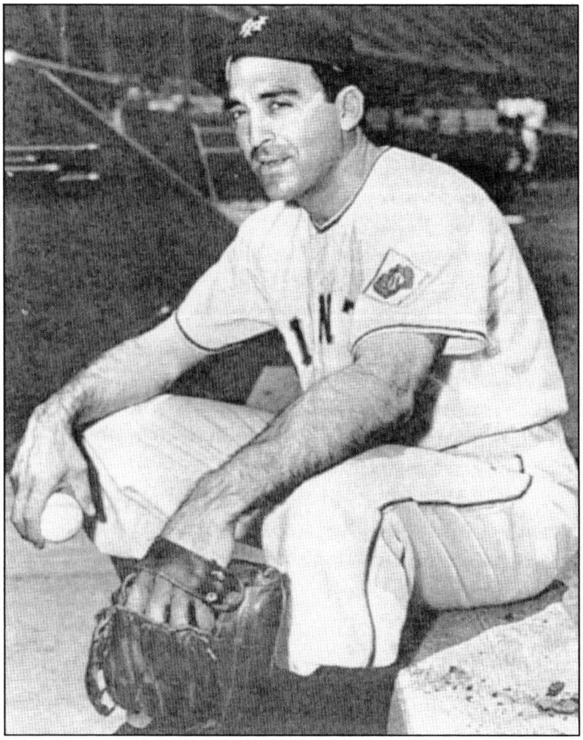

A CLOSE SHAVE. Sal "the Barber" Maglie earned his nickname from his habit of dusting off batters, a wicked philosophy of pitching that resulted in a league-low 2.71 ERA in 1950 and a league-high 23 victories in 1951. Philadelphia's Andy Seminick recalled once stepping out of the batter's box to protest the antics of second baseman Eddie Stanky, who was jumping up and down, trying to distract him. "After I complained to the umpire, Maglie drilled me in the damn ribs."

HOYT WILHELM. Until Jesse Orosco broke his record in 1999, no big leaguer had pitched in more games than Hoyt Wilhelm. Of the knuckleballer's 1,070 appearances on his way to the Hall of Fame, few were more memorable than his debut. On April 19, 1952, he hit a home run in his first major league at-bat. In 21 seasons, he never hit another. Wilhelm was 15-3 as a rookie reliever and led the league with a 2.43 ERA.

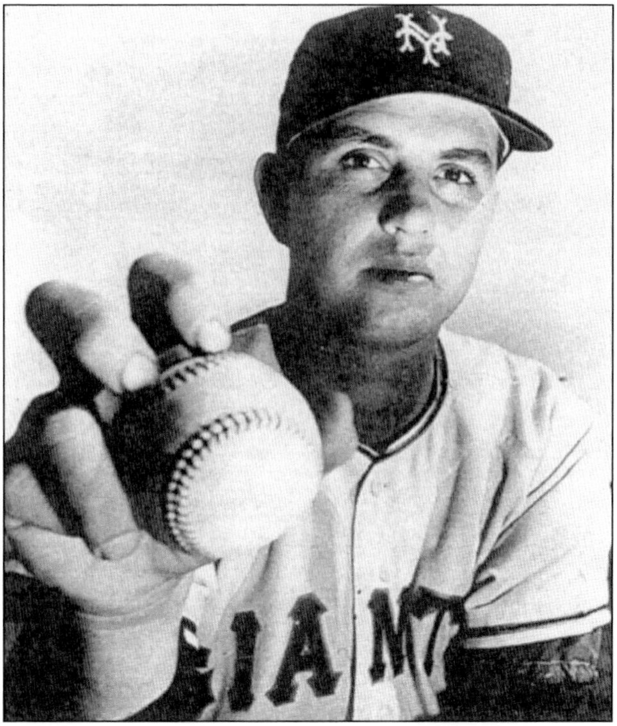

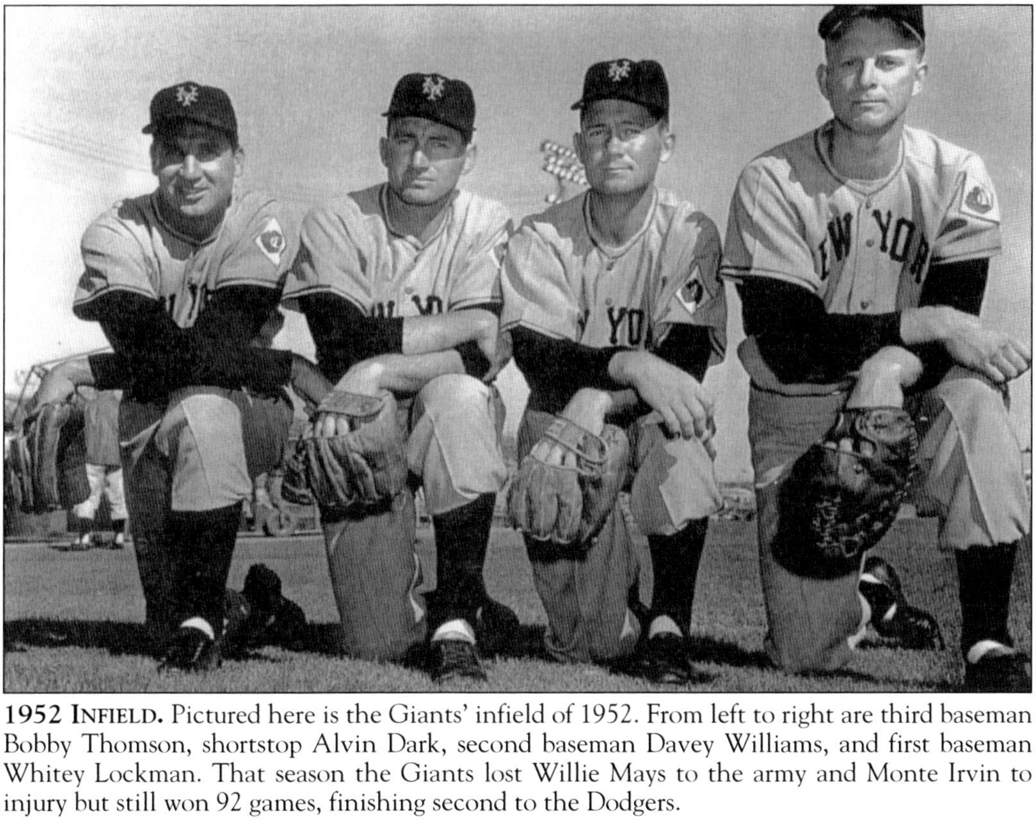

1952 INFIELD. Pictured here is the Giants' infield of 1952. From left to right are third baseman Bobby Thomson, shortstop Alvin Dark, second baseman Davey Williams, and first baseman Whitey Lockman. That season the Giants lost Willie Mays to the army and Monte Irvin to injury but still won 92 games, finishing second to the Dodgers.

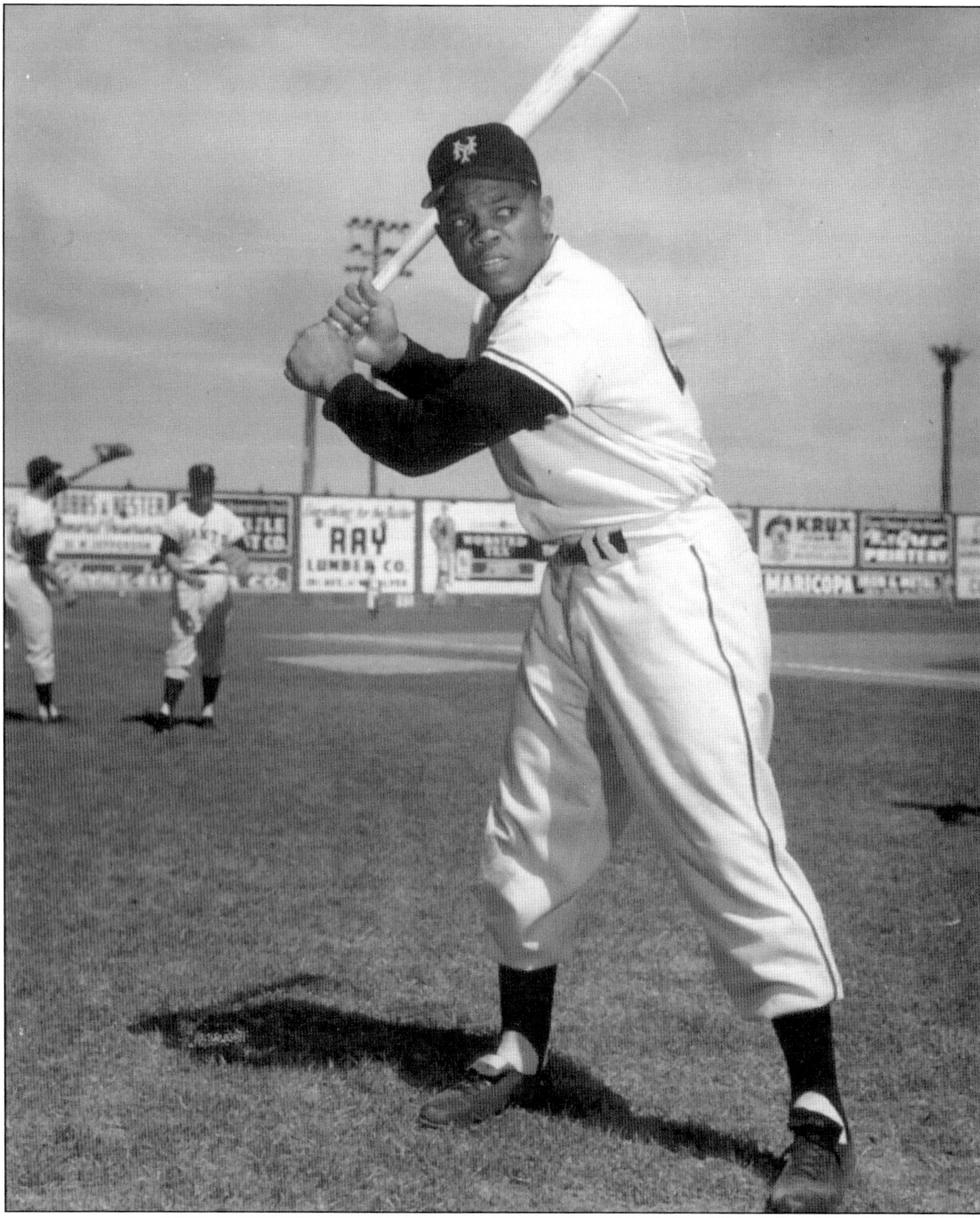

WILLIE MAYS. There are millions of fans who consider Hall-of-Fame center fielder Willie Mays the greatest all-around ballplayer of all time. Mays, an Alabama native who broke in with the Giants on May 25, 1951, won four home run titles, led the loop in stolen bases four straight seasons, banged out 3,283 hits, and ran and fielded spectacularly. Only Hank Aaron and Babe Ruth hit more than his 670 home runs. "What is there to be said about Mays that hasn't been said 100 times before," Gil Hodges said as Mays wrapped up his 22-year career in 1973 with the New York Mets. "He's simply the best."

WILLIE HAULS DOWN ANOTHER. "To play with Willie Mays and watch him every day was a treat," said teammate Johnny Antonelli. "I loved how he ran the bases or ran down long flies or got a base hit or home run we needed. He was just a great, great ballplayer."

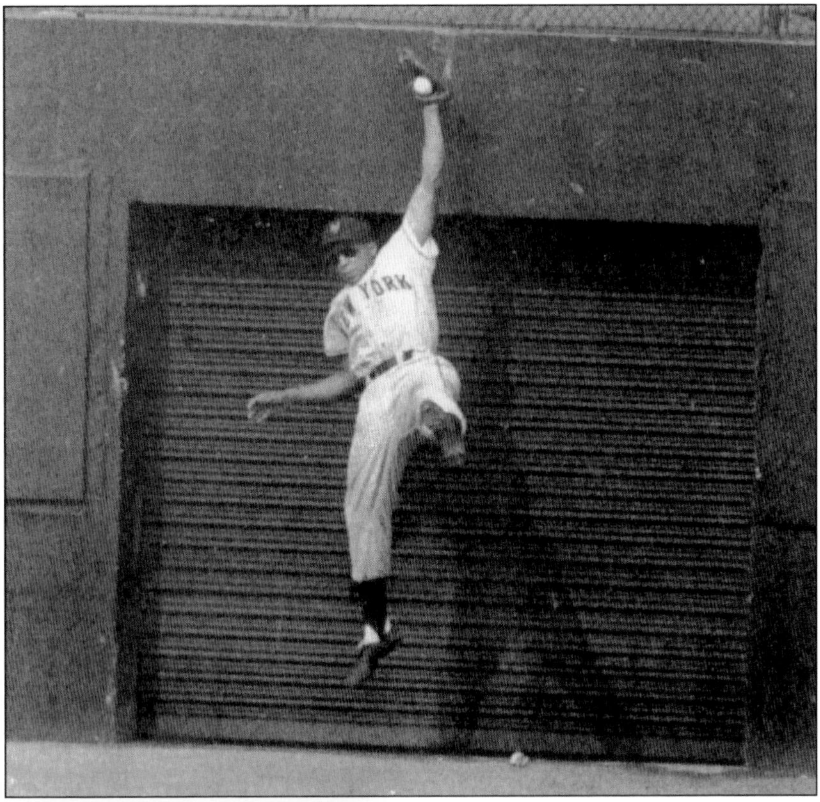

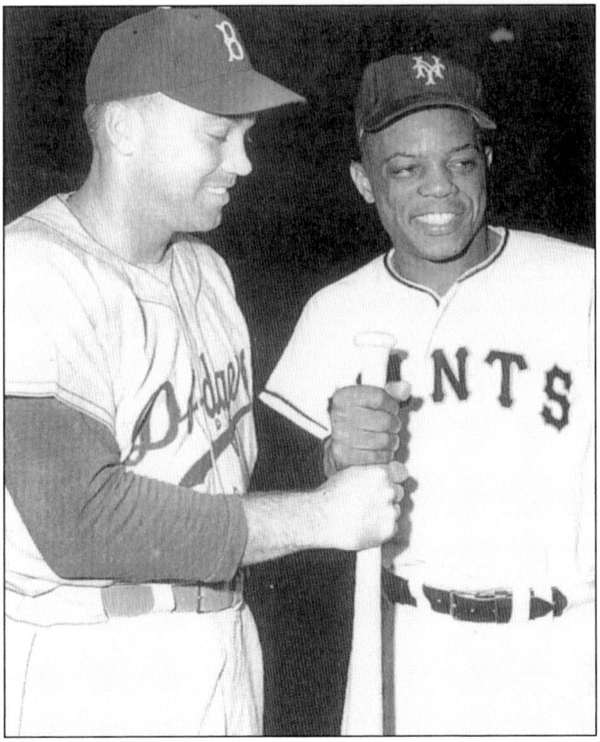

WELCOME BACK. In 1954, after spending two years in the army, Willie Mays returned to lead the Giants to their final pennant at the Polo Grounds. The 23-year-old wonder beat out teammate Don Mueller and Brooklyn's Duke Snider (left) on the last day of the season for his only batting title. Mays' all-around excellence earned him his first Most Valuable Player award. He would win a second in 1956.

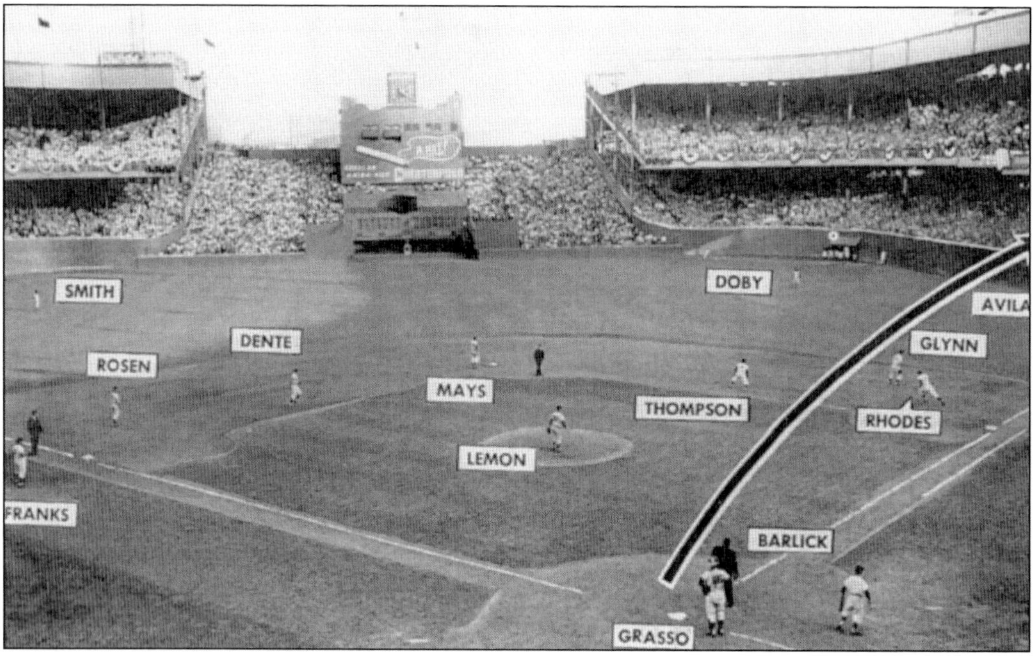

WORLD SERIES FOLK HERO. Cleveland, coming off an American League record 111-win season, was the favorite in the 1954 World Series. But the Giants shocked observers by sweeping the Indians, due largely to the devastating bat of James "Dusty" Rhodes. In the first game, the part-time outfielder pinch-hit a 260-foot fly ball that plopped into the seats in right (above) for a game-winning home run. The celebrating continued as Rhodes delivered timely hits in the next two games, winding up with a .667 average and seven RBIs.

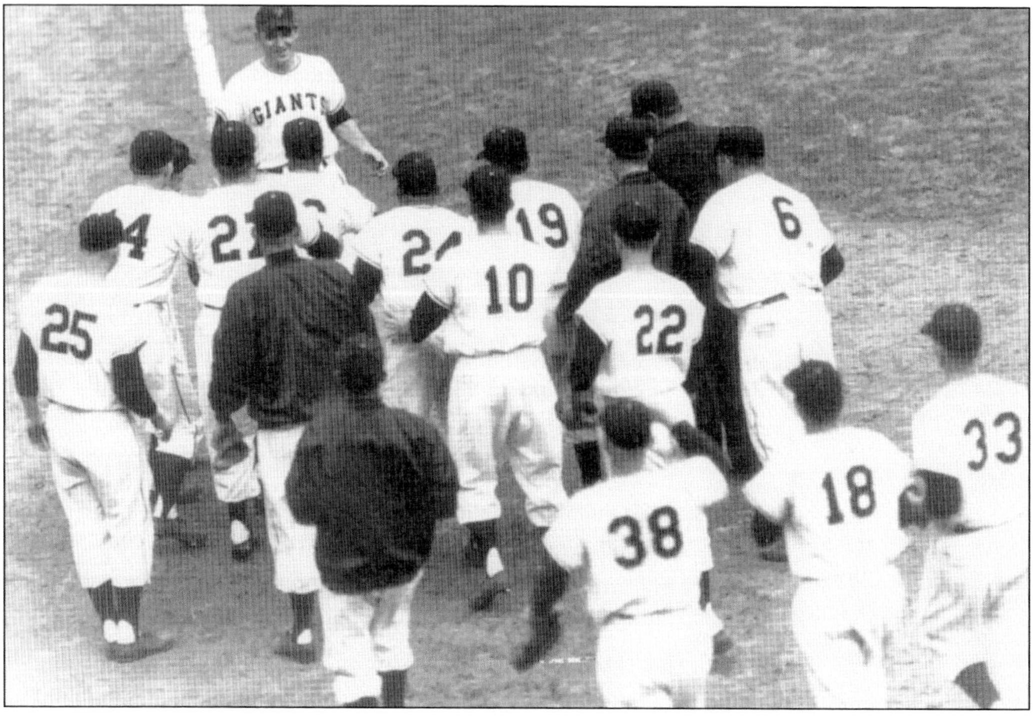

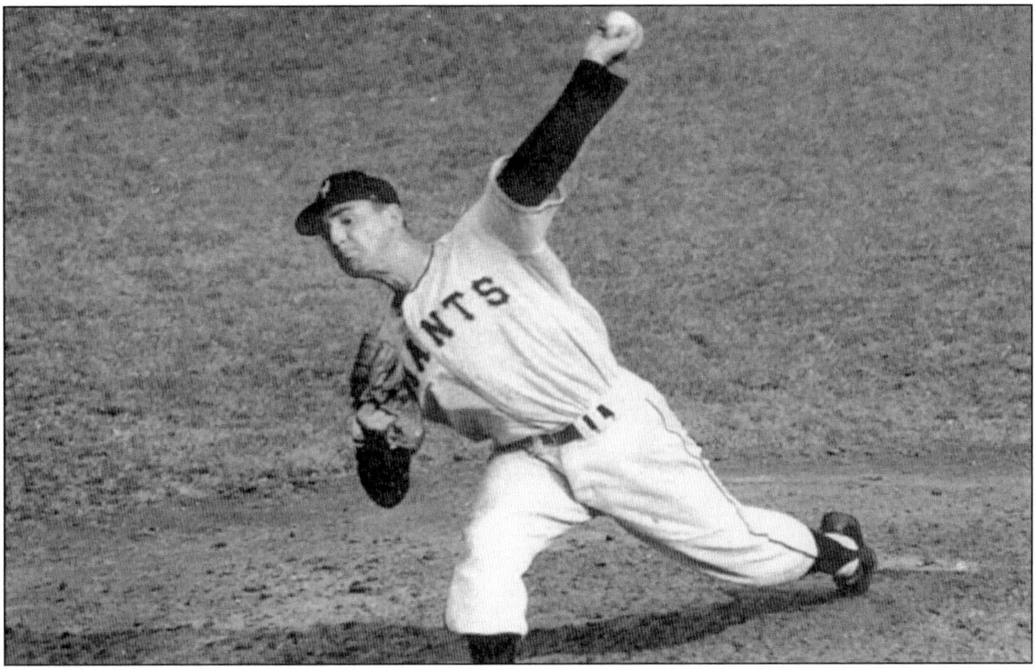

JOHNNY ANTONELLI. Johnny Antonelli came to the Giants from Milwaukee and rang up a 21-7 record in 1954, his first season in New York. He also led all National League pitchers with six shutouts and a 2.30 ERA. "The Polo Grounds was a friendly ballpark for me," he said. "I made them hit the ball straight away and I had Willie Mays to track it down." In the World Series against Cleveland, he started and won game two, 3-1, and saved game four, a 7-3 victory that gave the Giants their last world title.

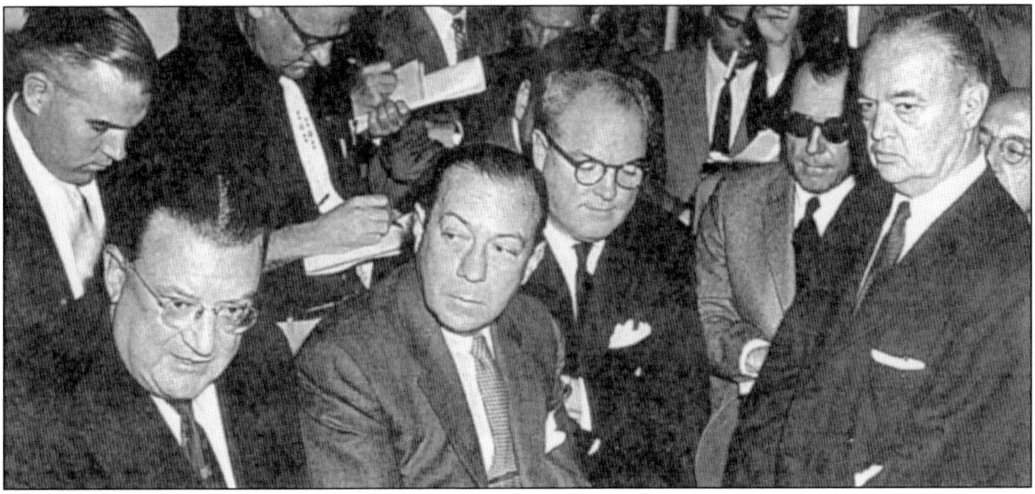

THE MOVE WEST. On August 19, 1957, Giants president Horace Stoneham (second from left) announced the decision by the board of directors to move the team to San Francisco after the season. That October, Brooklyn owner Walter O'Malley (left) announced that the Dodgers were relocating to Los Angeles. Both teams cited sagging attendance and deteriorating parks as their reasons for moving. The departure of the two old-line franchises was a seismic change for professional baseball and left New York with only one team, the Yankees, when the 1958 season opened.

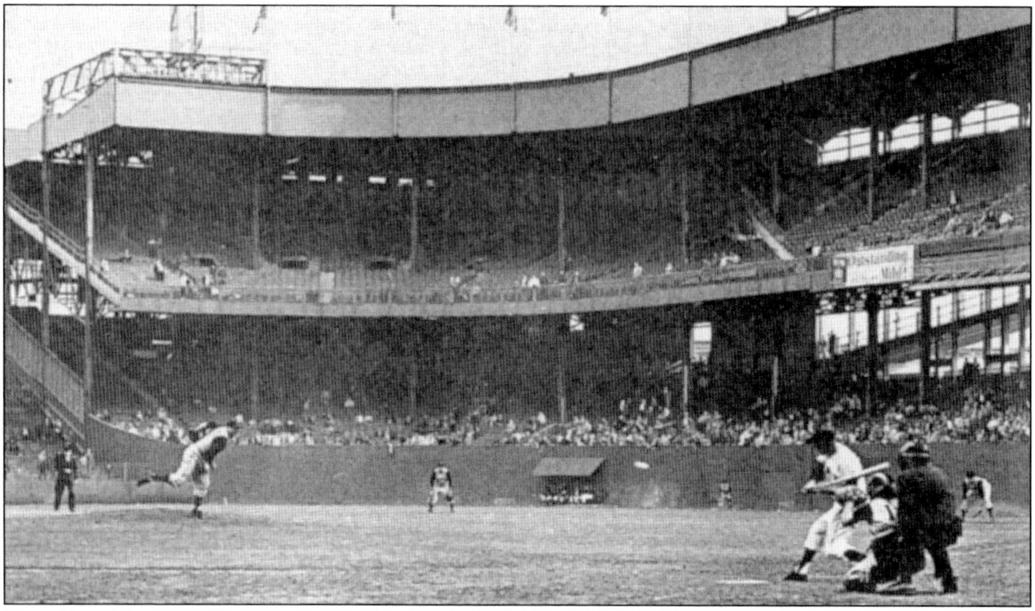

THE END OF AN ERA. On September 29, 1957, the Giants closed out 75 summers in New York by dropping a 9-1 decision to Pittsburgh in front of 11,606 fans. Pictured above, Dusty Rhodes is about to hit a ground ball for the final out. Pictured below, players run up the centerfield stairs for the last time, past a sign that pleads "Stay Team Stay." "We're sorry to disappoint the kids of New York," said Horace Stoneham, "but we didn't see many of their parents out there at the Polo Grounds in recent years."

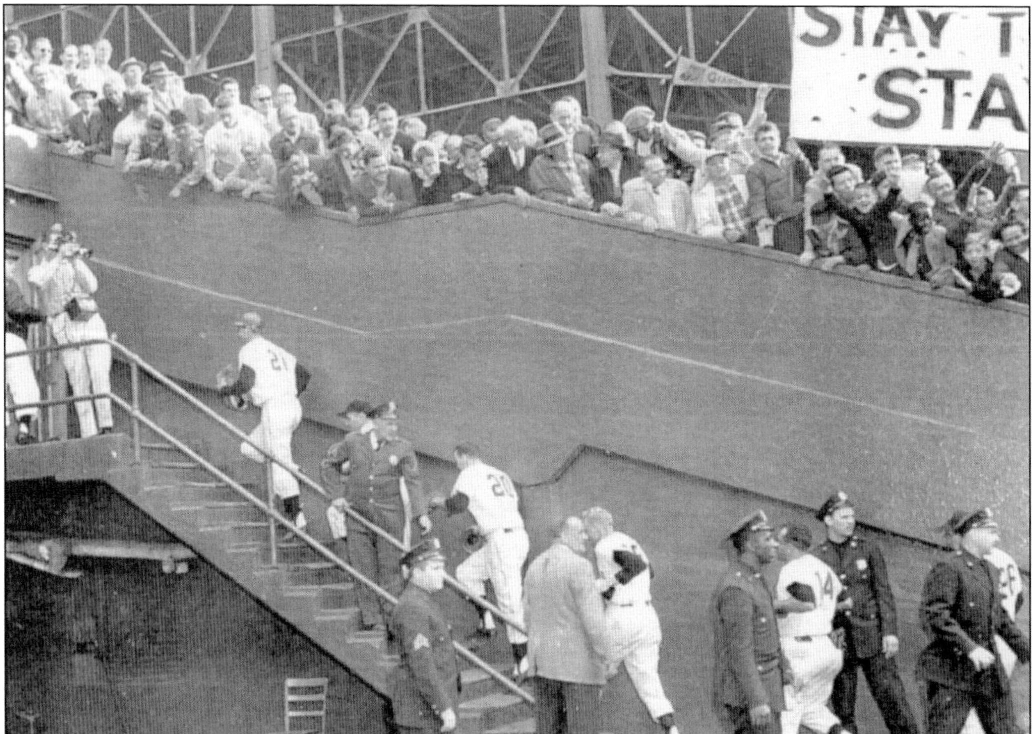

Five

UNDER COOGAN'S BLUFF

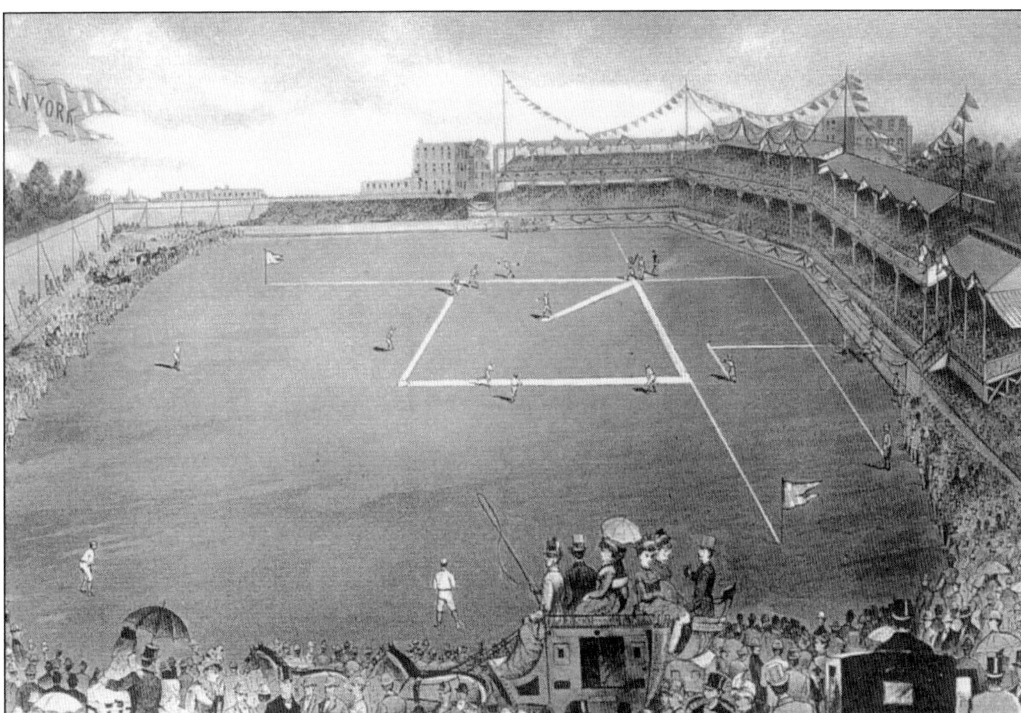

THE ORIGINAL POLO GROUNDS, 1887. In the 1870s, polo was played at a field adjoining the northeast corner of Central Park. In 1883, a ballpark was built on this site (from 110th to 112th Streets west of Fifth Avenue) to accommodate the Giants. In 1889, city expansion forced the team to leave what had become known as the Polo Grounds.

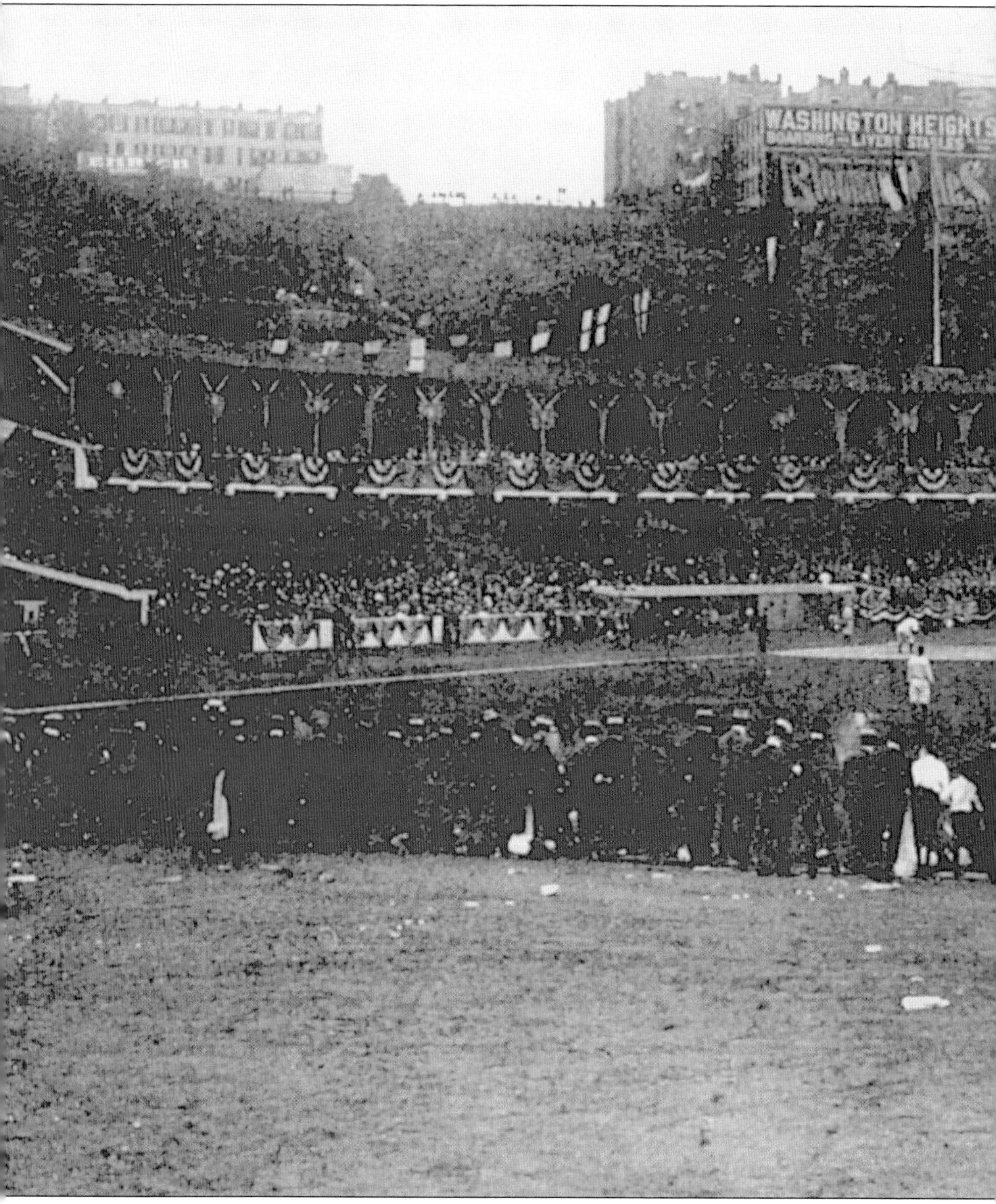

POLO GROUNDS, C. 1905. On April 22, 1891, the Giants began playing at a park between 157th and 159th Streets, in the northern half of Coogan's Hollow. The wooden facility, which had been built the previous year for the upstart Players League, was named the Polo Grounds after the original 110th Street Polo Grounds. A horseshoe-shaped double-decked grandstand

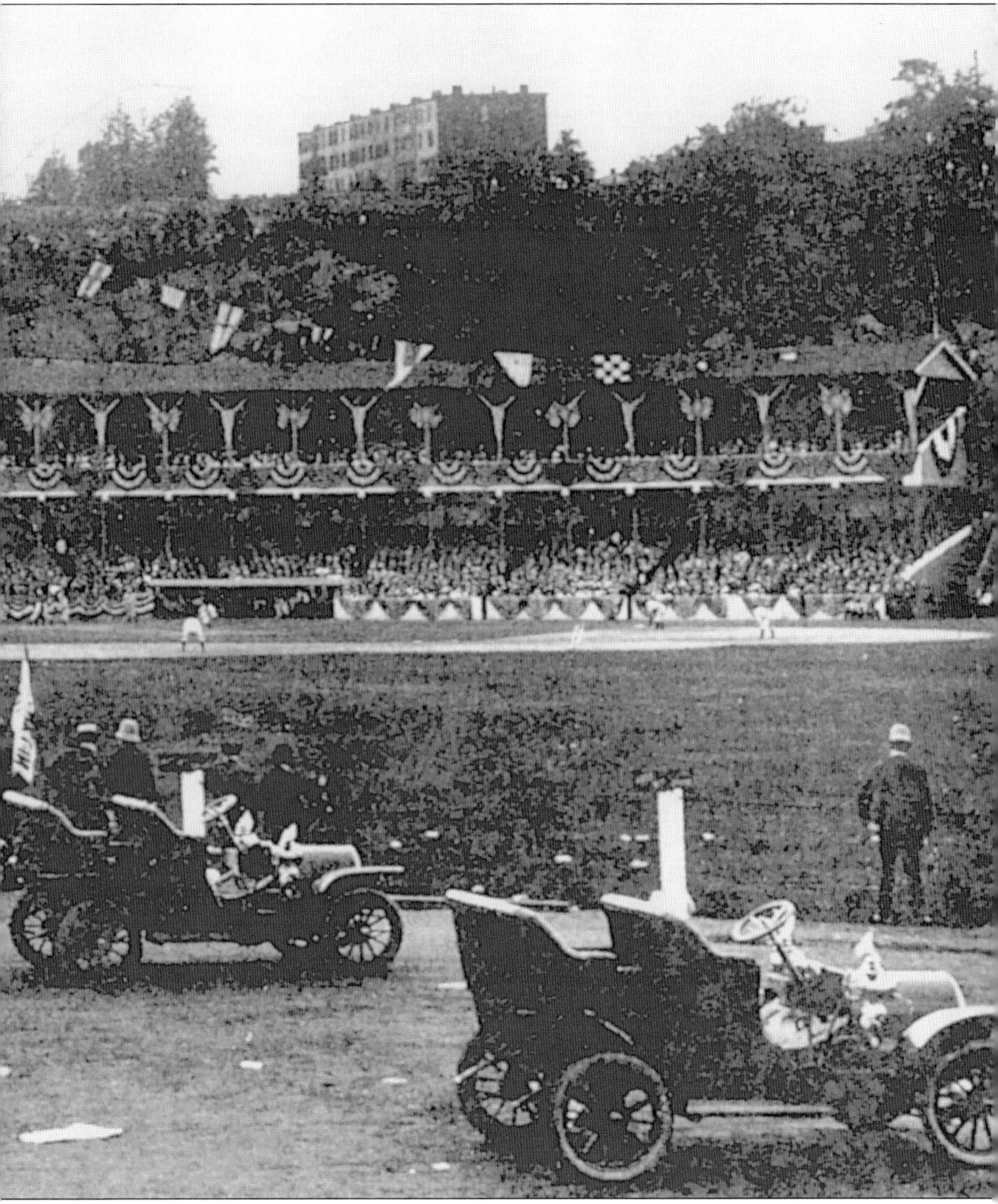

curved around home plate, while uncovered bleacher sections ran down both foul lines. By the time of the 1905 World Series, capacity had been raised from 16,000 to 23,000 by adding bleachers in the outfield. Although the look of the park would change over the years, the playing site would remain the same for 67 years of National League action.

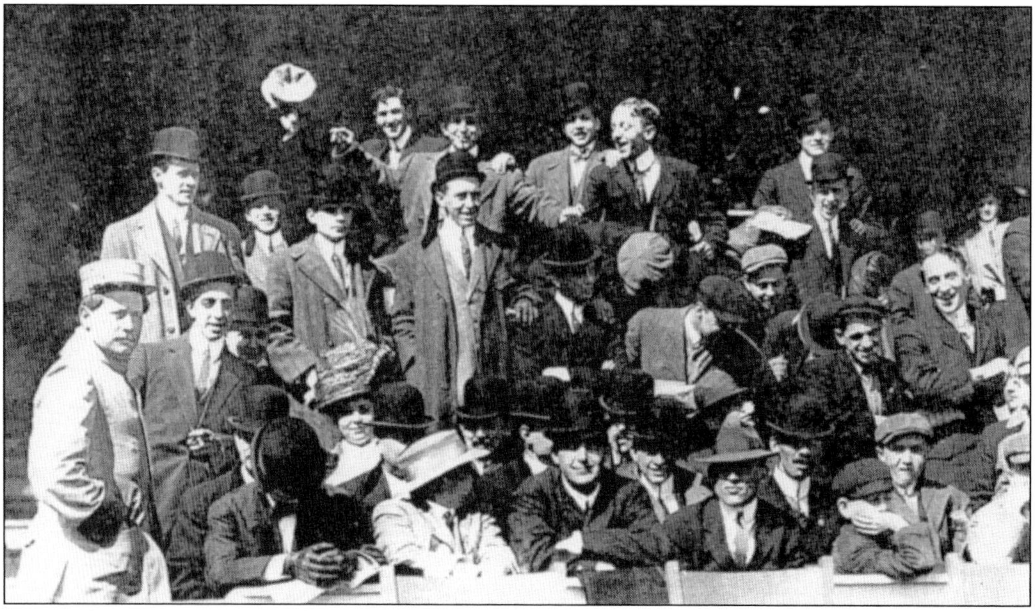

EARLY GIANTS FANS. Until Babe Ruth's Yankees stole their thunder in the 1920s, the Giants dominated the city's society pages, sports columns, and turnstile counts. "I was always a New York Giants man," wrote Harry Golden. "The Giants represented the New York of the brass cuspidor—that old New York which was still a man's world before the advent of the League of Woman Voters; the days of swinging doors, of sawdust on the barroom floor, and of rushing the growler."

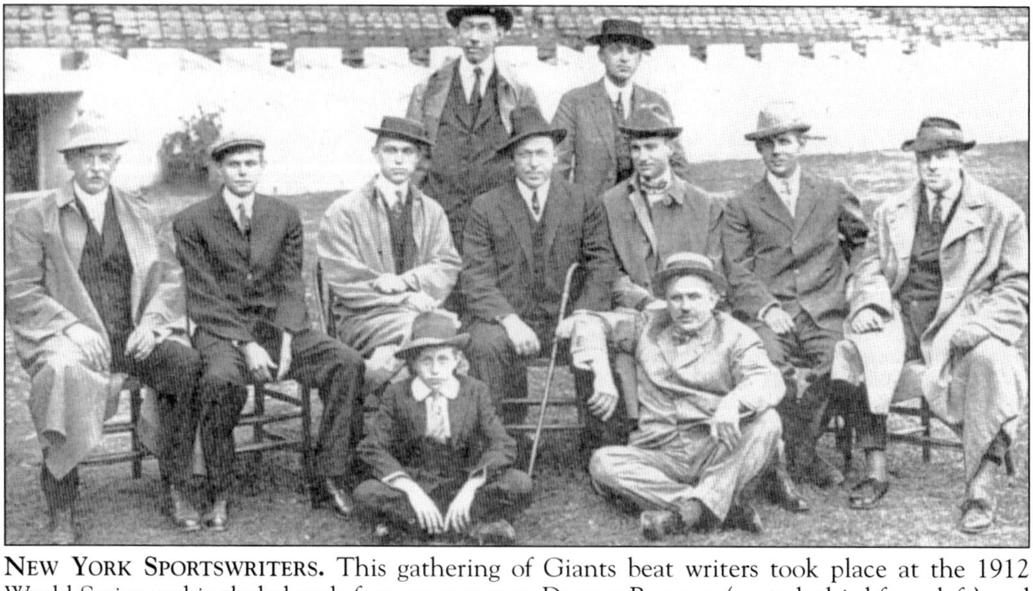

NEW YORK SPORTSWRITERS. This gathering of Giants beat writers took place at the 1912 World Series and included such famous names as Damon Runyon (seated, third from left) and Grantland Rice (seated, second from right). In the right foreground is concessionaire Harry Stevens, who one day in 1901 at the Polo Grounds came up with the idea of placing a frankfurter inside a roll. Thus was born the hot dog, a staple of ballparks ever since.

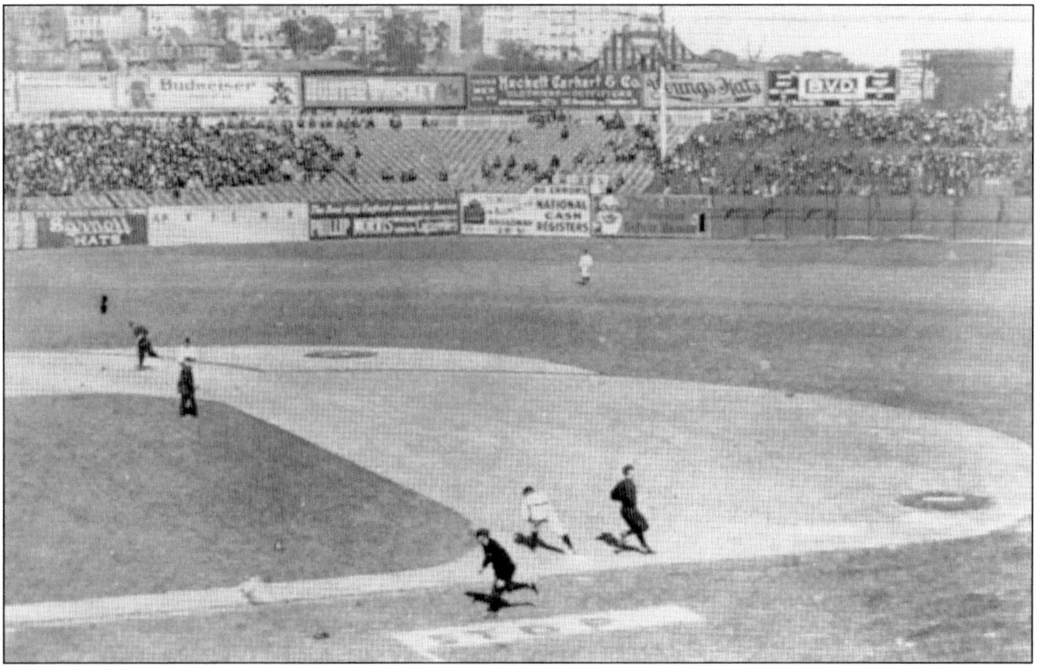

THE POLO GROUNDS, C. 1908. Seen here are two pictures of the Polo Grounds. The top shows the field from the perspective of someone sitting in the first-base stands. The bottom illustrates the vantage point of those atop Coogan's Bluff, the hill rising behind the home plate area of the grandstand. "An open space below the roof of the stadium made it possible for me, and for others crowded together on the rocky hill, to peek at part of what was happening on the field," one older fan recalled of those days.

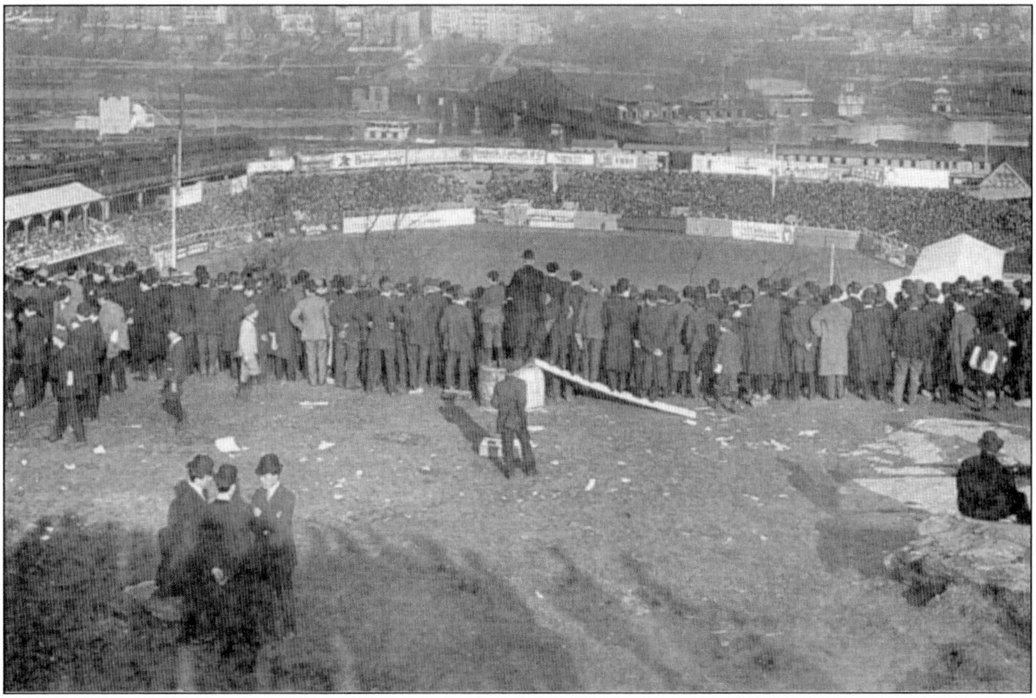

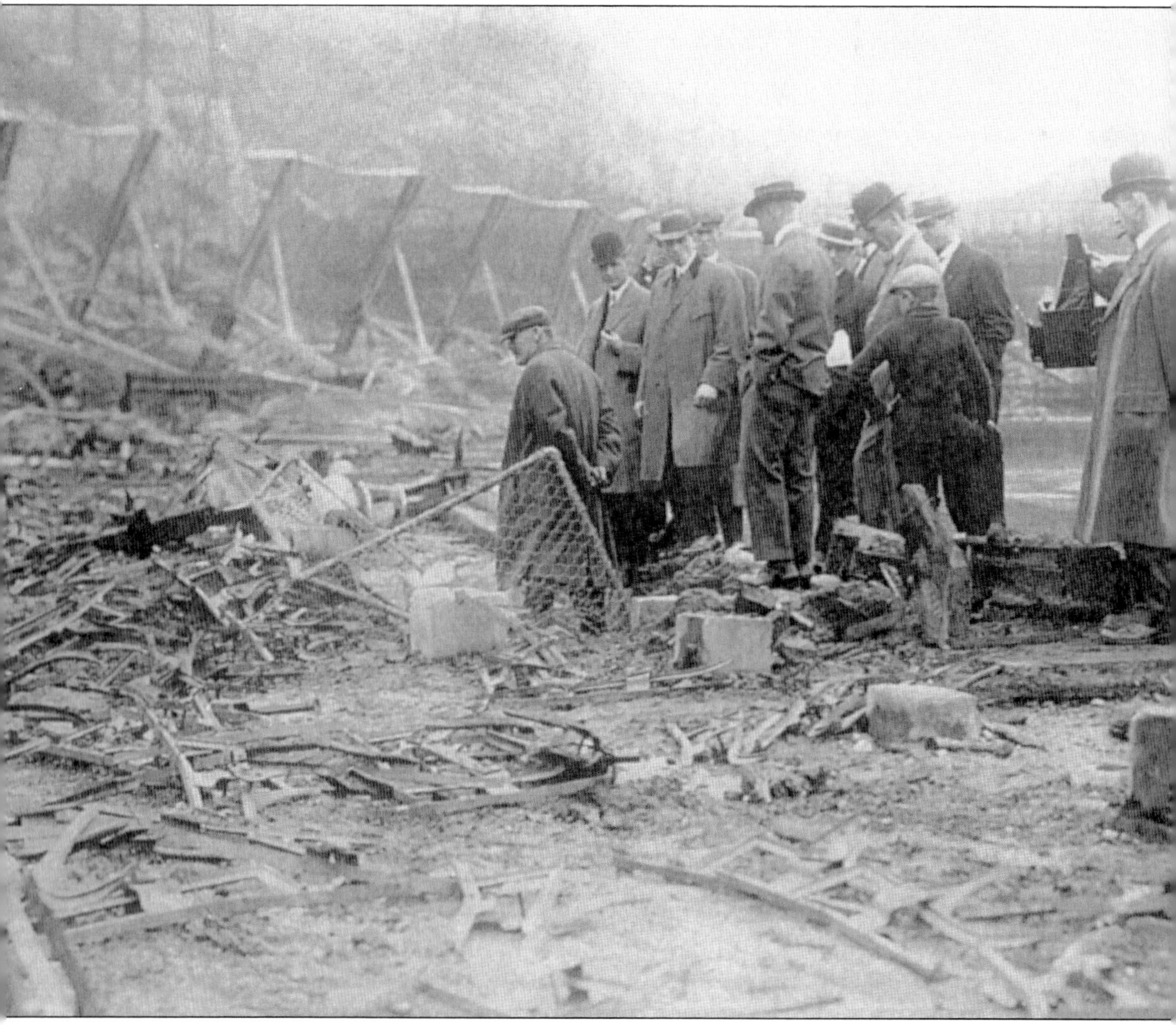

RISING FROM THE ASHES. In the early morning hours of April 14, 1911, a fire destroyed most of the Polo Grounds. While the Giants accepted the Yankees' offer to temporarily share Hilltop Park, contractors hurried to rebuild the Polo Grounds into a modern concrete and steel facility. In late June the Giants moved back home, although work continued throughout the summer. The completed structure, finished in time for that October's World Series, could seat 34,000 in its main double-decked grandstand and the uncovered outfield bleacher section. No big-league park held more people.

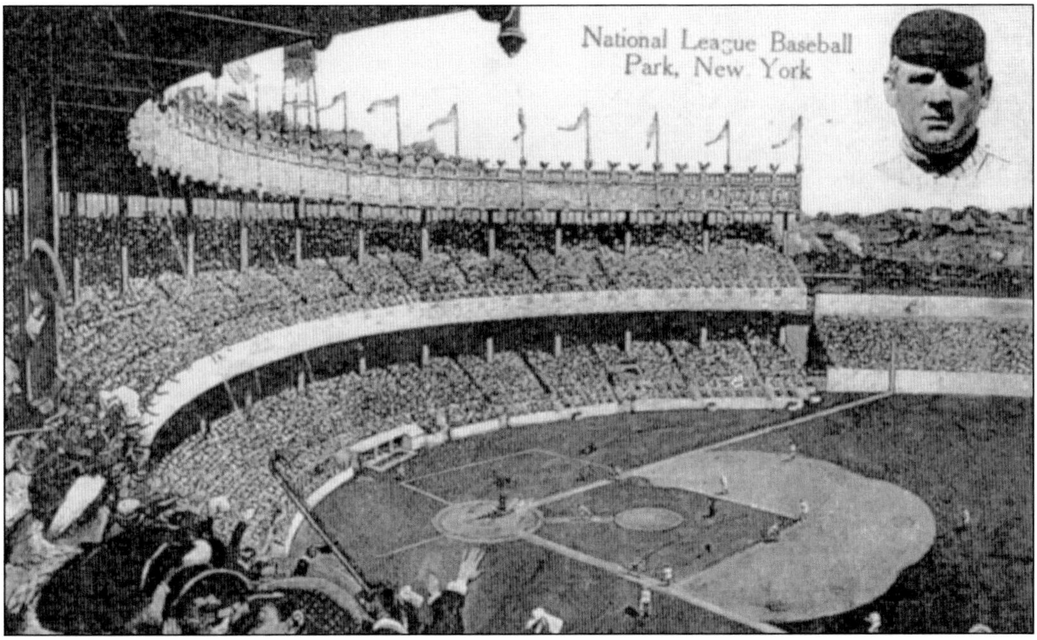

THE NEW POLO GROUNDS. A postcard of the rebuilt Polo Grounds reveals some of the decorative work on the upper and lower deck facades. Pictured below, a 1911 program from that year's World Series called the facility Brush Stadium, after owner John T. Brush. But New Yorkers continued to call it by its old familiar name.

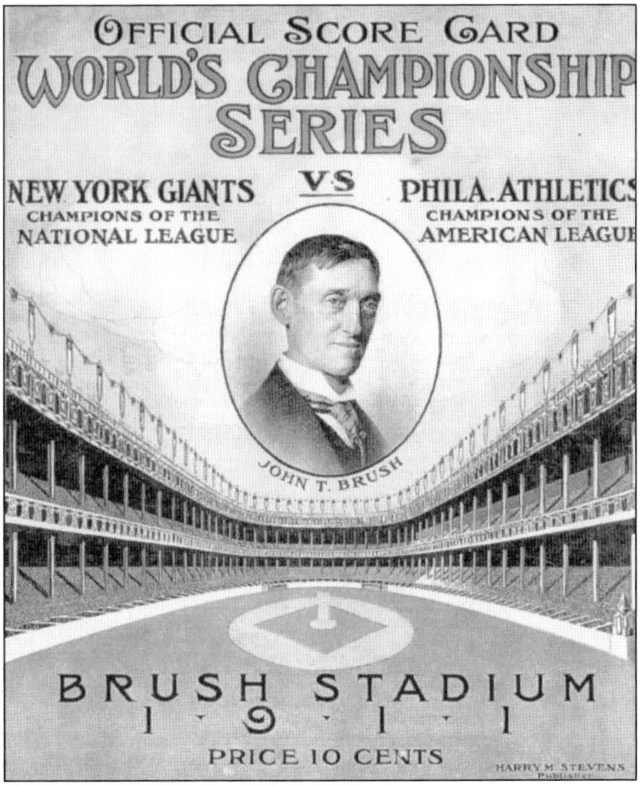

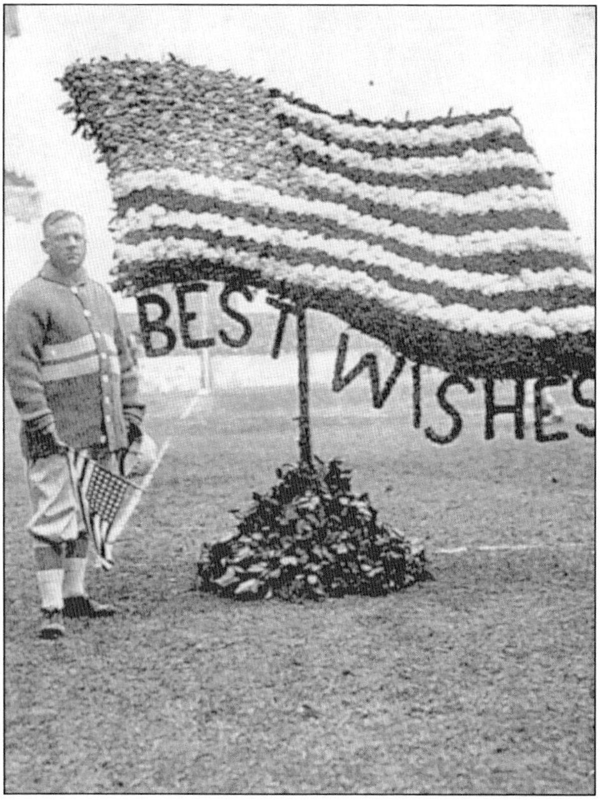

GOOD LUCK FROM THE LAMBS. Each April, opening day at the Polo Grounds was alive with optimism and festivity. Here John McGraw poses with a giant floral flag, compliments of the Lambs Club. McGraw was a member of the exclusive Manhattan social club until 1920, when he was expelled after a drunken brawl.

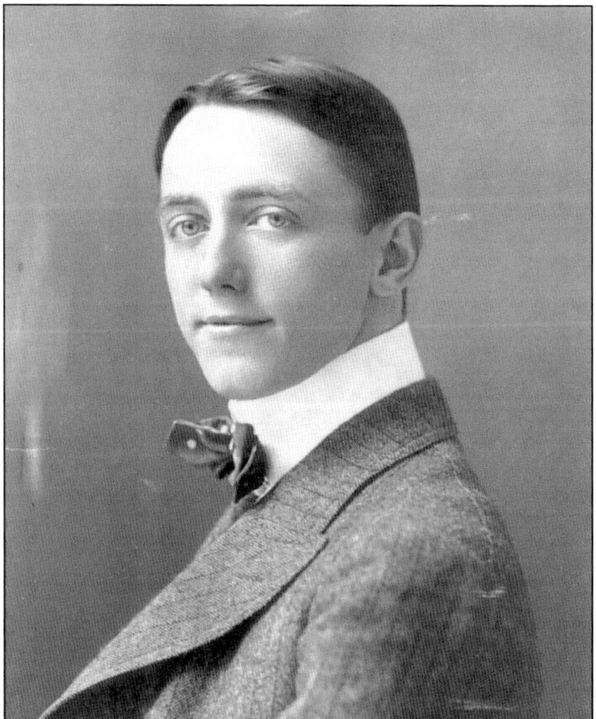

SINGING THE GIANTS' PRAISES. One of the most rabid fans at the Polo Grounds was George M. Cohan, pictured here. The legendary song-and-dance man, a good friend of John McGraw, often hired actors based on their ability to fill a position on the teams he organized after work. In 1908, the sight of fans rushing to the Polo Grounds inspired fellow New York songwriter Jack Norworth to compose the classic "Take Me Out to the Ball Game." Ironically, Norworth had never been to a baseball game.

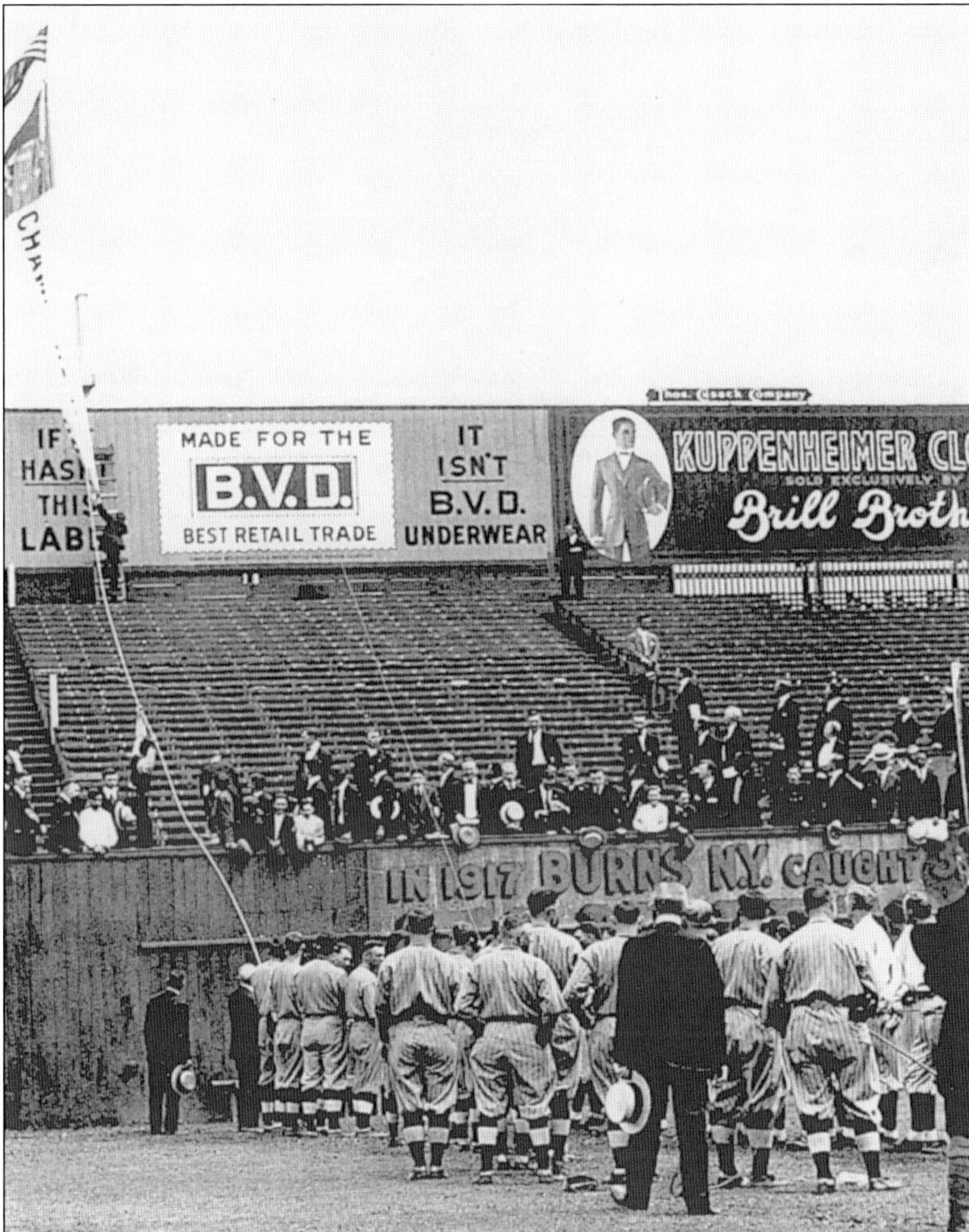

Flag Raising Ceremony, 1918. With appropriate hoopla, the Giants and their supporters unfurl a giant flag before the 1918 home opener, indicating that they are the defending National League champions. Harry Golden recalled "a lady with a very large black picture hat sitting in the front row of the center field bleachers . . . and just as the Giants took the field you could hear her battle cry in every corner of the Polo Grounds—'Come on, Artie!'—and the shortstop Arthur Fletcher would wave his glove at her, everybody would applaud, and then the first visiting batter would step up to the plate."

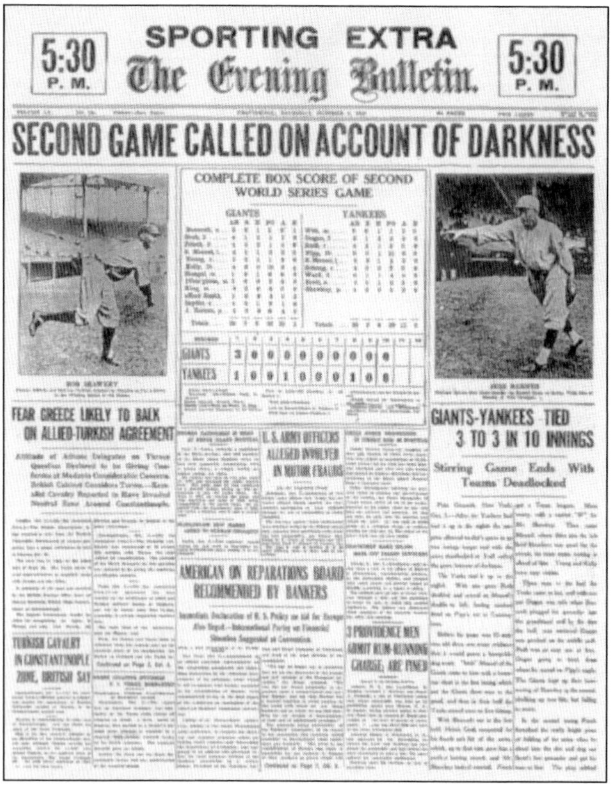
SPORTING EXTRA

5:30 P. M. The Evening Bulletin. 5:30 P. M.

SECOND GAME CALLED ON ACCOUNT OF DARKNESS

COMPLETE BOX SCORE OF SECOND WORLD SERIES GAME

	1	2	3	4	5	6	7	8	9	10	11	12
GIANTS	3	0	0	0	0	0	0	0	0	0		
YANKEES	1	0	0	1	0	0	0	1	0	0		

FEAR GREECE LIKELY TO BALK ON ALLIED-TURKISH AGREEMENT

U. S. ARMY OFFICERS ALLEGED INVOLVED IN MOTOR FRAUDS

GIANTS-YANKEES TIED 3 TO 3 IN 10 INNINGS

Stirring Game Ends With Teams Deadlocked

AMERICAN ON REPARATIONS BOARD RECOMMENDED BY BANKERS

TURKISH CAVALRY IN CONSTANTINOPLE ZONE, BRITISH SAY

3 PROVIDENCE MEN ADMIT RUM-RUNNING CHARGE; ARE FINED

NIGHT AND DAY. The Polo Grounds was home to many memorable moments, including this pair. On October 5, 1922, umpires unaccountably called the second game of the World Series "on account of darkness," even though it was only 4:30 in the afternoon and the sun was still in the sky. It was called a 3-3 tie after ten innings and the receipts given to charity. And on May 24, 1940, the first night game there was played, with the Giants whipping Boston, 8-1, before 22,460 curious fans.

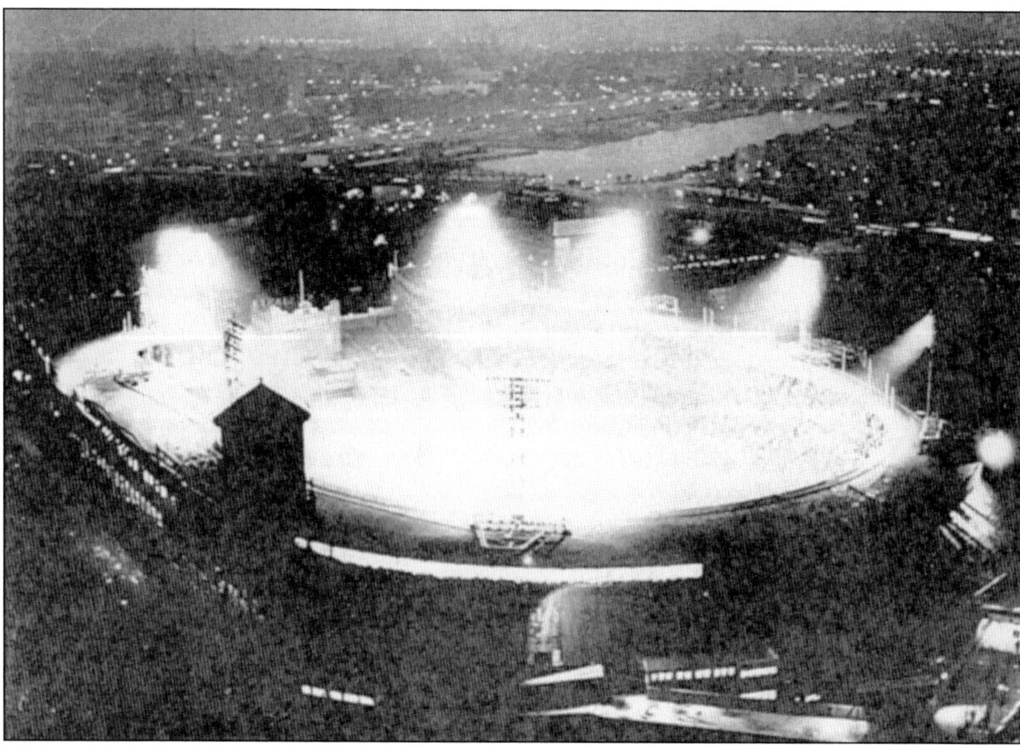

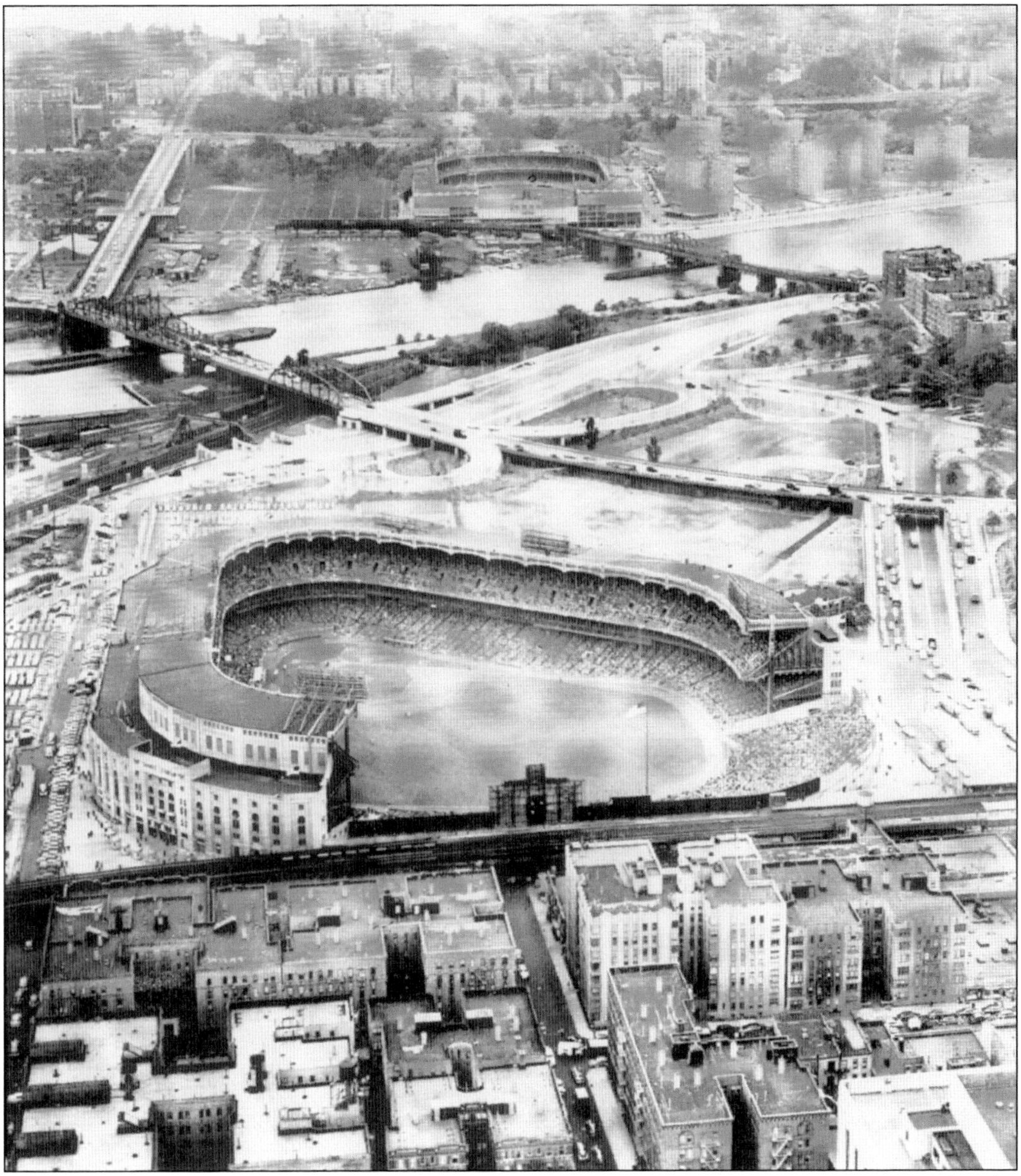

SUBWAY SERIES. The Polo Grounds and Yankee Stadium (foreground) were separated by the Harlem River and were only a 10¢ subway ticket apart. During the many years the two storied stadiums co-existed, the Yankees beat the Giants in the "Subway Series" every time: in 1923, 1936, 1937, and 1951. The Giants vanquished their American League rivals in the 1921 and 1922 World Series, when the teams shared the Polo Grounds.

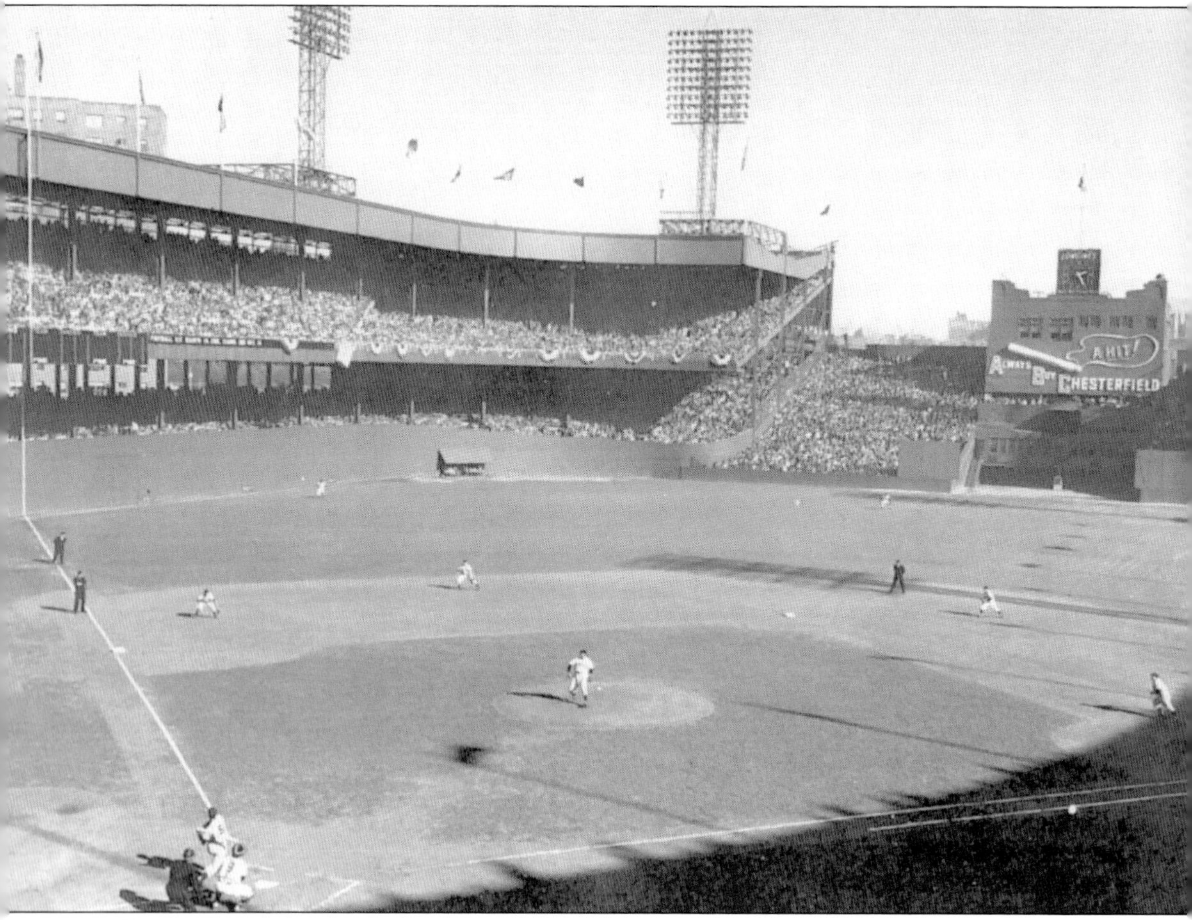

THE LONG AND SHORT OF IT. The yawning expanse of center field at the Polo Grounds was dominated by a giant sign for Chesterfield cigarettes and then later by Knickerbocker beer. This shot is from the fourth game of the 1951 World Series and shows the Yankees' Joe DiMaggio belting a Sal Maglie pitch into the upper deck of the left-field stands for the last home run of his career. Note the impossibly long power alleys—447 feet to left center and 440 feet to right center. Over the years, hundreds of cheaper home runs plopped into the seats along the abbreviated foul lines of the bathtub-shaped park, including a number hit by Babe Ruth during the years the Yankees shared the place with the Giants.

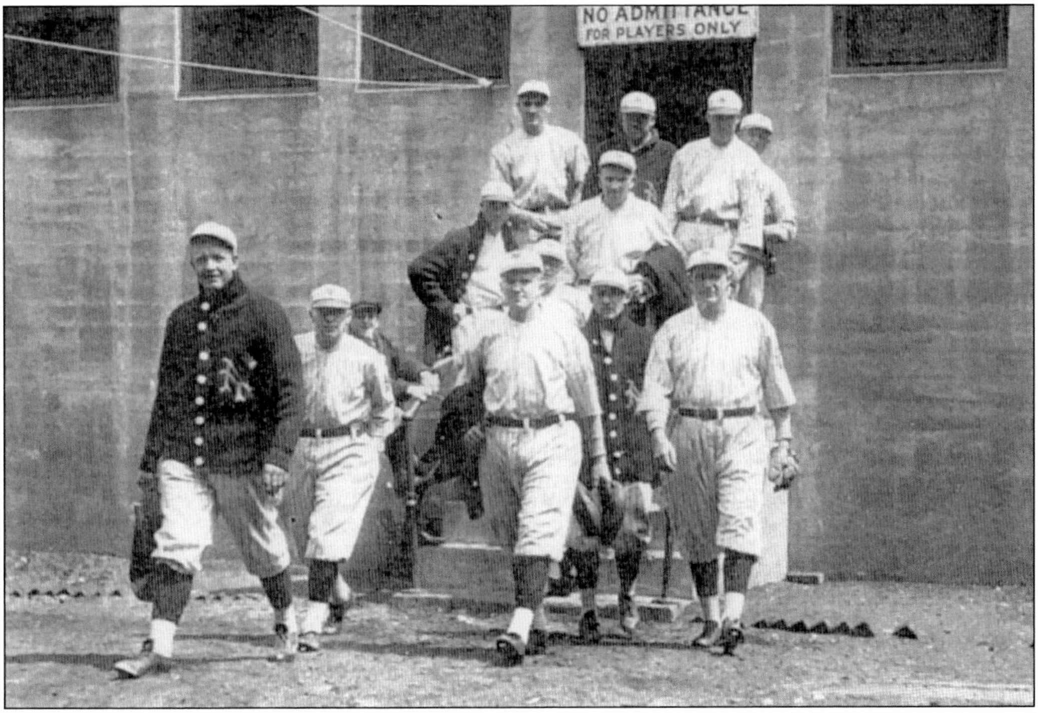

STEPPING OUT. At the Polo Grounds, the Giants' and visiting team's clubhouses were located in deep center field. This photograph of New York players emerging from the locker room dates from the early 1920s.

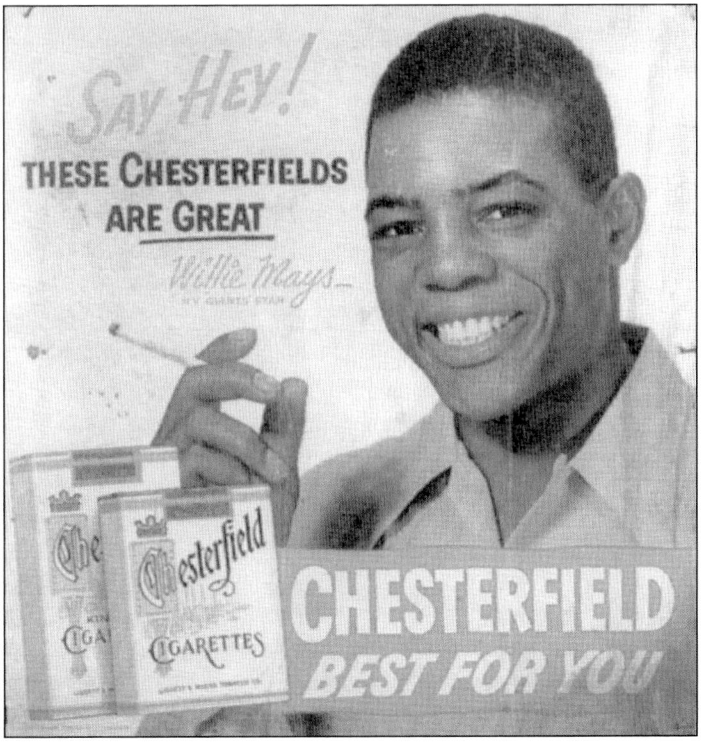

WILLIE MAYS CIGARETTE ADVERTISEMENT, C. 1954. The image of a famous athlete enjoying a good smoke was a common one in advertisements of the era. Chesterfield ads could be found all over the Polo Grounds, from inside scorebooks to the giant sign in center field, much to the dismay of parents and Little League coaches.

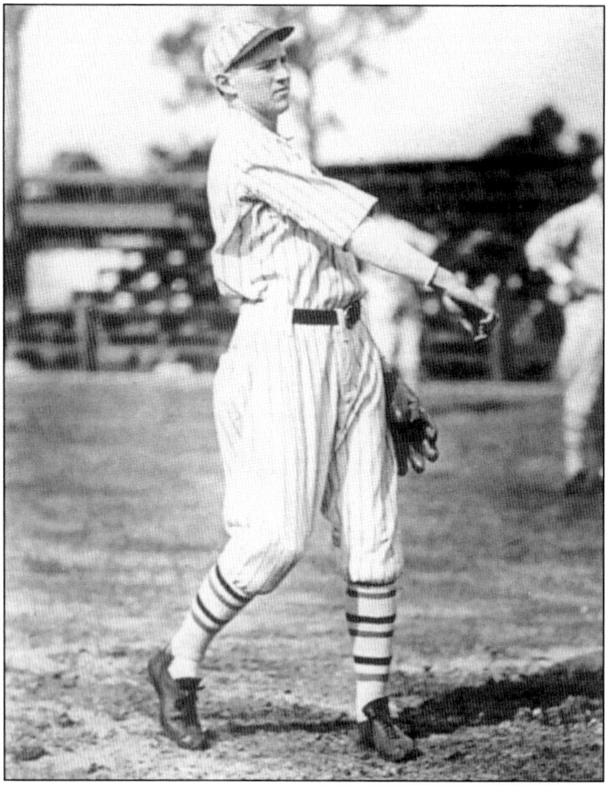

NEVER AGAIN. Freddy Lindstrom, who batted as high as .379 during his nine summers as a Giant, played the last game of his Hall-of-Fame career in 1936 at the Polo Grounds. This time he was wearing a Brooklyn uniform. "Somebody hit a pop fly into short left and Lindstrom came running in, the shortstop went running out, and it was 'I got it, you take, who's got it'," recalled Buddy Hassett. "The ball dropped in and both runs scored and we lose the game. Lindstrom came into the clubhouse and said, 'I heard about these things happening in Brooklyn. I never thought it would happen to me, and I tell you, it's never going to happen again.' He took off his uniform and never put it on again."

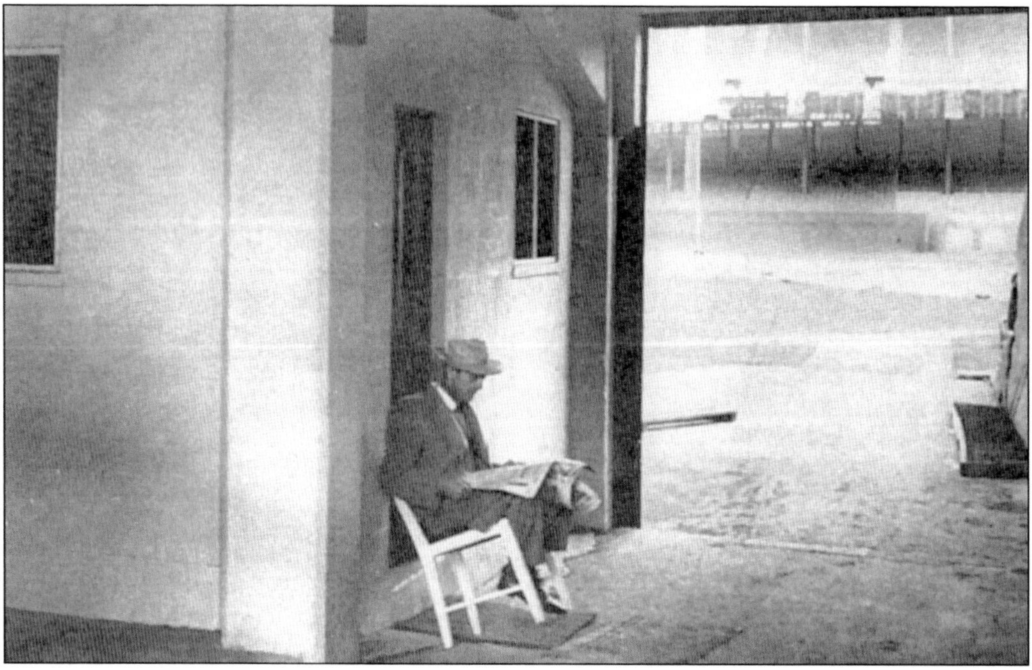

HOME, SWEET HOME. Groundskeeper Matt Schwab and his family were a familiar sight around the Polo Grounds, especially after the Giants built an apartment for them under the left-field stands in 1945. Here Schwab relaxes on the "front porch" of the family home.

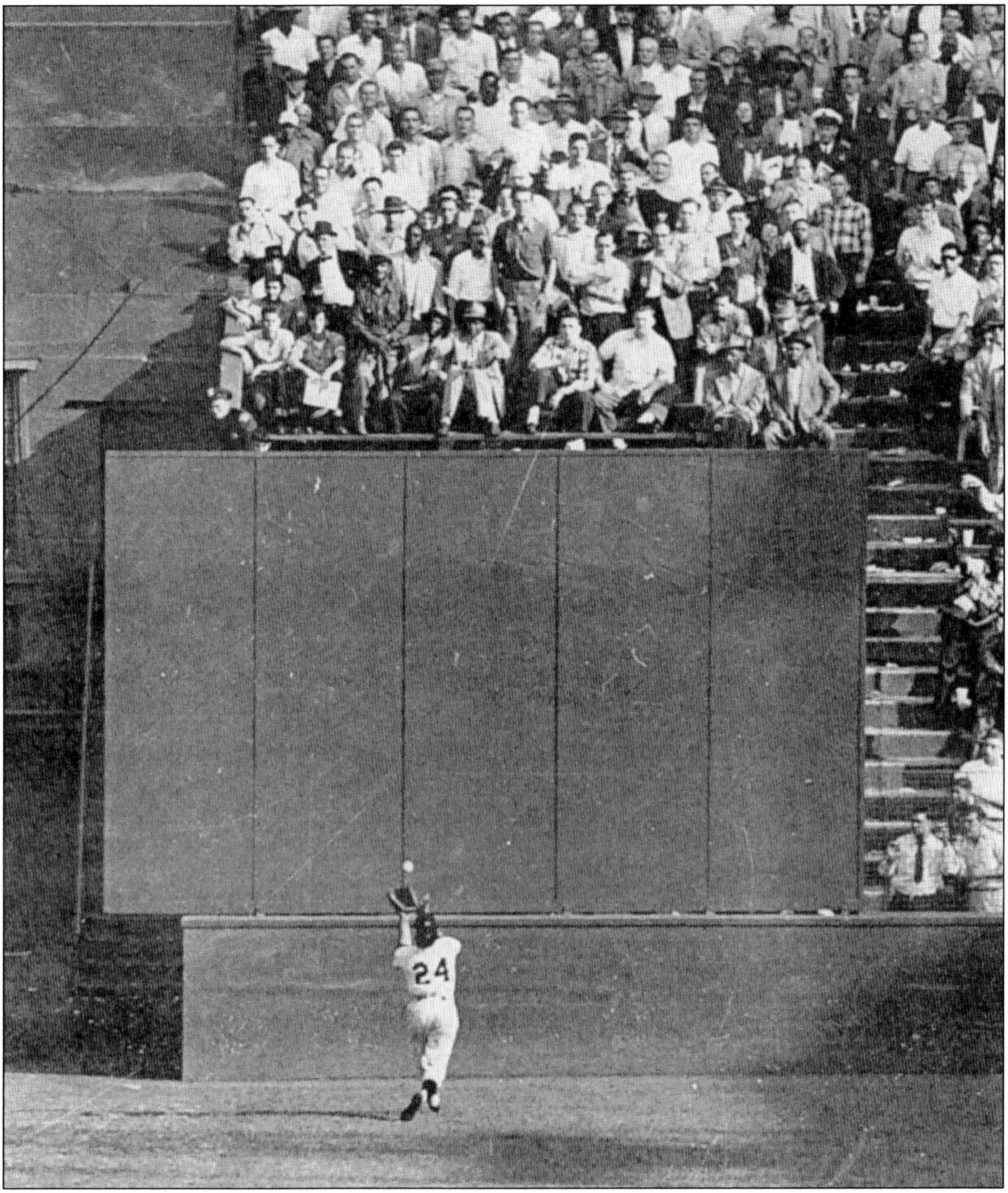

THE CATCH. The Polo Grounds was the scene of the most famous catch of all time. In the eighth inning of the opening game of the 1954 World Series, with the score tied and two runners on base, Cleveland's Vic Wertz scorched the ball towards the deepest part of center field, some 460 feet from the plate. Unbelievably, Willie Mays ran down the drive, reaching over his left shoulder to make the catch and squelch the rally. "I never thought he had a chance to get even close to it," said Monte Irvin, who was in left field. "I was going out there to play the rebound, hoping to hold Wertz to a triple. That ball was hit! But Willie caught it. Don't ask me how. But there he was, going a mile-a-minute, his back to the plate. When the inning was over and we were on our way in, I said to him, 'Nice going, roomie. I didn't think you'd get to that one.' Very casually, he said, 'I had that one all the way. Had it all the way.' And I said, 'Oh, you did, huh? Well, okay'."

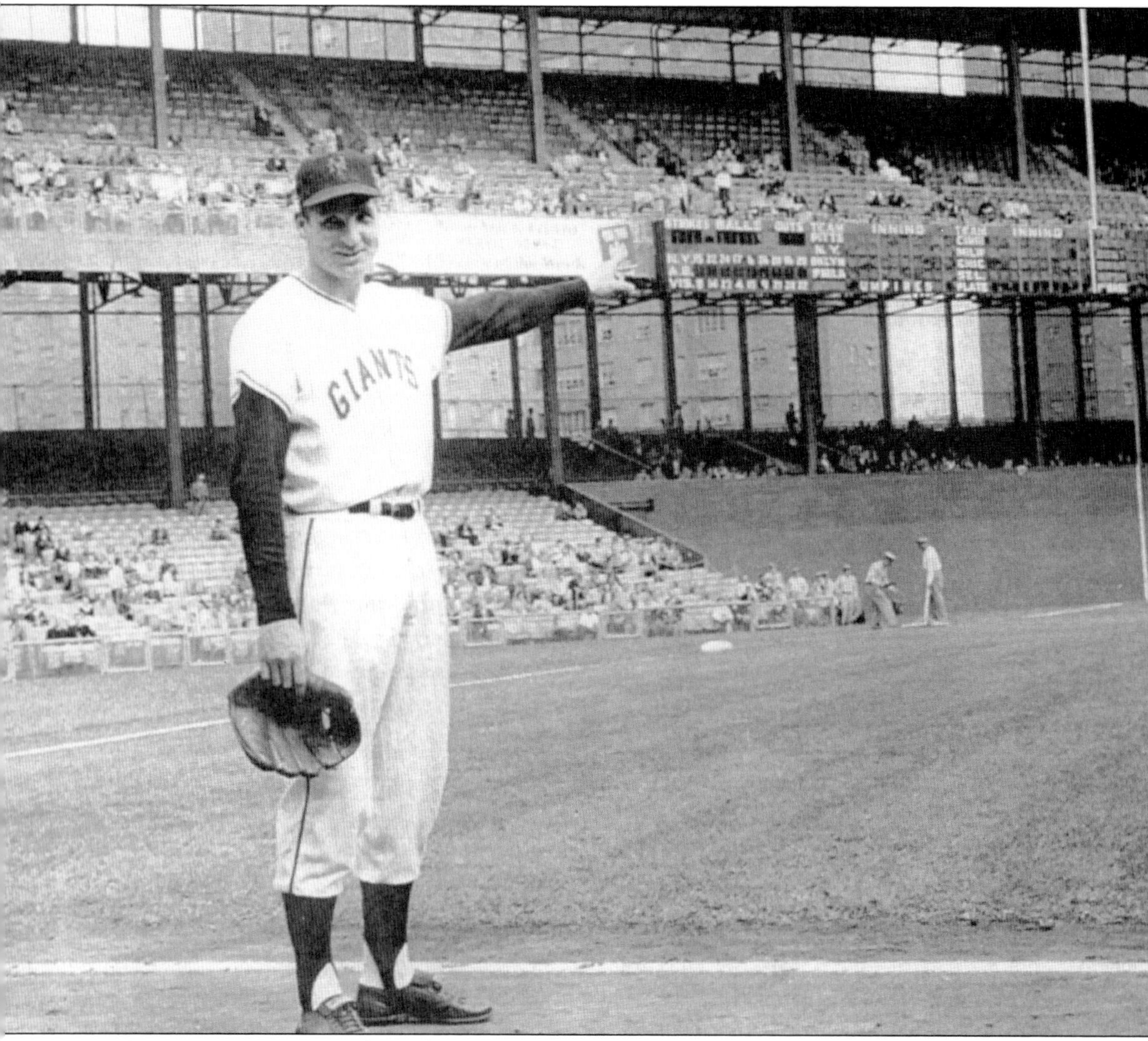

NEVER THE SAME. Before the Giants' final game at the Polo Grounds, Bobby Thomson pointed to the spot where his famous home run landed. The last person out of the park that sad September afternoon was John McGraw's widow. "I still can't believe it," she said of the team's move to San Francisco. "This would have broken John's heart. New York will never be the same." A new National League franchise, the Mets, would move into the Polo Grounds in 1962, managed by none other than former Giant Casey Stengel. The Polo Grounds were demolished in 1964. Despite the Mets' eventual success and citywide popularity, thousands of old-timers who remember the days of Mathewson, Terry, Thomson, and Mays still agree with Mrs. McGraw's verdict: New York without its Giants has never been quite the same.